LIBRARY SCIENCE TEXT SERIES

Introduction to Public Services for Library Technicians. 3rd ed. By Marty Bloomberg.

Introduction to Technical Services for Library Technicians. 4th ed. By Marty Bloomberg and G. Edward Evans.

Immroth's Guide to the Library of Congress Classification. 3rd ed. By Lois Mai Chan.

Science and Engineering Literature: A Guide to Reference Sources. 3rd ed. By H. Robert Malinowsky, and Jeanne M. Richardson.

The Vertical File and Its Satellites: A Handbook of Acquisition, Processing, and Organization. 2nd ed. By Shirley Miller.

Introduction to United States Public Documents. 2nd ed. By Joe Morehead.

The School Library Media Center. 2nd ed. By Emanuel T. Prostano and Joyce S. Prostano.

The Humanities: A Selective Guide to Information Sources. 2nd ed. By A. Robert Rogers.

Introduction to Library Science: Basic Elements of Library Service. By Jesse H. Shera.

The School Librarian as Educator. By Lillian Biermann Wehmeyer.

Introduction to Cataloging and Classification. 6th ed. By Bohdan S. Wynar, with the assistance of Arlene Taylor Dowell and Jeanne Osborn.

Library Management. 2nd ed. By Robert D. Stueart and John Taylor Eastlick.

An Introduction to Classification and Number Building in Dewey. By Marty Bloomberg and Hans Weber.

Map Librarianship: An Introduction. By Mary Larsgaard.

Micrographics. By William Saffady.

Developing Library Collections. By G. Edward Evans.

Problems in Library Management. By A. J. Anderson.

Problems
in
Library Management

PROBLEMS
IN
LIBRARY MANAGEMENT

by
A. J. Anderson

1981

LIBRARIES UNLIMITED, INC.
Littleton, Colorado

LIBRARIES UNLIMITED, INC.
P.O. Box 263
Littleton, Colorado 80160

Library of Congress Cataloging in Publication Data

Anderson, A. J. (Arthur James), 1933-
    Problems in library management.

    (Library science text series)
    1. Library administration--Case studies.   I. Ti-
tle.   II. Series.
Z678.88.A53   025.1   81-8153
ISBN 0-87287-261-0   AACR2
ISBN 0-87287-264-5 (pbk.)

Libraries Unlimited books are bound with Type II nonwoven material that meets
and exceeds National Association of State Textbook Administrators' Type II
nonwoven material specifications Class A through E.

For the memory of my father

PREFACE

Problems in Library Management comprises 22 case studies structured to meet the experiential learning needs of students and the facilitative teaching needs of instructors. It is the result of more than 10 years of sustained interest in and experimentation with the adaptation of the case method to the study of the management of libraries, media centers, and information systems. It is based on the belief that the acquisition of a body of functional knowledge and a set of professional skills cannot be developed solely by the traditional lecture-reading-discussion-term paper format, and that, in order to become effective managers, students must be afforded the opportunity to translate principles and theories into prescriptions for practice.

Instructors who teach management courses in schools of library and information science may debate how such courses should be taught, but few would question their necessity. No course on management would be complete without articulating the principles of management (i.e., planning, organizing, staffing, directing, controlling), and none would be complete if it did not attempt to instill an appreciation for a self-developed philosophy of management based on behavioral theories. However, most books and articles, which are the usual source material for management courses, provide only generalized statements of principles and theories, leaving virtually untouched the consideration of those principles and theories in operation. It is for this reason that the cases in this book have been written. Their goal is to relate abstract management principles and theories to actual management practice, and to help narrow the gap between the classroom and the real world. By approaching "lifelike" situations where principles can be applied and theories tested, students are given the opportunity to develop human relations concepts, problem solving skills, and decision-making acumen so that they will become more understanding, more useful, and more responsible members of a library or a media center or an information system, whatever their capacity. Experience indicates that student interest in assigned readings is heightened and classroom participation is increased when principles and theories are related to the type of situations emerging students-to-be-managers will soon be experiencing.

Each case in this book is drawn from an organization of practicing librarians, media specialists, and information scientists. The specific organization may be an academic library, a school media center, a public library, a regional center, or any other type of organization. The situation described may have its physical locus in the reference division, the serial department, the adult services section, or the director's office. The problems and assignments presented are real problems and assignments, and the people involved are real people, all suitably disguised to protect their identity. A case typically is a record of a situation which actually has been faced, or could be faced, by librarians, media specialists, and information scientists, together with surrounding facts, opinions, and prejudices upon which decisions have to depend. In other words, it is a record of both the rational and irrational aspects of an episode representing an actual situation experienced by real people, and it challenges its readers to use their knowledge of management principles and theories, their techniques of analysis, and their decision-making skills in the solution of the problems and assignments presented. A significant feature of the cases included herein is that the problems and assignments encountered reflect the fact that students are about to graduate and take jobs. Hence, they have been written with a view to enabling them to more readily identify with the situations and the people involved in them.

Additionally, the cases are designed to illustrate concepts that fall under the classical categorization of management principles as described by Robert D. Stueart and John Taylor Eastlick in their book, *Library Management* — planning, organizing, staffing, directing, and controlling — although their classification under these headings is not rigid. (Organizational behavior in practice — and cases are a form of practice — does not fall into neatly non-overlapping categories; the elements of any single case may point to numerous concepts.) Because of this, *Problems in Library Management* is designed as a companion volume to *Library Management*, but it can be used independently with any material that takes a functional approach or process orientation to management. And it can be used in management courses in schools of library and information science, but also in less formal settings, such as workshops, conferences, in-service training programs, and the like.

In *Library Management*, Stueart and Eastlick seek to bring together existing knowledge regarding the basic processes of library management, to state this knowledge in a practical and useful form, and to add new insights and interpretations that will assist librarians, media specialists, and information scientists in managing their various organizations. They divide management into the following processes:

Planning — that is, determining what is to be done. As used in their book, planning covers a wide range of activities, including establishing policies, clarifying objectives, and making decisions.

Organizing — that is, grouping activities necessary to carry out plans, defining relationships among departments and employees, and evaluating organizational structure.

Staffing — that is, building the organization through the selection and development of staff, describing jobs, evaluating employees, and administering salaries.

Directing — that is, getting employees to perform tasks efficiently and effectively to fulfill their own and the organization's goals and objectives.

Controlling — that is, establishing standards, and seeing that operating results conform as closely as possible to predetermined plans.

The cases in *Problems in Library Management* are loosely arranged under the above headings.

So many colleagues and students contributed ideas and suggestions for the cases in this book that it would be impossible to thank them all personally by name. However, a number of students contributed so substantially that they must be singled out for special mention and sincere thanks: John J. Adams, Robin Adams, Robert E. Wagenknecht, Janet R. Williams, and Kenneth Yamashita. I am also especially indebted to colleagues James M. Matarazzo, Nancy E. Peace, and Robert D. Stueart for their helpful comments. A special word of thanks is also extended to Patricia G. Oyler and to Kay Leary for all their assistance. No simple statement of appreciation to my wife, Victoria, would be adequate. She has been most tolerant and helpful in her cooperation during the more than 20 years the author has had the privilege of being married to her.

A. J. Anderson
Simmons College
Boston, Massachusetts

CONTENTS

PLANNING

A newly hired reference librarian in a small college library
is called upon to develop goals and objectives statements
and to think about the value of participative management.

A computer components manufacturing firm librarian is
presented with the opportunity to design a new corporate
library system, and gets a few pointers on corporate
politics.

An applicant for the directorship of a medium-sized public
library is asked to explain how he would conduct a community survey and demonstrate how he would plan library
programs.

A recently appointed adult specialist is called upon to
come up with a collection development policy for a large
urban library, and has a difficult personal decision to
make.

A young librarian is presented with the challenge of designing a model public relations campaign, and is given some
advice from a co-worker on how to deal with his supervisor.

ORGANIZING

STAFFING

INTRODUCTION

> "When I hear, I forget
> When I see, I remember
> When I do, I learn."
> — Chinese proverb

Briefly, this book takes a "learning by doing" approach to the education of librarians and media and information specialists as managers. It seeks to illustrate certain important principles of management — planning, organizing, staffing, directing, and controlling — by confronting its users with assignments and problems in these areas, and forcing them to devise plans of action to deal with them. It also seeks to illustrate certain important theories of management — authoritative, participative, situational — by demonstrating how they are frequently exercised.

The rationale behind the development of the book is that managers of libraries, media centers, and information systems must not only know the principles and theories of management, but must be able to apply them in a variety of settings and situations. In the course of a typical day, librarians and media and information specialists are called upon to make a number of decisions and solve a number of problems. To make these decisions and solve these problems they require an ability to analyze situations, balance conflicting requirements and demands, identify and combine options, select courses of action, and design plans for effectively implementing the desired actions in terms of the most favorable combination of probabilities; and, equally important, they require a knowledge of management principles and concepts, a philosophy of thought, a system of values, and an understanding of themselves and their effects on others, and of others.

THE PURPOSE OF THIS BOOK

The purpose of this book, then, is to provide students of library and information management with the opportunity to develop the perspective, method of thinking, and abilities required to cope effectively with problems and assignments by exposing them to life-like approximations of the kinds of problems and assignments that characteristically arise in the complex and continually changing milieu of libraries and media and information centers. (In order to avoid cumbrously constructed sentences, the term "library" henceforth will be used in this introduction to encompass "libraries," "media centers," and "information systems.")

As most of those engaged in teaching library management are aware, there is a paucity of library management case material to accomplish these purposes. This book is designed to fill that vacuum. It consists of 22 case studies in the form of narrative statements, which are either close to actual situations many librarians have experienced, or are close to situations many soon-to-be librarians may expect to become involved in. The cases are concerned with decisions that were made, or that have to be made, with difficulties that were resolved or are still unresolved, with what people said or did or failed to say or do that led to problems, with how they interpreted or evaluated something or someone, with how they talked or behaved in particular circumstances. They are more than mere historical records of things that happened; they are oriented toward the future in that each concludes with the need for subsequent decisions and actions on someone's part.

RELATING THEORY TO PRACTICE

The belief has long been held by management educators that, short of learning a limited number of abstractions and generalizations through traditional teaching methods (i.e., through lectures, assigned readings, questions posed in class, and term papers), the way in which management is best learned is through complementary practical exercises simulating, as nearly as possible, specific problems in real conditions: witness the growth and use of visual aids, role-playing exercises, case studies, and in-basket techniques. In other words, students cannot be "lectured" into becoming effective managers. What is learned in the traditional classroom does not transfer automatically into practice. Learning takes place in one environment but is put to work in another, and the learner is left to make the transition. How can the learner be helped in changing from the one environment to the other? According to learning theory, transfer of knowledge is facilitated when learners are given the opportunity to perceive similarities between what they are learning in theory and the situations in which they are to apply it.

What this suggests is that methods are needed to provide a functional relationship between theory and process, between principles and practice, between the printed or spoken word and the actual process of doing. To new managers faced with their first assignment or problem in the real world, the complexity of facts, the uncertainties of how to proceed, and the impalpable nature of human relations can add up to a situation that bears little resemblance to the logical and ordered material discussed in class. Through some form of simulation technique, students can gain a better understanding of human roles and relationships and how to apply theory and principles to concrete action and practices. Through active involvement, both cognitive and affective learning can take place, and the all-important difference between *learning about* management and *learning* management can be experienced. By reading and studying Stueart and Eastlick's *Library Management* they are made aware of the important principles and major theories of management; by solving the cases in *Problems in Library Management* they are given the opportunity to see how they would practice management.

THE CASE METHOD—A POINT OF VIEW

For those who are willing to look upon education as something of an adventure, the case method offers at least a partial answer to the aforementioned considerations. The method introduces a dimension of reality into the classroom by giving live demonstrations of textbook operations. Organizations are figuratively brought into the classroom and students are allowed, in imagination, to place themselves in the setting. Experimenters have found that situational cases, drawn from carefully selected bits of experience and skillfully written, can present problems and human relationships in such a way as to challenge the thinking and feeling of those who are capable of projecting themselves vicariously into real-life issues and circumstances.

A case-teaching veteran, the Harvard Professor of Business, Malcolm P. McNair, calls cases a "distinct literary form." The aim of that literature, according to McNair, is to create:

> ... the willing suspension of disbelief. In other words, the willingness to take at face value the situation which the case presents, forgetting that it is artificial, so to speak, forgetting that this is a classroom, being willing to take the situation at face value and become the person concerned with it—that is the ideal that a case discussion ought to achieve.[1]

A good case is a text that participants take seriously and with which they can identify. According to McNair, cases are good when they are communicating a clear "time structure," "narrative structure," and "plot or expository structure." A plot or expository structure is needed because:

> A case isn't just a bland narrative where there's no question or issues. A case involves a problem of some kind and the more you can build that up, the more you can develop the interest of the drama of the clash of ideas or maybe the clash of people, the better the chance of getting the kind of student commitment that makes for good classroom discussion.[2]

To meet this requirement, case writers will sometimes employ the techniques of the fiction writer. They will use the device of "flash-backs" and the device of "breaking the time sequence," and, as another case-teaching veteran, Andrew R. Towl, advises, they will remember that "the ordering of cases is a pedagogical sequence, not necessarily the same as the logical exposition of the subject."[3] Towl states that case writers are advised to present factual information in a factual way, but that when somebody thinks or feels something, this should be included: "Opinions of people in a situation are helpful to include, and should be tied to their source."[4]

One significant difference between a piece of fiction and a case, however, is that cases are written in the form of problems without solutions, rather than as complete narratives which carry a story to the end. A problem is the *sine qua non* of a case. It is up to the case analyst to supply an ending to a case. (For this reason, it might be more accurate to speak of "the problem method" rather than "the case method.") Another distinguishing characteristic is that cases are "real" in the sense that they have their origins in events and problems that have actually occurred, or something very like them have occurred. Usually case writers will draw upon a wide range of factual occurrences, sometimes combining several to produce an account of a problem or problems which will meet a given training need. And like fiction writers, they will attempt to imbue them with life and meaning and value for the people who are investing their thoughts and time in their analysis. They will try to reflect the underlying attitudes, prejudices, and sentiments of the central characters – attitudes, prejudices, and sentiments which have such a profound effect both in bringing about the situations and in their outcomes that they cannot be ignored. All these bits of raw material – these "chunks of reality" as McNair calls them – are encapsulated in a carefully organized and well-rounded whole, which the reader must pull apart and put together again.

Stated in its simplest terms, then, a case is a written account of a problem or issue, or a series of problems or issues, to be investigated and solved. It contains sufficient information about a set of events and the people involved to allow for careful, systematic investigation. To accomplish this objective, it will present enough historical and physical background information to establish a social and environmental context; it will include relevant policies and descriptions of technical processes to allow for an understanding of the total environment within which the problems or issues are taking place; and it will report interactions between people, including their conversations and the influences that act upon them – their thoughts, actions, and decisions – in sufficient detail to allow readers to diagnose why the characters are behaving as they are.

FEATURES OF THIS BOOK

Problems in Library Management is a rather unique book, quite distinct from any existing in the library management field to date. Hence a few observations in addition to those found in the preface seem to be in order.

In short, the book is designed to enlarge the scope and usefulness of the case study method. The cases consist of "assignments" to be completed, "problems" to be solved, and "issues" or "areas" to be investigated. It has been written primarily to meet the needs of two groups of people: students who are studying library management in formal courses in library school; and experienced managers, who are looking for training material for management workshops, staff meetings, conferences, and in-service programs.

To facilitate its study and use, the 22 cases have been grouped in five sections according to the classical categorization of managerial functions as delineated by Stueart and Eastlick – planning, organizing, staffing, directing, and controlling – in a kind of contrapuntal design. But since many of a manager's activities include elements of all of these, and it is difficult to trace the sequence and isolate their components, the cases could fit equally well in more than one area. For example, a case with strong planning features may have equally strong aspects of staffing or organizing. A case centering largely around performance evaluation can also involve questions of policy making or of supervision. And since each case concerns people and their interactions, numerous behavioral features have been included. In other words, the elements of any single case may point to several concepts; in this sense, the cases are like icebergs – more is hidden than appears on the surface. Still, despite this overlap of involvement, a classification of cases by function serves the useful purpose of highlighting areas of major emphasis.

Most people would probably agree that one definition of management might be the process through which these functions are exercised in the attainment of the objectives of the group or of the enterprise. And most people would probably agree that analytical ability and a high degree of insight, the capacity to discern and evaluate facts and inferences in complex systems of relationships, and the possession of a fund of knowledge and a set of professional skills are not the attributes only of those in the top positions of a library. The practice of librarianship requires performance of the same management functions irrespective of position. But virtually all business case material has a "top-management" skill orientation; too little of it emphasizes the kinds of substantive and organizational problems that arise at the lower and middle levels of management.

The argument usually put forward for taking a top-echelon viewpoint in case material is that this is the level at which planning, organizing, staffing, directing, and controlling are integrated. But in reality integration should take place at all levels. When lower level managers are not expected to exercise management theories and principles, albeit on a smaller scale, then the organization is not functioning as efficiently as it might. When cases are brought down from the heady director and board of trustees atmosphere, students in particular and analysts in general begin to show some interesting tendencies. They have a feeling of relatedness with the material and they project themselves more easily into the roles of the characters who must frequently attempt to influence their superiors, rather than hand down decisions. A unique feature of this book, then, is that the cases emphasize the kinds of problems recent graduates encounter in the early years of their careers.

While it is true, as stated earlier, that management principles and theories are applicable at all levels of an organization, the types of problems and assignments are not necessarily the same at all levels. This book attempts to reflect that fact. But what is also true is that all managers, regardless of level, number among their most frequent problems those having to do with people. The vast majority of management problems, even those which seem at first glance to be wholly planning or organizing or controlling problems, usually turn out to be bristling with ticklish human relations problems. One distinctive characteristic of this book is that the "people problems" are interwoven into the cases as they are in actual situations. Unlike many management case books that view management as only a series of "people problems" and disregard what managers do the rest of the time—which is most of the time—this book tries to put them in context.

The intent of the book is not to accumulate a large number of cases; rather, the intent is to develop a set that illustrates the principles and theories of management in action. Some case books take the approach of multiple exposure: if 1 case is good, then 101 must be better. This does not follow. What this book seeks to communicate is not an index of cases practicing librarians can file through later in their professional lives on the off chance that lightning will strike twice and that they will be able to locate an elegant solution to a somewhat similar experience. Instead, it seeks to communicate a confidence that as problems come along and assignments are undertaken students will be equipped to handle them because the mental process of effective problem solving will have become second nature. The transfer of classroom solutions to daily operations is not accomplished directly. The hope is that silently, between all the details of the cases, the power of judging will have built itself up as a possession that will never pass away, and a point of what might be called management sophistication will be reached.

While it is important that students solve the problems and complete the assignments in the cases, it is just as important — no, more so — that they develop skills in analysis and persuasion. The cases are "rehearsals" for more serious problems elsewhere, and if ever students are to become their own effective problem solvers they will need to "recognize the cases" in their surroundings and will need to be able to devise appropriate abstract organizing ideas to help them solve them. It is the method by which classroom cases are approached, analyzed, and solved that is important. It is the "method" that must be transferred to real-life managerial situations.

The proper study of library management is library managers. Their daily experiences provide grist for the case-writer's mill, from which insights concerning management processes may be gleaned. Truth in the library field — as in every field of endeavor — is indeed stranger than fiction. The exigent demands library managers face often result in highly dramatic events. The cases herein are attempts to capture a large measure of the reality of numerous management scenes that are acted out daily on the stage of different kinds of libraries across the country — scenes that include conflict, emotions, prejudices, misunderstandings, and unreasonableness, but also kindliness, humor, friendliness, and goodwill. They are drawn from actual happenings. The people involved are real people and the problems and assignments are real problems and real assignments; however, any exact correspondence to actual and specific, persons, places, and events is purely accidental. They derive from a variety of sources: from professional colleagues and students who have willingly contributed their own experiences; from research in the areas of human relations and management; from consulting work done by faculty members; and from the author's experiences. Each is an account of the management process as it moves through a series of significantly related events, culminating for the central characters in the cases in cliff-hangers of various sorts — i.e., problems or assignments that require making succeeding decisions or developing plans of action. The decisions to be made and the plans to be developed do not necessarily represent crises, or even spell success or failure for the library, but they do usually involve characters in situations that call for the exercise of good judgment. It will be readily apparent as the events unfold in some of the cases, however, that librarians are sometimes called upon to make painful decisions.

Every effort has been made to avoid the "once-in-one-person's-lifetime" type case — the highly abnormal or unusual problem. Real life situations are always unique, however, in that each contains at least some elements that are quite literally new or novel — they have never happened before in exactly the same context and never will do so again, even for the person who has experienced them. But, too, many situations appear to be the same as others, so much so that careful examination may be necessary to discover the uniqueness underlying the similarities. Complex relationships and implication must sometimes be dug out. It goes without saying that case writers are obligated to try to present the type of experience that will cause the reader to say: "These are the kinds of situation I might well experience when I start working," or "Something like that happened to me at the 'X' library when I was there," or "I've known people like that," or "We have our own version of the character in that case at our library."

Another point to be made is that questions have not been appended to the cases. In some instances, an action question is explicitly posed by a character in the case, but as a rule analysts are left on their own to ferret out useful and appropriate areas to be investigated. People who have used cases in teaching know from experience that some person or persons will give an entirely new interpretation to case data and will pick up as significant some detail that others have overlooked, and so give a case a new twist. Indeed, groups of people have been able to find in them many things of interest that others did not even suspect. One argument against including a list of questions is that often analysts will think they are the only questions that might be asked. But no one — neither instructor nor student — can ever know or predict *all* of what may be discovered in the examination of a case. As in real-life management situations, participants usually reflect different perceptions of the situations, of the people involved, and of the interpersonal relations, and reflect their own frames of reference and ways of putting things together. So, too, in a case. A case is partly a function of who is viewing it. In this sense it is reminiscent of the cunningly drawn pictures of our youth. The reader will recall them: objects hidden in the scenery, contrived in such a way that one had to turn the picture at all angles to find the camouflaged items. In this way, a case becomes an inexhaustible source of possibilities. Thus analysts are encouraged to identify their own areas of investigation and to ask their own questions — as they are required to do in life.

The cases also serve particularly well as "springboards" to more generalized discussions about issues, values, hypotheses, research findings, points of view, and so forth. For example, "hidden" in the narratives are clues to broader areas of investigation (i.e., the mid-life crisis, overcoming resistance to change, motivational factors, learning theory, assumptions about human nature, and such) which will assist in understanding and analyzing the problems and dilemmas and in their solutions. Doing research and reading on some subject introduced in a case thus becomes purposeful and meaningful. The case provides a practical framework for the discussion of research findings; analysts talk about their findings as findings but also as they relate to the particulars of the case. With the case as target, analysts relate general observations to specific situations.

ON USING CASES — SOME SUGGESTIONS FOR INSTRUCTORS

All that instructors interested in using cases need to do is to start using them. All they need is a willingness to experiment a bit and to try out a pedagogical method others testify to being of some value. Indeed, the method's very persuasiveness is one way of explaining its widespread use in various fields of *practice* — business and public administration, social work, law, medicine, and other clinical disciplines. The value of the method for class discussion, for written reports, and for research has long been acknowledged.

Decisions as to the way to use cases need not be made at the outset, or ever with absolute finality. Instructors should not expect them to be perfect at their inception; it takes time for things to set themselves in order and to attain their proper shape. It is suggested that instructors get a "feel" for them and their possibilities before making an analysis of the pedagogical implications for themselves.

The method is sufficiently flexible to allow for wide modifications; and like any other teaching technique, effective use demands a degree of expertness that comes only with experimentation and experience. The method does not develop without careful nurture. There are six or so ways in which cases can be used: 1) supplementary reading; 2) assigned reading for discussion groups that are an integral part of the course; 3) illustrative material in conjunction with lectures; 4) discussion material in courses where there is formal and informal discussion for a portion of the class period in addition to lectures; 5) basic material for lectures and discussions that take up the major amount of class time in a course; and 6) basic material for discussions that constitute the entire course. In other words, they can be used with any method of instruction where the educational objective includes the comprehension of professional management subject matter, awareness with regard to subject matter sources (textbooks, periodicals, leading authors), and the development of skill in the art of managing.

Whichever procedure is selected, it is the duty of instructors to make clear their objectives at the outset. No two instructors will follow the same pattern in introducing a case to a group for the first time. In orienting a group, however, it is important to bring out certain points so that students will understand their roles and that of the instructor. The manner of this initial presentation is important because it will establish the tone for the discussion that follows. Some points that might be brought out include the following:

First, the purpose. This has been elaborated above, but to state it succinctly, one might say that cases are written descriptions of real-life situations — "chunks of reality" — brought into the classroom to be worked over by the class and the instructor. They present actual problems and provide students with information concerning their background so that they can make those reactions that will be demanded in real management situations, situations they would not otherwise have access to. They approximate real-world decision making while remaining once removed from real-world involvement. For this reason, it is probably not inaccurate to say that the case method of teaching is the closest substitute for actual on-the-job experience that exists.

Second, the information given. When cases are first presented some students may complain that they need more facts than some of the cases provide. No case can give *all* of the facts and *all* of the opinions. As McNair says, they "represent selections from a situation."[5] They are the presentation of a few facts out of the total dynamic process of organizational and human behavior, and they focus on one particular aspect or a few aspects that require judgmental decision making. This is not to suggest that important information is deliberately withheld. Much of it simply is not available. This is precisely the situation managers find themselves in most of the time. To quote Towl, cases "are not an actual snap-shot or sound movie of 'what really took place.' Rather they provide 'realistic' educational experiences both for mature executives in advanced management programs and for students beginning their study of business administration."[6] Case-writers are the students' proxies on the scene.

In anticipating requests for more information, instructors should make sure that students have read the cases thoroughly and have not missed anything, and they should encourage the students to make the most of the available data. More often than not there is enough information for them to make a decision. But the incompleteness of information can be turned into an asset by challenging students to specify what additional information they would like and how they would attempt to get it. The second is often much more difficult than they generally suppose. Another way is to have them make assumptions and in effect "rewrite" portions of the case, thereby supplying the other information they consider necessary. They may have to invent some data in the process. But they should be impressed with the fact that in real life managers seldom have all the information they require to make decisions; managers must make the best use of the combinations of facts, half-facts, opinions, and secondhand information they have available to them. Part of their skill as managers derives from their ability to know what additional information they need, and to obtain it. The ability to ask relevant questions is at least as much a skill in analysis as answering those already raised. Students must also be impressed with the fact that frequently in the actual world there is not time to get additional information.

Third, there are no "right" or "wrong" answers. Although through careful analysis, research, and discussion there should evolve alternative courses of action that are more appropriate than others, it should be stressed that there is not *one* determinate resolution to a case, and that a wide range of resolutions is normal. Since the method is concerned with the development of each student's own independent, maturing judgment, individual solutions to specific cases are, in the final analysis, of less importance than the process by which they are reached.

Fourth, the instructor's role. If instructors can begin each discussion with the attitude that they still have something to learn, they will find the reciprocal exploratory effort of case analysis to be most rewarding. Thus it is recommended that they refrain from trying to force their solutions on students. Instructors presumably have a somewhat larger background in management, and particularly in the problems of trying to learn it, than most of their students; they also have longer acquaintance with the cases, and have had the benefit of analyses and discussions made by previous classes; but they should be especially careful that they do not dominate by insisting upon their approach and their conclusions. To do this is to thwart the goal of eliciting genuine dialogue — candid, searching, and purposeful discussion — and motivating students to think, to study, to weigh ideas, and to develop their own solutions. Instructors, like students, should have their opinions and solutions, but they should remain just that: their opinions and their solutions, but not *the* opinions and *the* solutions. This is not intended to imply that their ideas and views should be forever withheld, but to say that their ideas and views should be subject to the same scrutiny as those of the others. They can certainly enrich discussions by sharing anecdotes from their own or others' experiences — as can any discussant — but they must guard against trying to make students clones of themselves. They should be ever mindful that their role as instructors is to give students opportunities and occasions for learning. This is something quite different from giving them the answers.

The cases themselves are not solely responsible for the success of the method; the success depends heavily on the quality of students. Students who slight pre-class preparation are a drag on the class; they will not know what is going on and if they speak at all will frequently attempt to wrest the discussion away from the case to more comfortable topics. For this reason, many instructors require brief written reports on every case. This is the minimum level of preparation. These reports consist of what students see to be the main problems, assignments, and issues or areas of the case, the primary action alternatives, the recommended solutions, and the relevant principles and theories involved. Thus, in order to ensure the success of the method, students have an obligation to familiarize themselves thoroughly with the facts and opinions and the general context of the case; instructors similarly have that obligation and the further one of directing the discussions to as many problems and issues as time allows. Sometimes one hears of case sessions that end only with the conclusion that an interesting discussion took place. It is up to instructors to ensure that the points they want brought out are brought out. It is up to them to guide discussions into elucidation of the principles and theories which should be made.

Case discussions differ materially from ordinary classroom discussions. In case discussions, interest is focused on the task of determining what is going on in a particular case; in ordinary discussions such a task is seldom present. In case discussions, many arguments can be resolved by direct reference to the case data. Unlike many classroom discussions, students are not given general theories or broad hypotheses to discuss; rather, they are given specific instances and situations to discuss. In case discussions, students are not asked how insubordination in general should be handled, without a frame of reference; rather, they are asked what they would do about the question of this particular instance of insubordination under these particular circumstances in this particular library. When students talk about a case they are more likely to talk about it in both concrete and abstract terms than when they talk about a broadly phrased question without details, such as "How should people be promoted?" or "How should a difficult employee be handled?" or "How should a training program be set up?" Cases keep discussion grounded on certain persistent facts that must be faced, and keep a realistic rein on airy flights of academic speculation.

For best discussion results, the atmosphere of the group should be conducive to view sharing. The respective roles of students and instructor should be made clear early in the course. Basically, the pattern should be a progression from structure to freedom. Instructors should be most directive during the first few case analyses, stating their analytical framework explicitly, showing by example how it works, holding the balance between participants, dealing, if necessary, with questions of fact and procedure, reinforcing desirable student behavior, demonstrating theories and principles in action, summarizing as points emerge. Once students begin to grasp the use of the framework, instructors should become less directive. Students will begin to see that the emphasis of the course will soon be theirs rather than the instructor's, and they will begin to show signs of being able to organize themselves. The instructor's major function at this stage should be to serve as a classroom traffic officer, keeping everyone from talking at once and recording the flow of analysis and conclusions. Instructors may sharpen a difference of opinion between two students; they may divert discussion from unprofitable avenues; they may ask students to consider the consequences of a proposed action; they may tactfully cut short long-winded contributions; they may draw attention to facts being overlooked; they may build linkages to the theories and principles, and to other courses and to other cases; and so on. They can add perspective, can interject color and fun, spark and focus. But they should be careful during this critical stage not to become intrusive elements. They should be cautious not to "pull rank" and interfere with the learning process by stepping in and taking over. They should participate, but no more than seems necessary. Eventually, they should be able to "hand the chalk over to the students" and take a back seat. They will know they have succeeded when they can walk in and sit down and participate like any other member of the discussion. They will disappear out of the students' lives as Virgil and Beatrice disappear out of *The Divine Comedy*. They will have achieved the objective of all good teachers: to make students self-reliant. The students are "finished products," who are able to transfer their self-confidence and knowledge to their jobs.

These are the principle techniques that are used in a case-class. Their pedagogical purpose is to shift responsibility to the students for problem identification, analysis, and the task of applying the management process to carefully derived solutions. Looked at from the point of view of the instructor, a case-class is a most demanding and exacting form of teaching. It is a very different kind of activity from lecturing. It requires intense concentration on what students are saying. In case discussions, the task of understanding specific material is as present as it is in any lecture and provides information about various principles, theories, policies, and procedures — but it is done as they are applied in concrete administrative situations. Since case studies pose a dilemma or problem to be solved, time and effort is not wasted in simply discussing ideas at a remote theoretical level. It is often remarked by students that exposure to cases creates a new interest in textbook material.

APPLICATION TO THE CLASSROOM

The enemy of the case method is time. Instructors have to keep an eye always on the clock to ensure time does not run out before the essence of the case has been extracted. Those who plan to use a case as a basis for a lecture or as an illustration should choose one that will not start too many trains of thought in diverse directions. In this book some cases are quite short — three or four pages. Others are longer, and some are very long, running to dozens of pages. Some are simple, some are complex; but the short ones are not necessarily the most simple, nor the long ones necessarily the most complex. Some are concerned with broad policy issues, while others are less encompassing and present some of the narrower problems that cross the library manager's desk. There is a useful place for both long and short cases, for both simple and complicated cases. What this suggests is that instructors must be thoroughly familiar with their contents, and must know exactly what they are attempting to accomplish.

In this book, cases 11, 12, 14, 16, and 18 might be used early in the course as introductions to the method. With these the instructor might begin the discussion by asking students what they see in the case. "What is going on here?" or "If you were this character, what would you do now?" or "What aspect of this case do you think we should discuss first?" — such questions usually elicit several comments and suggestions, which can be listed on the blackboard. The instructor's most potent armory for such a purpose is a list of questions that can be dropped into the discussion at appropriate points. Discussants in case-classes say over and over again that they are surprised at how much there is to talk about.

Instructors who plan to use cases involving a large number of considerations and factors should plan to devote two-thirds or all of the class time to their analysis. There must be adequate time for individual students or groups of students to present their analyses, and permit discussion to evolve in desirable directions. When the point is reached at which the instructor begins to fade into the background, individual students or groups of students can be assigned or can select cases to analyze and solve on their own or in groups before the class period, literally pulling them apart and putting them together again — "working them to death." They will then present their conclusions and solutions for the class's appraisal. Student participation and involvement can be further increased by dividing class members in accordance with their views and conducting debates, by having teams prepare competitive analyses, and by culminating discussion in role-playing exercises. The cases provide a rich mine of role-playing material. Role-playing requires participants to unravel the motivation and behavior of the *dramatis personae*, and affords them the opportunity to scrutinize their own communication processes; students who have to defend themselves by role-playing their proposed actions gain insight into the effect their normal behavior has on others.

THE STUDENT IN CASE ANALYSIS

From the students' point of view, the case method of instruction involves putting forth intensive intellectual effort, not only to increase their knowledge of management principles and theories, but, more important, to use that knowledge effectively in critical analysis of specific problems, assignments, and issues presented in the case. Analysis is a weighty word for the mental process people use when they make decisions. For some decisions explicit analysis is unnecessary; however for difficult and complex ones, the search for solutions is so crucial that anything short of careful, thorough, and systematic analysis must be considered totally inadequate. The purpose of analysis is to help decision makers formulate and then sharpen their judgment. Stated more analytically, its purpose is to compel students to face rationally a particular situation, to evaluate all of its aspects, to identify possible courses of action along with predictable results, and to select the best course of action.

In analyzing cases, students are encouraged to consider themselves, if they can, as part of the situation, so that they will develop an increased appreciation of the difficulties encountered by the key figures. They are encouraged to try to project themselves into the position or role of the character with whom they identify most strongly, and to do the assignments and to solve the problems from that person's point of view. By doing this, there is a greater likelihood of committing themselves to a course of action, whatever it might be. Additionally, it is interesting to discover which of the characters they most dislike, and then to analyze why this is, attempting in the process to try to understand the pressures and pulls affecting those most disliked people.

If students find it impossible to step into the shoes of any character in the case, thereby becoming that person, they are advised to select a character for whom they would be willing to serve as a "consultant." As consultants they would make recommendations to that character on what to do about his or her problems and/or assignments, developing solutions in precisely the same manner as if they assumed the role of that person. They are asked to imagine that the character they select to serve as a consultant to has approached them and related the case story to them and sought their advice.

As stated earlier, the purposes to which cases can be put vary almost without limit, and there is no "correct" technique for using them, no formula to be offered to ensure success. The cases do, however, have a higher probability of adding to the managerial skills of analysts when they are approached in a focused, purposeful manner. The following suggestions are based upon the author's own teaching experiences, and are offered as guidelines or frames of reference.

A quick once-through reading to "find out what is happening" is a good way to start, but several readings are usually necessary to get to know the case so thoroughly as to engender the feeling of having lived through it. As the case is being read, it is helpful to take notes on the personalities and relationships, on the basic facts, on the various appendixes (the cases are divided into two basic parts: text and appendixes), and on other critical factors and elements.

Next, the case should be reread with a view to identifying and listing the problems to be solved, the assignments to be completed, and the issues or areas to be investigated. It will be found that the cases consist of many such. Analysts should not stop to reflect on the importance or significance of each at this stage, but should concentrate on getting them down — no matter how frivolous they may appear to be at first glance. This point should be emphasized: while jotting down the problems, assignments, and issues or areas, no attempt should be made to evaluate them or to determine whether they are big or small, significant or insignificant, practical or theoretical, and so on; they are merely being generated at this time and nothing should be done to stop the flow.

After analysts are satisfied that they have identified every conceivable problem, assignment, and issue or area, they should review their lists and categorize them under their appropriate heads: "Problems to be Solved," "Assignments to be Completed," and "Issues and Areas to be Investigated." Only when analysts have structured the case by breaking it down into manageable pieces can they begin to see what has to be done. Each item, which should be stated as concisely and unambiguously as possible, can then be taken one at a time, and a situation that might have appeared confusing and overwhelming can be subdued. Analysts are then ready to begin to work on them.

The "Assignments to be Completed" should be further defined in terms of their objectives, and analysts should complete the assignments as if they were the characters in the case (or consultants who have agreed to complete the assignments for them), doing whatever research and report writing are necessary in order to satisfy the desiderata of the assignment.

The "Issues or Areas to be Investigated" should be explored fully. Analysts should dip into selective readings and examine and pull together different points of view relating to them. The instructional objective is for students to prepare and present their findings on these issues and areas based on outside readings and other sources of authoritative information.

The "Problems to be Solved" might be approached by using any of a number of problem solving models. An approach including the following steps of activity has proved to be a logical and satisfactory method for analysis, problem solving, and discussion. It is composed of nine steps:

1. Statement of the main problem

2. Statement of the facts

3. Listing of the "cluster" problems

4. Statement of the alternative courses of action

5. Identification of the advantages and disadvantages of the alternative courses of action

6. Selection of the best alternative, and statement of why it is best

7. Follow through

8. Discussion of the "cluster" problems

9. Documentation

Step 1: Statement of the Main Problem. Analysts should review their list of problems and select what they consider to be the "main" or primary problem. Widely accepted scientific and philosophical dogma says that "a problem well stated is more than half solved." Hence too much emphasis cannot be given to the importance of isolating and articulating the main problem. The "left-over" problems become "cluster" problems to be discussed in Steps 3 and 9. Analysts are frequently tempted to try to encompass all the problems in the case in a problem solving model, but this should never be attempted. Only the main problem will be analyzed in the manner outlined below.

Once analysts have singled out the main problem, they should word it in the form of a question beginning with the words "How" or "What": "How should ...?" "How could ...?" "What should ...?" "What could ...?" To illustrate, let us imagine that the head of a public library, Mary Smith, has asked one of her reference librarians, John Jones, to become the young adult specialist, and he refuses. That might be the main problem in the case once it is boiled down to its essence. The problem might be stated thus: "What could Mary Smith do about the fact that John Jones has refused to become the young adult specialist?" or "How should Mary Smith handle the problem of John Jones, who refuses to become the young adult specialist?" The wording is important because analysts will be generating a list of alternative courses of action in Step 4, viz.: "She could accept his refusal and appoint someone else, if someone else is available," etc.

Step 2: Statement of the Facts. Here analysts should offer a quick review of the pertinent facts of the case, viz.: what the situation is, who has been asked to do what, etc.

Step 3: Listing of the "Cluster" Problems. Having extracted what appears to be the main problem, the analyst should now list the "left over" problems, which also require attention but which will not be subjected to this rigorous analysis. They will be discussed in Step 8.

Step 4: Statement of the Alternative Courses of Action. *All* possible means of resolving the problem should be identified. There are always a number of workable courses of action, spanning a spectrum of extremes, and if they are not all listed the best may not emerge. Analysts should give free rein to their imaginations and not discount even the wildest possibility. Frequently it turns out that the most bizarre alternative will contribute to a highly workable solution either in whole or in part. For convenience, the alternatives should be numbered, but not necessarily in terms of their desirability.

Step 5: Identification of the Advantages and Disadvantages of the Alternative Courses of Action. The next operation is to anticipate the consequences and implications of the alternative courses of action. Each alternative course of action should be taken separately and probed in terms of good and bad consequences, known and suspected pros and cons. Analysts should make every effort to anticipate *every* palpable reaction to the alternative courses of action, and list them. None should be neglected.

Step 6: Selection of the Best Alternative and Statement of Why It Is Best. In order to select the best alternative, analysts should review their alternative courses of action and their respective advantages and disadvantages and select the one with the greatest net advantage or least net disadvantage. They should also provide a full justification of the factors and elements that have been taken into consideration, stating clearly why they feel the alternative they have selected as best *is* best. Their "best" alternative will also outline exactly how they plan to implement it, and provide step-by-step details of exactly what they would do. They must guard against selecting as best alternatives solutions that are practically without meaning as directions for specific action. Such "solutions" as "Mary Smith should have a talk with him," or "Mary Smith should try to bring him around to her way of thinking," or "John Jones should be made to cooperate" *are not solutions at all*. They are "no solution facades." After going through Steps 4 and 5, analysts must state precisely what should be done: "Mary Smith should ask John Jones to come to her office. Therein she should tell him that he is to become young adult specialist. If he refuses to come to her office, she should go to where he is and tell him that. If he still refuses to become young adult specialist, she should tell him she will ask the trustees to agree with her that he be dismissed. If the trustees refuse to agree that he should be dismissed, she herself has several options (not "she should consider leaving"; that is too unprecise): she could resign, she could accept their decision, ...," etc. And the whole cycle starts over again.

Step 7: Follow Through. Steps 6 and 7 are interrelated to a certain extent, and some of the "follow through" is identified above. Basically, what analysts are doing here is pursuing every possible reaction to their best solution. In other words, they are saying "If my best alternative, which is ..., is not acceptable, then I would fall back on alternative course of action number 3, which is...." "If this course of action does not work, then I would fall back on alternative course of action number 5, which is...." It is in this way that students gain "experience by proxy" and get a "feel" for handling problems in the flesh-and-blood world; it is in this way that the cumulative effect of case analyses improves the students' capacity to "think in the presence of new situations." The process lends itself nicely to role-playing. If analysts recommend that an employee be fired, they should have to fire him or her. In other words, they should be encouraged to put their decisions into effect to demonstrate how they would actually proceed. Few experiences are more eye opening than to see how difficult it sometimes is to accomplish one's objectives.

Step 8: Discussion of the "Cluster" Problems. Here analysts return to Step 3, where they have listed the "cluster" or "left-over" problems, and discuss them one by one in terms of what they would have the characters do about them; they may also at this time present the results of their research.

Step 9: Documentation. Finally, in giving their analyses students are encouraged to focus attention on management principles and theories, keying their assigned and supplementary readings to various aspects of the case. They should read and prepare themselves extensively, giving illustrations and analogies to support conclusions.

As discussed above, the minimum level of preparation should be brief reports. The maximum level should be thoroughly documented and detailed written reports that could be handed in to instructors after oral presentation to the class. The ability to communicate and defend one's position before one's peers provides another realistic simulation of actual conditions. In this laboratory situation, students' analyses and programs of action may undergo some modification as collectively the class debates alternatives and discusses findings. Students should also be encouraged to prepare extra copies for distribution in class of any forms they may have designed, any floor plans they may have developed, any outlines they may have prepared, and so on.

A FINAL WORD

The foregoing discussion is not intended to imply that the thoughtful study analysis of situational cases is a panacea for all the problems encountered in the practice of the management of libraries, media centers, and information systems. It is, however, one very valuable means of attaining the "management frame of mind" so necessary in the preparation of students for careers as managers. Many students, after working with cases, have testified to the help they received in developing a firmer grasp of the management process, a sharper ability to make objective analyses of situations, and a clearer concept of the dynamics of human relationships in organizational settings.

REFERENCES

[1]"McNair on Cases," *HBS Bulletin* 47 (July-August, 1971), p. 10.

[2]"McNair on Cases," p. 12.

[3]Andrew R. Towl, "Case-Course Development," mimeographed report, 9-358-003 CR108R2, distributed by Intercollegiate Case Clearing House, p. 9.

[4]Towl, "Case-Course Development," p. 3.

[5]"McNair on Cases," p. 12.

[6]Towl, "Case-Course Development," p. 3.

PLANNING

1

GARSCHINE ON MANAGEMENT

Emily Tournquist had just returned to the reference desk when the telephone rang.

"Em?" a voice inquired. "This is Ruth. Would you come up to Mr. Garschine's office right away? It's urgent."

"I have a couple of students waiting to see me," answered the reference librarian. "Could I make it in 15 minutes?"

"I'm afraid not," replied the secretary positively. "He wants to see you right away. Get someone to replace you, okay?"

"Okay! I'll be there in a moment."

Tournquist called the head cataloger, who said he would send one of the cataloguing clerks who sometimes sit in for her during lunch hours and breaks to replace her. As she ascended the staircase to the library director's office, she tried to fathom the reason for the imperious summons. Surely she hadn't done anything wrong in the two weeks she had been there, she thought to herself. What did he want? Quickly recognizing the futility of trying to decipher the purpose of the call, she dismissed it from her mind and continued on.

Peckham College is a moderately small (1,600 students) accredited private co-educational college in the mid-Atlantic region of the country. Its academic departments are divided into four groups: art, foreign literature and languages, natural sciences, and social sciences. The curriculum is of sufficient scope to provide the student with a foundation for a professional career, for business, or for home life. The highest degree awarded is the master's.

The library staff consists of 6 professional librarians (with MLSs) and 11 clerical workers, all of whom are held firmly in line by the forceful personality of R. Boyce Garschine, a retired military colonel, who at 59 has been director for eight years (Appendix I). He might be classified as a benevolent autocrat. His benevolence is manifested by his friendly, comfortable, and at times almost fatherly manner with students, faculty members, and library staff; his autocracy by his demand that subordinates be completely obedient to him, by his use of coercive tactics to achieve results, and by his unwillingness and inability to delegate responsibility and authority. With one or two exceptions he is respected by the staff; however, of late most have found remaining on good terms with him to be something of a challenge, even when at their most submissive. He is frequently given to black and terrible furies. Tournquist reckoned herself fortunate to have escaped being the object of his irritability at any time during her short stay.

When she reached the director's outer office, the secretary beckoned her to go in. Garschine, who had his back to the door and was looking out of the window when she entered, swung around. His face had an ashen quality, and his voice lacked its usual robustness. He motioned for her to sit down.

"Well, Em," he began, trying to manage a smile, "I've just returned from the doctor's office. I'll be going into the hospital this afternoon for another back operation tomorrow morning. I injured it seriously many years ago when I was in the military, and it's plagued me ever since. It's what drove me out of the service, actually. I was forced to take an early retirement. I don't know whether I told you, but I took a military pension at 50, went to library school for a year, and then took this job. I've had to curtail my ambition because of this back problem. I thought it was improving, but then a few months ago it began acting up. And now another operation. I'm told I'll be out for 8 or 10 weeks this time."

"I'm sorry to hear about this, Mr. Garschine," Tournquist said, in the gentlest and serenest of accents, "I'm sure everything will turn out all right."

Garschine smiled grimly in his fatigue, and muttered something about hoping she was right. Then he said: "I'll tell you why I've called you in. I want you to be in charge when I'm gone."

The statement startled Tournquist. She knew from her interview with him that she would be expected as reference librarian to fill in in his absence, but she hadn't expected to assume the responsibility quite so soon. Summoning up her most agreeable tones, she asked if it might not be wiser to ask someone whose experience far exceeded her own two weeks to substitute for him.

"No!" was his definitive answer; it was apparent he would brook no alternative suggestions. "Look," he said, observing that she had misgivings, "there's not that much to it. Ruth can take care of the day-to-day affairs. I just want you to be available to handle any emergencies that might come up."

The telephone rang. Garschine cupped his hand over the mouthpiece. Some muffled words. Tournquist stood up and signaled that she was prepared to leave. Garschine signaled her to stay. "My wife," he told her, pointing to the phone, "I'll just be a second." More muffled words. "I have to leave fairly soon," he said as he returned the receiver to its cradle, "so let's get down to business."

Tournquist realized that her only course was to accept the situation, so she thanked him for his confidence in her and sat down again.

The director then said: "As you know, we have a new president — Dr. Tai. She started in September, the same time as you. Well, she wants all departments to give her an annual report, and a statement of our goals and objectives, and our long-range plans — *in writing*. Old Langeford — God bless him! — didn't feel this was necessary and always found ways of circumventing the issue when some agency or body would request them. Don't ask me how he did it, but he did. What a man! As competent as anybody I ever encountered in the military. He got and went his own way at all times. Crafty! He wanted nothing to do with the straitjacket of guidelines and so-called standards; he wanted to be free to develop the school according to his specifications, not someone else's, and he wanted to be able to expand in any way he saw fit. He always got around accrediting agencies somehow. Anyway, those agencies leave a lot to be desired. Since they're composed of colleagues from other colleges, which of them is going to seriously fault a school when they know their own school might be visited by a team made up of people whose programs they criticized? Human nature is vindictive. Cross me up in some way and I'll find some way to get back at you. At best they rap people's knuckles. The accrediting process is ludicrous. Read some critical articles on it sometime. They're eye-opening."

He paused. A wistful look appeared in his eyes as he lingered over memories of President Langeford. "I guess Dr. Tai will be instituting some changes," he murmured, almost inaudibly.

Emily Tournquist hesitated whether to speak or not to speak. An expression of surprise and uneasiness came over her face as she argued with some wild thoughts in her own mind. What was she to make of his comments? Was this the time to present other points of view? And what about the assignments he's given her? What did she know about what they've done in the past — if that's the sort of thing that goes into annual reports? And what did she know about their goals and objectives? Why, she'd never heard them mentioned in regard to the Peckham library, and then Garschine had said the former president had obviated their need. And what about future plans? She still didn't know her way around the collection, let alone what will be happening five years hence....

Garschine must have sensed her thoughts, for he said, with doubtful reassurance, "Don't worry! Here's all I want you to do. I want you to investigate annual reports and tell me the kinds of thing that are usually included. The same for long-range plans and goals and objectives. I started working on a goals and objectives statement yesterday and was planning to finish it today, but ... well, you know why I can't. I'd like you to tell me what you think of it and finish it." He handed her a sheet of paper (Appendix II). She accepted it, and observed that he had stopped a sentence in the middle.

Then he made a remark that struck her as almost iconoclastic. "What purpose do these damn things serve anyway?"

The recent graduate had assumed they were a "given" — at least that's what she had been taught in library school. She looked at him quizzically as he pressed on. "I think goals and objectives statements are all interchangeable. They don't guide day-to-day behavior. Look at what I've come up with. It's so vague and general and all-purpose that you could superimpose it on another library's and no one would be the wiser. You'd just change the name of the college from Peckham to something else. Consultant reports are the same, too. They're exercises in futility, a waste of precious time. I defy anybody to tell me that each college has a different mission and an absolutely unique set of goals and objectives. They're all trying to accomplish the same things. I'll bet you find that out when you start investigating them."

Tournquist did not know what to say. But under his smug and even slightly amused gaze, she felt obligated to come up with something. "Won't we need a statement of this sort for the next college accreditation visit?" she ventured, on a new track.

"That brings up another point," he responded. "The school'll be visited early next spring. We haven't been visited for nine years, the year before I came. I guess you better start preparing for that, too."

"Well, do we have anything from the last visit? — The report we must have had to prepare?" She put the feeler out cautiously.

"*It's* useless!" he fired back quickly. "There's nothing of value in it. Ask Ruth to dig it up for you. I've never been able to find what my predecessor must have submitted to the team that headed the college self-study. It's lost. Gone. I've looked for it a couple of times. All we have is what the college decided to include in the final report (Appendix III). I can't believe that's all they thought important to include, but Langeford must have known what he was doing. Anyway, look it over." He drummed on the desk. "Yes," he said absently, "you might as well start working on that. I'd like to be ahead of Tai on that one. Do the other assignments first and then tackle that one."

Tournquist made no remark.

"I guess you should locate the ALA's new standards for accreditation and tell me about the sort of self-study questions we should be preparing for the team of evaluators." He lowered the corner of his lips to indicate his opinion of accrediting evaluators.

She still made no remark. The secretary appeared at the door. "Dr. Tai's on the phone," she announced.

"Do you want me to leave?" Tournquist inquired politely.

The director shook his head from side to side.

"Good morning, L. Y.," he said cheerfully as he picked up the receiver.

Tournquist settled back in her chair, trying tactfully not to read any of the papers which littered his desk.

"Well, I guess I knew this would happen sooner or later," she heard him say. He leaned back in his chair.

There was a pause while he was listening. "The doctor says 8 or 10 weeks," were his next words. "Emily Tournquist. She's our new reference librarian.... T-O-U-R-N-Q-U-I-S-T. Emily.... I was just now asking her to do some preliminary work on them. She'll do the groundwork.... By October 29th? That gives us about six weeks. No problem.... Well, I'll have her mail what she puts together to me in two weeks.... No, no. It's all right. Really. I plan to get a lot of work done anyway. Like material selection. My secretary will be in touch with me every day, and she'll be dropping things off to me every two days or so.... No, really. I want it this way. Do you think I'm going to start watching soap operas!.... We'll meet that deadline. Don't worry.... This will be good training for our new reference librarian.... She started with us two weeks ago.... It'll test her mettle!.... Do you have any format in mind? Any suggestions on how we should write them up?... Okay. We'll try to be creative!... We've anticipated you on that one! We're also getting ready for the self-study.... (He winked at Tournquist).... Thanks for calling.... At Prince of Peace Hospital.... That would be very nice.... I'm sure everything will be all right. Thanks for offering.... Thanks again. Bye."

He hung up the receiver. "You heard, Em? She said she'd leave it up to us as to how we present what she wants. She wants the reports by October 29th. I'd like you to give me the outlines by October 1st. That gives you two weeks. I'll need the rest of the time to fill in any gaps with specifics. I'm glad we had talked about the self-study!"

"I don't want you to worry, Mr. Garschine," offered the reference librarian, trying to muster up a confident air. "I'll get right on this and get what I come up with to you in two weeks."

"You're sure you know what to do?"

"I'm sure," she replied, with a confidence still slightly feigned.

"You'll have to do all this as an overlap activity while you're at the reference desk, you realize. But get one of the other professionals to spell you as much as possible. Now don't forget, you don't have to know about this library. You're going to find out what goes into college library annual reports. The same thing for goals and objectives – what do they consist of? And long-range plans. And tell us what we'll need to know to get ready for accreditation. Got it straight?"

Emily Tournquist said yes, and rising to leave indicated that one of the first things she intended to do was call a meeting of the staff to see if they had any ideas and if they could help.

Apparently, the director had not expected such a statement. He stared coldly at her for a moment, then spat out: "Bah! You're in charge. It's up to you to see that things are done."

"I thought I might take advantage of their experience," she defended herself, somewhat nervous and abashed by his formidable stare.

"You're in charge," Garschine repeated without comprehending.

"Yes, but I believe in involving people in matters that affect them," Tournquist tried diplomatically to explain.

"Look!" he growled angrily. "I don't hold with all this participation stuff. To me it's just abdication. No one's ever been able to convince me that participatory management works. All that stuff about working in groups. It takes too much time, and most people don't have anything to contribute anyway. I've seen people clamor for a say, and when it's given to them they don't take it."

Then a pause occurred, very brief but uncomfortable, while Garschine inspected her curiously. She resumed her seat.

"Since we're on the topic," he sighed, massaging his temples, "let me share a few other thoughts with you. Behavioral scientists have fallen into the error of assuming that employees resent job structuring and autocratic leadership, and that if they're given a high degree of freedom they'll be stimulated to improve their work and their morale will improve. That simply doesn't jibe with sociological and psychological facts. Most people want — and need — an idealized father figure as a leader. I accept the world and people as they are and don't have any rosy, unrealistic assumptions about human beings in organizations. I question whether people are naturally good and capable of disciplining themselves. The only way to be a good administrator is to be born a good administrator."

Tournquist hesitated before she asked:

"You don't think that leadership skills can be learned from a book or taught in the classroom?"

Garschine flinched as if he had been hit. "Right!" he shot back forcefully. "Books on management and management training programs and courses are largely a waste of time and money. I refuse to accept the notion that employees can pick up skills and change their attitudes and values by formal training. In fact, I would go so far as to say that people do not change. After some sort of formal training, they flaunt the so-called basic rules of management, but if they don't have true leadership qualities they're simply hacks as managers. Their basic nature has too strong a hold on them and they remain basically the same. You can't alter people's knee-jerk reactions to stimuli. Do you realize that a 22 year old has lived 180,000 hours of life, and that a 44 year old has lived 360,000 hours of life, and so on. Are you trying to tell me that the exposure of an hour or 2 to a book, or even 20 hours as in a course, is going to significantly alter the ways of thinking and doing of a lifetime? C'mon, Em! That's not realistic."

He broke off and looked at her, as if to indicate that the balloon of her argument had suddenly had a pin stuck in it, and was expiring with a hiss. His words rolled out with no effort, which meant to her that he had worn them smooth from constant turning in his mind; they were rote-familiar. She wanted to say: "Your mind has stagnated. Make it fluid again. If the muscles of our brains receive daily exercise, they become different. If you make a conscious volitional effort to change, you *can* change." But she could not bring herself to do so. She said, rather, "I've seen a study that indicated that decision-making groups make a more accurate assessment of a problem, which results in a solution superior to that formulated through individual effort. The group has access to more extensive resources than a single person. The polling of individual judgments often eliminates random error, and the group will come up with more diversified alternatives to consider. Someone's off-the-cuff idea may be the clue that will tap another's thought and lead to a successful solution. The conditions must be right, though. People must be made to feel that they and their ideas count."

Her listener, vaguely stroking his chin, mused a moment upon this; then he said, almost as if he had not heard:

"All successful managers are autocratic to some degree. Give me some examples of leaders who practiced democratic-participative leadership and kept their organizations afloat. It can't be done. Even the much-touted Douglas McGregor, the guru of the collaborative decision-making set, said there is much evidence to support the claim that communication aimed at changing people is effective only to a slight degree."

All at once Tournquist's vision narrowed and she saw everything as if it were happening in a small room far away, or as if she were looking at it through the wrong end of a telescope. She sat there, saturated in depression, as if she had lost her faith. Participative management was part of her religion, beyond and above argument. Was everything she learned for naught? She felt extinguished. Blotted out, scattered, lost. Her impulse was to rush out of the office. But no! She had, suddenly, a new feeling, like a tardy response to the stimulus of an unfamiliar drug. He was drumming on his desk with exasperated fingers, his mouth quirked at the corners, as if saying: "Wriggle out of that!" She was determined that she would do her best to wriggle out from under the dunce cap he was trying to place on her. She wanted to say: "You are a conceited, obstinate, inflexible, manipulative, pompous, close-minded, insensitive, abrasive, opinionated platitudinous oaf!" But the words were frozen on her tongue. Instead she substituted: "So all you need to be a good manager then is to select the right parents." She waited like Saint Sebastian for the arrows to begin piercing her. Sure enough they came. His face turned unnaturally red, as if his blood pressure had risen.

"Listen!" he growled, in a tone so dry, sarcastic and acrid that not another word was needed to indicate that he was not about to be upstaged by a 24 year old. "I've been around a long time, much longer than you, and I've learned a great deal that is not found in management textbooks. I've witnessed management problems compounded over and over by the suggestions and theories of behavioral scientists. What I've learned I've learned by trial and error and not out of some book or from some course. The negativism we've seen in recent years toward autocratic managers has been nurtured by the literature of the participative-democratic exponents. This presumptuous and naive literature is making it harder and harder for managers to do their jobs. They have to keep contending with young whippersnappers who would rather make a country-club out of their organizations than work. Managers have to keep worrying about the poor darlings' feelings, and sensitivities, and delicate egos. They all have persecution complexes."

She was completely composed now, caution quite gone. She wanted to say: "The trouble with you is that nobody can tell you anything. All truth is contained in the compass of your mind. Open your mind and let the world in." But what came out was: "Are you saying that books and courses that encourage wholesome questioning and explore wider circles of experience have nothing of value to say to us? That we should put up a "No Admittance" sign to ideas that don't comport with our simple worlds of stereotyped images? That's to deny the influence of education."

He took her meaning. "I suppose in an indirect way you're trying to tell me something, and if I had more time I'd pursue it with you more fully. Well, let me tell you this before I leave. From my experience, most people have only limited management potential. Oh, I've experimented with other approaches from time to time. But I've always found that if I sent a decision down the hierarchy ladder, it almost always came back up for a final decision. I subscribe to Hobbes' view of people rather than Rousseau's. From my observations, most employees are inherently fearful and immature. Like little children they're selfish, demanding, and dependent. They have strong needs for security above all, and need forceful authority to gratify their needs to be submissive. You haven't been around the working world long enough to realize this. I'd like to be able to talk with you in 40 or so years to see how you feel then."

"The ultimate put-down," Tournquist thought of saying. "To label me ignorant because I'm young. Where youth and age meet, not where they differ, wisdom lies. I hope when I'm your age I'm not wrapped up in a kind of finality of self-congratulation. I hope I will not have reached a final stage of thinking, something that I'll call 'the truth,' to which nothing can be added. To feel that one has reached a stage as final as that means that the mind has stopped work. It has closed up shop and turned out the light. I hope there'll be air and space in my mind, and that people won't have to gasp for breath when they talk with me." But she opted instead for: "If people want regimentation which relieves them of responsibility, how then do you explain parents reaching out for control of schools, disdaining the help of experts. Students themselves want an influence in what and how they are taught. Consumer resentment against insensitive product design contains an element of the drive toward greater participation. Submission of political questions to voter referendums is another example. Even today's military reality is different from the almost total subservience that was expected of those who served in the past. How do you explain these things if all people want is to be submissive and relieved of responsibility?" Her tongue was unloosed now, and she gazed at him questioningly, piercingly.

"Good grief!" he cried, catching sight of the clock. "11:30! I've got to go. We can pick up this discussion some other time, after you've armed yourself with ammunition! I'll give you one more thing to think about though. If people aren't submissive, why do they take all sorts of nonsense from their bosses? That's all I want to say right now."

He rose. Apparently the discussion was over. In a sense she was relieved, because, while she thought that she had acquitted herself reasonably well, she wanted next time to be better prepared. He extended his hand and added: "I have some tidying up here to do before I leave in a few minutes. We'll get back to this topic. Believe me!"

She rose, took his hand, wished him well, and quitted the room.

As she stood by the secretary's desk waiting for her to terminate a telephone call, she continued to wonder why he has asked her to take his place and to do these assignments. There were several librarians who had been around longer and who knew more.

When the secretary finished the call, she said that she would be glad to help in any way possible. This was good to know, because she had been around quite a while and was familiar with much of the director's work. Tournquist asked her for the library's portion of the college's self-study and to notify each member of the staff about the meeting she was calling for 2:00 that afternoon. She then walked slowly and thoughtfully back to the reference desk.

The anxiety she felt about appearing before the staff soon disappeared. Everyone expressed concern over the director's operation; and they seemed neither surprised nor jealous that she was appointed acting director. She outlined the tasks she had been assigned and mentioned that if any emergencies came up she was the person to bring them to. There was no discussion, only expressions of commiseration for her and wishes of good luck. When the meeting finished, she informed them that she would be calling on them periodically. To a person, they said they would be glad to respond, but other than that they had little to offer. The professionals said they would staff the reference desk for her when she needed them.

From this encounter and subsequent discussions with individual staff members, she came to realize that the course of this meeting did not vary appreciably from those Garschine usually held. The librarians were not accustomed to meetings in which any significant decisions were made. At the rare meeting called by the director, announcements were usually made by him and insignificant items discussed. He always made important policy and procedural decisions without consulting them. She was soon to realize that while the secretary knew what was to be done, she, too, had never been permitted to take care of other than routine matters. No one on the staff was accustomed to accepting responsibility or making decisions without clearing every detail with Garschine.

As she sat alone in the staff lounge at the end of her exhausting day, she reflected grimly that she was on her own as far as the assignments were concerned. She looked incredulously at the single photocopied page from the last self-study report. Garschine was right: it was of no use.

She lolled far back in the couch and stretched out her legs. A shaft of yellow sunshine fell across the carpet. She attempted to define to herself the thoughts that lay half-formed in the depth of her mind. How was she going to deal with R. Boyce Garschine? She, who believed in and attempted to practice a participatory form of management? Was she, too, destined to become as docile and obedient as the other staff members appeared to be? Must subordinates always adapt *their* personalities and behavior to their supervisors' styles? Is there to be no give on the part of supervisors? She actually had an impulse to go and tell the staff to cast off their chains; she did not, however, yield to it. The blame was not theirs that they were so lacking in gumption, was it? The blame could be laid squarely at the feet of R. Boyce Garschine. Heavy was the account she had against him. And yet, his methods worked! That was the irony. Her reason admitted the force of his arguments, but her instinct opposed it. No one complained about the library from the outside, and the staff went merrily about its business, apparently content. Ah! but were they? There was the rub. How would she find out? How could she involve them more? How could she change their attitudes? If she remained quiescent, business would revolve as usual, forever. The audacity of what she had done struck her now with overpowering force. She, crusading light, had made a move against him, entrenched darkness. She must be prepared to buttress her claims that people want more say, and that power is becoming more widely dispersed. She must try to convince him that no single individual, no matter how gifted, can any longer grasp the innumerable facets of modern corporate effort. She must try to convince him that we have come to an era where management is a group effort, involving group direction, group initiative, and group responsibility. But how? Like all narrow-minded people, he dwelt contentedly in the absolute belief of being right. The self-satisfied expression on his face was a proof of his certitude. He was never disturbed by doubts. How, then, could she move him from his authoritarian mode to where he could at least tolerate contributions and initiative from his subordinates? When Garschine says "Jump!" the staff merely says "How far?" Never "Why?" Or "Is there a better direction to jump in?" Who could help her? Rensis Likert? Chris Argyris? Harry Levinson? Carl Rogers? Where could she go to find ways of selling ideas so that he might welcome what she and the staff might propose? The literature of salesmanship? Psychology? Behavioral science? Why do people resist change? She remembered the psychological principle that no appeal to reason that is not also an appeal to a want can ever be effective. New ideas must be sufficiently tied to the old to be acceptable. When people do change, what do they change first — their attitudes or their behavior?

The light began to fail. Turning on a lamp next to the couch she continued the conversation with herself. She remembered how in *The Great God Brown* Eugene O'Neill has people wear masks to indicate when the "social" rather than the "real" person is speaking. When dealing with their bosses, few subordinates enjoy the luxury of integrity. The dependence on bosses for recognition, rewards, and advancement breeds an artificiality of relationship, a need to be polite and agreeable. The consequences of alienating their bosses are frightening. In spite of their protestations to the contrary, most bosses prefer subordinates whom they get along with, who support them, who make them feel that what they are doing is right, who have no criticism, who oblige happily when asked to undertake tasks, who cause them no anxiety, who quietly accept their decisions, who praise them. But does that mean total subservience? She could not bring herself to answer yes. She yawned, stretched herself, and allowed her gaze to wander around the room. Everything was real, unchanged.

She sat a long time on the couch, confused, questioning, pushing her thoughts into new latitudes. Her ideas were inchoate just now, but she would be ready for R. Boyce Garschine when he returned! By George, she would be!

APPENDIX I

PECKHAM COLLEGE LIBRARY
ORGANIZATION CHART

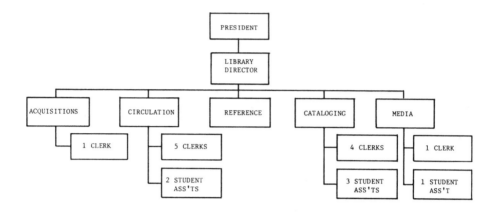

APPENDIX II

PECKHAM COLLEGE LIBRARY
GOALS AND OBJECTIVES

MISSION

The mission of Peckham College Library is to provide access to recorded knowledge consistent with present and anticipated instructional, research, and public service responsibilities of the college and to share those resources, insofar as possible, with those outside the college community.

OBJECTIVES

To select and acquire those informational materials most needed to support the instructional, research, and public service goals of the college.

To make available to Peckham College Library users those information resources required, whether from the immediate collection or through interlibrary loan or other forms of interlibrary cooperation.

To maintain materials contained in Peckham College Library in good physical condition.

To house the collection in facilities that expedite access to the collection materials and that safeguard their preservation and ensure their security.

To provide services to the user which promote utilization and understanding of the library's resources.

To develop and engage in constructive efforts to share effectively information resources with other libraries and to develop mutually useful policies for collection development.

APPENDIX II (cont'd)

To organize all materials acquired according to national bibliographic standards and in such manner as to facilitate patron access.

To develop and maintain constructive relationships with faculty, students and other members of the college to help assure development of

APPENDIX III

REFERENCE TO THE LIBRARY IN PECKHAM'S SELF-STUDY REPORT

2.14

interim basis. A faculty committee is reviewing the original purposes of the Career Planning and Counseling Center in anticipation of the resumption of a full-time program later this year.

IX. FACILITIES

During the past ten years, a major addition to the academic plant occurred with the construction of Dora Pratt Hall. It provided much-needed office and classroom space and relieved the intolerable pressure for space in the existing facilities, which also underwent extensive remodeling. The science laboratories have been re-equipped with the most advanced technological devices, and new language laboratory equipment has been installed.

Growth of Library Services. During the decade, library holdings have increased as follows:

	Ten Years Ago	*Present*
Volumes	114,970	128,760
Periodicals received	498	544
Films and slides	202	1,670
Filmstrips	158	274
Microfilms	488	678
Microcards	xx	340
Phonograph records	876	1,121

Dormitory Space. One additional residence hall was constructed during this period--Cockburn Hall, with a capacity for 150 students. This structure has consumed the remaining available space on campus.

APPENDIX IV

ENTRY FOR PECKHAM COLLEGE LIBRARY IN
THE AMERICAN LIBRARY DIRECTORY

C PECKHAM COLLEGE, Gifford Library, 116 Bruce St.
Founded 1922, Enr 1,600; Fac 98; Highest degree: Master's
Dir Boyce Garschine; *Tech Servs* Bernice Mayer; *Cir* Albert Croyden; *Ref*
Hannah Varga; *Cat* Daniel Egan; *Media* Alice Goodwillie. Staff 23 (prof 6,
cler 11, student assts 6) Inc $299,972 (inc fed $7890). Exp $103,816, Bks
$48,376, Per $39,852, Bd $6890, Micro $4826, AV $3872; Sal $196,111
(prof $109,750, cler $63,874, student assts $22,487) Bk titles 103,600, vols
199,680; Per sub 698, vols bd 16,000, micro 2973. Micro Hldgs: Fiche 450,
Ultrafiche 210, Reels 2056. AV: Rec, A-Tapes, V-Tapes, Flm, Fs, Slides,
Ov tr. VF 12.
Special subjects: Art, music, relig, soc & behv sci
Special collections: Women; 20th Century American Wit & Humor

2

GREASED LIGHTNING

The hallway outside the library at Technicomm, Inc. grew noisier as the coffee-break lines snaked out of the cafeteria. Mary Ann Hawthorne hated to close the door, fearing people would assume the library was not open, but she had no choice. Back at her desk, she turned again to the report she had written. It was an outline of the progress she had made in her brief six months with the computer components manufacturing firm. When Forrest R. Jay, head of New Product Engineering, and W. Lane Patterson, vice-president of Engineering, his boss, had interviewed her for the position, it was clear that neither man had any idea of what to expect of a professional librarian. All they were looking for was someone to take responsibility for the small collection of old journals, books, and reports the Engineering Division had accumulated over the years. Jay's secretary had started to organize the small, 11x10-foot room, but it soon became too much for her to handle along with her other duties. Her sister-in-law worked as a school librarian, and so she convinced Jay to hire a professional to do the job.

Some of Hawthorne's friends from library school thought she was making a mistake taking what seemed to be a "dead-end" job. But she considered it a challenge: she saw a lot of potential for starting a full range of library services within the company. During her interview she had talked animatedly about the wonderful things she foresaw happening with the library at Technicomm, Inc. As a matter of fact, she was certain it was her enthusiasm that won her the job, since she had no previous professional experience. She was convinced that passionate faith could move mountainous executives. And she was grateful: there were not many library jobs in the outlying suburb where she lived, and the job at Technicomm, Inc. paid very well.

Still, the young librarian sometimes wondered if she had made a wise choice. The first few months proved to be a difficult transition from school. There had been no problems organizing the collection of "hand-me-down" materials; it was small enough that within a few weeks she had every item cataloged and labeled; but she felt it just wasn't a library — it was more a stagnant collection of potentially useful information that no one seemed to use very often.

Mary Ann Hawthorne thought perhaps the problem was that she was not being taken seriously. Most of the engineers in her department had no idea she had a master's level education, or that she was anything other than a file clerk hired to give some sort of order to the room. As she tried to figure out how to change her and the library's image, she made some interesting observations. She noticed that the secretaries and other "non-professional" employees tended to take their coffee breaks or lunches together, and at slightly different times than the "professional" staff and executives. She also noticed that the relative status of an employee was often predictable by the way that person dressed. So she dipped into her meagre savings and bought herself a suit, a blazer, and a couple of conservative shirtdresses. She re-arranged her schedule so that she appeared in the cafeteria during all the different groups' coffee-breaks and lunches — professionals, secretaries, salespeople, maintenance personnel.

One of the immediate results was that she struck up a friendship with Jeffrey Gordon, a young consultant assigned to the R&D section. Rumor had it that he was being wooed by Technicomm, Inc. for an unspecified executive position, and that he was giving the matter serious thought.

During his relatively brief career as a corporate tactician, Jeff Gordon, a lanky 32-year-old who retains a touch of the "aw shucks" manner of his native southland, has chalked up some substantial achievements. A voluble talker, he is known as a person with a large talent and a large ego. Everywhere he has gone he has undertaken ambitious reorganizations, and has rescued many a company from the jaws of disaster. He boasts that he has never left a company that has not continued to do well after he's gone. He is quick to spot "deadwood" among chief administrative officers, and has no qualms about recommending whose "head should roll." But when he believes in a person and what he or she is attempting to accomplish, he is noticeably aggressive on that person's behalf. He invariably gets his way.

Gordon quickly perceived that Hawthorne did not fully appreciate the significance of everything she saw, and he offered to help by explaining some of the finer points of corporate politics. At first the neophytic librarian was mildly shocked by his revelations, and sometimes her heart gave a jump when he described some of the bitter struggles that went on constantly between individuals or departments. But soon she began to accept the rivalries and competitiveness as standard fixtures of business life.

She did stir uneasily however when one day he exhorted her to be careful whom she was seen with, and when he advised her to remember that in her new and different setting people who fail to observe unwritten rules of acceptable behavior are in some people's eyes expendable. He could not or would not particularize. He had told her this in the library. But what was he trying to convey? A book lay open on her desk; but she could not follow the sense of a single line. She must try to divine his message. She was exceedingly perturbed. Wherein had she erred? Try as she might she could think of nothing. Was it because she took coffee with "nonprofessionals?" Surely not! But it was all she could come up with. She would at least consider his warnings. Hitherto she had been stringing along with the notion that honesty and hard work were all that were needed to achieve success. But now she was beginning to wonder if there was any truth to the old adage that "It's not what you know, but who you know." She became an arena where all the confusions of which a human being is capable began to struggle. Must she fortify herself with an arsenal of stratagems in order to survive? Must she henceforward associate only with the "right" people? Must she become a master at the art of corporate gamesmanship? The word reminded her of a book by that or some similar title which she had seen advertised some years ago. Was it gamesman? Yes, she thought so. Yes, *that* was the title — "The Gamesman." Perhaps she would be well advised to consult it and others of its ilk to see if she could learn something about surviving in the corporate world. That way she would at least understand what motivated the different types of boss she was likely to encounter. (When she confronted Jeff Gordon with his cryptic disclosure one day at lunch, she learned that Forrest Jay had a grievance against her because she socialized with mortals who were not "professional." It was not *de rigueur.* Shades of the professional/nonprofessional debates of the introductory course at library school! But she was experiencing it!)

Twilight was deepening. Suddenly a yawn surprised her and recalled her to the existence of her body. "Time to wrap it up," she said to herself.

Jeff Gordon took an active interest in the library. He had worked at several companies where well-established libraries were an integral part of the company's operations. He began feeding her reference questions and bibliographic research; he also told his co-workers how dedicated and skilled the librarian was.

At the same time, Hawthorne came up with the idea of a newsletter to announce her presence and to more or less advertise her services. And it did attract attention. Heads started appearing in the doorway, muttering, "Oh! So this is the library." A few asked for novels or popular magazines. But the biggest impact was felt when boxes appeared, sometimes anonymously, filled with old books and magazines—mostly valueless. It seemed that as people cleaned out their offices to make more room, they were shipping their "surplusses" down to Mary Ann Hawthorne for her library. She welcomed the attention, but the inundation became a problem. Occasionally, someone would drop by and ask if she was using their material and where she had shelved it. And a few even requested tax deduction statements for income tax purposes, which requests she politely denied. But that was it: she would need a selection policy statement; it was the only way she could protect herself from the possibility of alienating the very people with whom she was trying to ingratiate herself. The statement became a top priority item.

Forrest Jay had not been down to the library for weeks. He had been wrapped up in a new project that was closely tied to the company's new growth. He came at Hawthorne's urging, but he seemed preoccupied with grave and heavy matters. Did it have anything to do with the fact that three of his engineers had been summarily terminated? Jeff Gordon had apprised her of this fact at coffee yesterday. Yet, he came.

Looking at the foot-thick carpet of serried and disordered books everywhere on the floor, he agreed that the library was outgrowing its accommodations. "I'm not sure what to tell you, Mary Ann," he said. "There just isn't any extra space to be had right now."

"I know Mr. Jay," she replied tactfully. "I'm not asking for any special favors. But the point is that people are finally starting to look at me as a librarian, and to this place as a library. If we don't get more room for the library and a decent collection, it will go back to being nothing. A lot of people are going to be disappointed."

Forrest Jay thought hard for a few moments. She was right; she had started something with her newsletter. To pull back now would make both her and him look bad.

"Well, if you can be patient," he said at length, "I'll see what I can do. Maybe we can get some space. But it will have to be justified." He halted and after a reflective pause added: "Tell you what. Write me a report of what you've done here so far, showing why you need more room. I'll see if I can swing it past Patterson at the next forecast meeting."

"Does that mean I might get a budget?" She bent her head towards him, looking into his face with a sort of eager expectation. She had become increasingly dissatisfied with the lack of a distinct budget for the library. She could only buy new materials if they were specifically requested for project-related support, and only for Engineering staff. Every purchase was carefully scrutinized by Jay or someone on his staff—she knew not by whom. When approval was granted, the material was forwarded by the supplier to her, but it quickly became the property of the engineers, who seldom returned it. In truth, she was little more than an order clerk when it came to building a collection.

Forrest Jay brushed aside her question with a wave of his hand. "I don't know. I've got to go now. We'll talk about it after you send me that report."

That was six weeks ago.

Hawthorne wrote the report and had it in Jay's mailbox within two weeks; but he had become busier and busier with that new project, delaying their meeting more and more. She suspected he hadn't even read it in time for the forecast meeting last week. But this morning his secretary called to tell her to be in Jay's office at eleven-thirty.

The librarian established herself in the large leather chair opposite Jay's huge mahogany desk. The small, fiftyish man looked tired and slightly worried as he scanned the folder that contained her report. Then he folded his hands and looked up at her. His anxious face broke as if by the loosing of a spell into a captivating smile.

"Well!" he began with pleasant satisfaction. "You certainly have been working hard. I have to apologize for taking so long to get back to you, but things have been pretty hectic. I guess I've been out of touch. I didn't realize how much you've accomplished in your six months here. You've been doing a great job. Did I tell you how pleased Mr. Patterson was with your little newsletter? Everyone was impressed."

She smiled charmingly upon him. There were moments when he could be almost affectionate, moments when his thoughts did not seen to be turned inward upon his own anxious solicitudes. She had a distant fleeting vision of a workplace in which people acted like free and sensible human beings, instead of like the martyrized and victimized puppets of a terrible system called "one-upmanship." How agreeable life could be if only people would stop mistrusting each other and learn to work for the common good instead of for their own personal aggrandizement. If only every chair could be a throne and hold a king or a queen....

He was waiting for her to say something.

"Thank you," she said, blushing slightly. "Yes, the newsletter did get a good response." ("But for what reason could he have employed the word 'little' to describe it?" she mused.) "As you've read," she went on aloud, "I've had strong indications from several departments that there is a definite need for a Corporate Library Service here. As a matter of fact, since I wrote the report I've had several more instances of good requests coming into the library: Marketing wanted financial figures on our top competitors; Accounting called for information on local college programs; and R&D had a few international patents that had to be tracked down. But do you know what?" She stopped and scrutinized his eyes with a faint apprehension. "I couldn't help them. I could not answer a single question because I don't have the materials I need." She was on the verge of saying: "And you know why? Because all I have is a pile of useless junk which people have given to the library instead of throwing out." But she stayed her tongue, and said instead: "I don't have the materials I need to do the kind of work they want done, and nowhere to put them if I did. I feel foolish when the best I can do is refer them to another library."

She braced herself, afraid that from some obscure motive of propriety or self-protection he would turn on her.

But he merely wrinkled his face into a distressed frown. "I know," he said lamely. "I know you want to do the best job you can—not that you haven't all along. But you have to understand the facts of life around here. There are certain budgetary restrictions we must adhere to. I can't justify spending money for things that don't relate to Engineering functions."

"What if we got the other departments to pay for their own services and materials?" she parried, seeing a faint ray of hope in the idea.

Her interlocutor shook his head. "No. What you're suggesting takes the approval of all department heads. You're asking me to go to each vice-president and department head and ask him to rewrite his budget. There's no way I can do that. No, I'm afraid it's out of the question right now. Maybe next year. Yes, maybe next year." Then a slight, pleased smile passed again over his features. "That ties in nicely though with why I called you here in the first place. I have good news for you. I just found out that the mail room will be moving to the basement at the end of the week. They're packing up right now. If we move fast, we can grab the space for the library. I went to work on Patterson this morning, and he's given me until two this afternoon to let him know." Then, with an elfin smile: "You see, I haven't been entirely unconcerned!"

The dramatic swiftness of the revelation stunned her. She scorned the idea. The mail room was at the far end of the building, away from most of the departments she saw using the library. The floor was poured concrete, and the walls dirty and an unpleasant color. There was no window. She looked at him, raising her eyebrows, and trying to screw her lips into a formal smile. "Is that the best that can be done?"

"It's that or your present location," he responded with a bewildered, unsympathetic air. His smile had vanished.

"Do I have to decide right now?" She had been hoping some other department might be moving, one with more desirable space.

"Look, Mary Ann," he said with a note of hard resolve. "I'll give it to you straight. It's that or nothing. But if it'll make you feel better you can have until one o'clock to decide." He consulted his watch. "I don't have any more time to talk right now. Go down there and look it over. Try to picture it as a library. You may have to modify it a little. Come back after lunch and we'll firm it up." His quick sentences had the tone of entreaty.

Hawthorne gave an uneasy laugh, which was merely the outlet for her disappointment. "I know for a fact that it has to be modified, and more than a little," she said, grinning awkwardly. "It needs paint, carpeting. I'll need furniture...."

"Okay," he said, as if clinching the affair. "Here's what I want you to do. I want you to move in as soon as the room is empty, at the end of the week. Take the stuff out of your present location and pile it in a corner." He paused to respond to her lack of enthusiasm. "Look, you want to do this, don't you?" he coaxed her. She nodded uncertainly. He went on: "It's considerably better than what you have now. And you've been asking for more space almost since you arrived." Again she nodded. He resumed: "Well, then, one thing at a time. First, let's get you into the room. Then come up with a full proposal—floorplans, growth charts, costs—showing what you think we should have in the way of a core collection and facilities. You can plan the whole kit and caboodle. Right from the word go."

His secretary stuck her head into the room. "Mr. Patterson's on the phone," she announced.

Jay rested his hand on the receiver. "See you at one o'clock," he whispered to Hawthorne as she rose to leave. And then he put the instrument to his ear and said: "Yes, Lane."

The young librarian was immensely depressed as she pattered down the hall towards the mail room. She was trying not to be bitter, but she couldn't help feeling that Jay could be more supportive if he wanted to be. In her frustration, she almost missed Jeff Gordon, between whom and herself there now existed a feeling of unmistakable, frank friendship, as he passed her in the hall. She asked him if he had a few minutes to spare.

In the cafeteria, she disclosed to him what had happened at her meeting with Jay. "He says we'll discuss it further after lunch. But I don't see the point. He seems to have made up his mind that I'm moving to the mail room."

"What if you say no?"

"I don't know. He's not in a very cooperative mood. He hardly even talked about the report he told me to write to justify everything. I don't think he even bothered to show it to Patterson. But, still, he is getting me the room. Barely."

Gordon played with his french fries a moment.

"I probably shouldn't tell you this," he said confidentially, "but you'll find out sooner or later. In the meantime, it's strictly q.t. Jay's in trouble. That new project he's been busting himself and everyone else over is way behind schedule. He's been trying to cover up his tracks; those engineers who got axed were his scapegoats. But Patterson's getting fed up. He's got R&D working on it right now, and he hired some new people to start next week to help bail out the situation. As a matter of fact, I wouldn't be surprised if you're getting the mail room next week so your office can be used by one of the new guys."

"Then he really could care less about the library. And that little bit about writing a full proposal was just another delay."

"I don't know if I'd go so far as to say that. But he's definitely in no position of strength right now. Anyway, things should clear up in a couple of weeks. But if I were you I'd take the mail room, and I'd prepare the best darn presentation possible for a library in that space. I'd detail everything I felt the library should have—*everything*! I'd shoot for the works—furniture, collection, painting, carpeting, you name it—and I'd hang the expense. But I'd give costs. It could be that someone else would be more sympathetic and persuasive with the chief honchos. That's all I can say right now."

He winked at her as he stood up. "I've got to get going. Patterson has called a big pow-wow for this afternoon. Good luck!"

Hawthorne sat alone at her table, mulling over Gordon's remarks.

"He's going to replace Forrest Jay!" shouted she to herself. The idea came to her in a flash like greased lightning. She could scarcely contain her excitement. "Yes, sir, I'll do it!" Her brain was activated by a thousand possibilities as she carried her dirty dishes over to the window—"the perfect library, a selection policy statement ... WOW!"

APPENDIX I

ENTRY FOR TECHNICOMM, INC. IN
KLOP'S DIRECTORY OF CORPORATIONS

page 1073

TECHNICOMM, INC., P.O. Box 385, Kleesdale
President: James B. Pierce
Chairman of the Board: Warren F. Adler, Jr.
Vice President of Administration: Arthur S. Chandler
Vice President of Sales and Marketing: William Kopacheck
Vice President of Engineering: W. Lane Patterson

Founded: 1968
Manufacturer of computer components for telecommunications, including specialized communications terminals
Annual Sales: $57 million
Sales offices located throughout the U.S. and Canada, as well as Europe and Japan
Headquarters location employs 1050

APPENDIX II

MAIL ROOM FLOOR PLAN

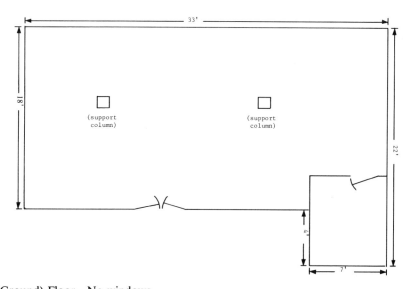

1st (Ground) Floor—No windows
Walls—Cinderblock
Floors—Poured Concrete
Ceiling Height—8½' (suspension-acoustic tiles)
Lighting—Recessed Fluorescent (excellent)

APPENDIX III

ORGANIZATION CHART

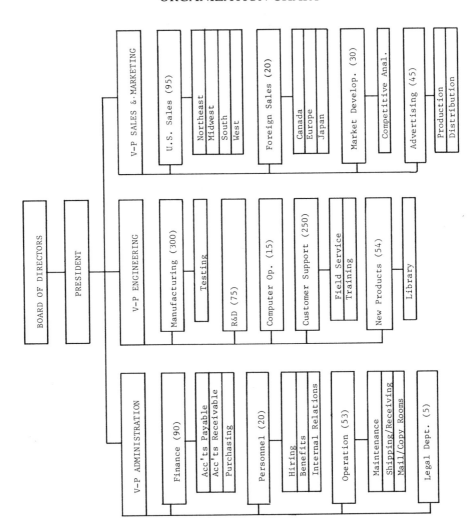

3

THE RED CARNATION

Today, with its population of almost 80,000, Wexler bears little resemblance to the roaring lumber center it became in the middle decades of the nineteenth century. It was hacked out of the wilderness by Caleb and Ephram Wexler, and for many years it stood alone in the forest, a halting place in the long stagecoach journey from eastern localities to the unknown West. News of boundless timber reserves spread, and before long lumberjacks from the thinning hardwood forests of New England swarmed into the uncharted area with no other possessions than their axes and brawn and the clothing they wore.

Soon the hills began to echo with the thud of the woodsman's ax. The forest wall receded. A sawmill was erected. And then another. And another. Here came every sort of human ingredient—sturdy homesteaders, skilled craftsmen, precious scoundrels. Here, too, came succeeding armies of immigrants—from Scandinavia, Poland, Germany, Italy, Russia, the Netherlands—drawn by the promise of a better life.

The town grew swiftly and without direction. And when, finally, the heavily timbered ranges had been pillaged almost beyond repair, many lumbermen pulled stakes and pushed westward. Others remained and revived the stripped acres with hand-reared trees, or turned to dairying. Whereas, before, the land was dense with stately white pines, now apple, plum, pear, peach, and cherry orchards stood in regimented rows. Cattle grazed peacefully.

And so, from its hardscrabble beginnings to immediate time, Wexler has lead a varied existence, changing from milltown to shipping point for fruit, and from resting place for travelers to dairy center. Now a thriving industrial city, it covers 40 square miles, has a population of 78,808, gives employment to 30,500 workers, and distributes an annual payroll of $640.6 million.

Unmindful of the epic moves that made it what it is today, Elwood Bibeau fastened his seat belt as his plane approached the Wexler airport. He was to be picked up by the secretary of the board of trustees, who would be wearing a blue blazer and a red carnation boutonniere.

A native of the Southwest and the assistant director of a public library serving a population of 40,000, Bibeau had not visited this part of the country before. He had consulted a map to find the location of Wexler, and had familiarized himself with the library by consulting the *American Library Directory* (Appendix I), but that was all he knew. He was coming to Wexler to be interviewed for the position of director of the city's public library—the Halvorsen Memorial Library. The incumbent director, who had held the position for 28 years, planned to retire as soon as the board found a suitable replacement.

He was to learn something of the history of the city from the secretary as they drove from the airport to the Three Willows Golf and Country Club, where he was to dine with four members of the board and the president of the "Friends of the Library" group. At dinner, he was to learn several other things as well, to wit: that the city was incorporated in 1901; that the Council-Manager form of government was adopted in 1919; that the board of trustees consists of nine elected members, who serve three-year terms with a turnover of three members per year; that the "Friends" group is very active; that the trustees had had a "phenomenal" response to their ad; that he was one of three people being brought in at the trustees' expense for an initial and then a second interview; that they had been very impressed by his credentials; and that no one from the Halvorsen staff had applied for the position.

As he and the secretary made their way along from the country club on the outskirts of the city to the library, where the interview with the entire board was to occur, Bibeau noticed that the streets were unusually broad and that century-old houses mingled on surprisingly good terms with modern bungalows and new apartment buildings. He commented on how attractive the city was.

The secretary admitted with a twinkling smile that they were passing through one of the most exclusive residential sections—the fashionable Silver Hills area—occupied by the more prosperous elements of the community. He went on to explain that while there were no unsightly slums, there was a fairly large district of rather nondescript homes intermingled with plain two- and three-family brick and frame dwellings, principally in the eastern reaches of the city. He added that in the early days of the city's development, the different ethnic groups had clustered in well-defined colonies, but that with the passage of time these cantonments have become blurred; the groups continue, however, to keep alive their heritages through festivals and cultural activities.

The secretary pointed out that all main approaches to the city lead to the courthouse square, the hub of the city's business district. Here, within an eight-block radius were the principal businesses, stores, and municipal buildings. Told to look to his immediate right, Bibeau saw a two-story marble structure, suggestive of an Italian palace. A sign on the lawn read: "Halvorsen Memorial Library," and gave the hours as "9 to 9 Monday through Friday," and "9 to 5 Saturday." "So here's where I may spend the next several years of my life," Bibeau mused.

On entering the parking lot behind the building, the secretary informed him that the library, which had been the Halvorsen residence, was bequeathed to the community in 1917 by Anna Lucciola Halvorsen as a memorial to her husband. In addition to contributing $20,000 for remodeling (it was considerably modernized in 1959), she established a $25,000 endowment fund. Lester J. V. Halvorsen, a Swedish immigrant who made a fortune in lumber, built the mansion for his Italian bride. The library opened its doors to the public in 1921. It is now one of 29 members of the Weymouth Pines Federated Library System.

After a quick tour of the facilities and after meeting a few staff members, Bibeau was ushered into the "Board Room," where he was introduced to the other remaining trustees. As the nearly hour long interview drew to a close, during which time they had roamed freely over an enormous range of topics, much of it in the vein of small-talk, Faith L. DeSmedt, chairwoman of the board, told Bibeau that as part of the screening process the trustees had decided to ask those who had successfully survived the initial winnowing—the three people being interviewed—to furnish them with tangible evidence of how they might perform on a specific assignment. She hastened to add that the trustees considered the choice of director to be one of their most important duties, further remarking that they were scrupulously committed to the clear demarcation of duties: the board establishes policy and the library director carries them out.

"What we would like you to do," she remarked, by way of commencing, "is to tell us in writing how you would undertake a community survey and a needs assessment survey."

Bibeau had his coffee-cup close to his face. At these words of Faith DeSmedt he gulped loudly, spilling his coffee recklessly, and then said, in a sporting tone: "Right now!"

Everyone laughed. "We'll give you 15 minutes!" the chairwoman said merrily. "No, really, here's what we have in mind. We've prepared a description of Wexler (Appendix II) on which we've assembled some information about the town—the number of schools, churches, recreational facilities, special events. Things like that. Please accept our apologies for it, but we didn't really know what sort of information to compile. What we'd like you to do is tell us how you would get to know the community. We'd expect our new director to be able to do this. He or she should be knowledgeable enough that we wouldn't need a consultant, whom I understand are engaged for that purpose."

"We've been thinking of doing this for some time," another trustee interjected, "and then when the present director announced that she would be retiring we saw it as an ideal time. It would give the new person an opportunity to learn about the community, and us an opportunity to review our services and see what we might do that we're not now doing."

Bibeau listened intensively. He was fascinated.

"Permit me to backtrack a bit and tell you how we've been approaching the business of selecting a new director." It was the chairwoman's voice. Bibeau glanced in her direction. "We studied the resumes of our applicants carefully, and sifted from them three people we're interested in. You're one of the three, of course. The resumes gave us the educational credentials and previous work records. We've paid careful attention to references. We view this preliminary interview as a way of securing additional information about the applicant and transmitting information about us, the library, and the town, and what we're seeking for the second interview. These interviews give both of us—you and us—a 'feel' for how we might work together and get along."

The secretary then spoke. "There's no question," he said, "but that an individual's past performance is a good indicator of how he or she will perform in the future. However, success on a job is not just a function of personality and abilities but of personality and abilities in a given environment."

Bibeau made no reply, but the comment set him thinking. He gulped down the last of his coffee.

"That's why we'd like you to address yourself to one of *our* problems," offered the chairwoman. Bibeau turned his head back to her, "the problem of getting to know the community."

"As you know," another trustee put in, "many companies are experimenting with putting their applicants through tests of various sorts—intelligence, aptitude, projective, sociometric, and such. Underlying each of these is some measurable advance prediction of how people will behave on the job. We're going to be experiencing a considerable turnover in staff in the next few months due to retirement. For instance, we'll be needing a new assistant director, a new technical services head, and a new reference librarian shortly after the new directed is hired—all professional positions. Then within the year we will need to replace the young adult librarian and several clerks. We want to avoid hiring people who won't succeed."

"Can you imagine everyone going at once like this," said the voice of another trustee mirthfully; and to Bibeau: "You'll have quite a bit of interviewing to do yourself, if you become director!"

"Sounds like it," exclaimed Elwood Bibeau, startled.

Another trustee spoke up. "Not one of us on the board has had to interview anyone for a library position," he said, "so we're novices at this!"

"That brings us to our next request," supplied the chairwoman. "We'd like you to outline for us what kinds of tests are available and would be desirable to use in our setting."

"More than that, Faith," said another. "We also need to know the kinds of questions we are legally restrained from asking."

"And the federal laws that apply," quickly added another.

"Well, that brings up another matter we had discussed among ourselves," DeSmedt said. "Are there selection evaluation forms we might be using?"

Said another timidly, nay, sheepishly: "You can see we need help, can't you Mr. Bibeau?"

Elwood Bibeau nodded and smiled weakly. (Somewhere within a voice was whispering, "You better believe it!")

The chairwoman resumed:

"Since we'll be requiring a new assistant shortly after you, I mean the new director"—she corrected herself—"is hired, we thought another useful assignment for our director applicants to undertake would be to identify the characteristics and qualities an assistant director in a line capacity should possess. And then, how can we determine whether applicants possess them—through the kinds of tests mentioned before? As I said earlier, we want to be as sure as we can be that the people we hire will succeed in their positions. There must be some acknowledged predictors to find out in advance."

A trustee who had not spoken before said: "Mr. Bibeau, our plan is to have the three contenders for the position, if I may use that expression, research these topics for us and then come back for a second interview and share their findings and thoughts with us."

Bibeau nodded comprehendingly. A person less confident than himself might have been astonished by their requests. But Elwood Bibeau quailed no more now than he had quailed at being assigned tasks in his present position as an assistant director. It is true that assignments were being heaped upon him with immense rapidity, but he would be able to sort them out and contrive solutions. It was not for nothing that he had learned to identify and isolate problems and to solve them.

"Let me see if I can state what we'd like you to do as succinctly as I can," the chairwoman was saying. "We'd like you to outline for us how you would go about undertaking a comprehensive community and needs assessment survey of Wexler—what you'd look at and study, and why. We'd also like to see how you'd involve the staff and us and the Friends—and any others you can think of. How would you distribute a questionnaire if you have one? And how would you tabulate the results? How would you work up a survey sample? Then, having done this, we'd like you to show how you would translate the information gathered to plan a library program or activity or service, using a hypothetical program, activity, or service, of course. How would you organize it? What would its goal be? What sort of timetable would you set up? Et cetera. This would be an opportunity for us to see how creatively you'd approach an assignment of this sort."

She stopped and looked hard into his eyes, as it were, appealing for approval. He greeted her look with a kindly smile which was entirely matter-of-fact — as though this assignment was just like any other assignment he had ever been given. Yes, he understood. No problem.

She went on:

"Then there's the whole question of the selection of a virtually new staff. We've narrowed that down to what you would look for in the case of an assistant director. How would you determine whether the person possesses those qualities or attributes? Would you use tests of some sort? What kinds are there? Are there questions employers are legally prohibited from asking? What major federal laws must we be aware of?"

"I think I get the picture, Ms. DeSmedt." Here spoke the absolutely confident applicant, the young man equal to this or any other task.

"That's splendid," she beamed. Then something compelled her to blurt out: "Are you interested in the job?"

"We haven't frightened you off, have we?" ejaculated another, with a nervous laugh.

"Very much so" — he told the truth in reply to the question from the chairwoman. "And not in the slightest" — he said this in response to the other trustee. For not merely was he struck favorably by the board's naiveté and obvious interest, but he was convinced that there was a job to be done in Wexler and he was the one to do it. As a director of a public library he should be able to do and to know what they were asking. Their methods might be unorthodox, but the requests were certainly not. He saw nothing wrong with them. To hire as director someone who could not do what they wanted and did not know the answers to their questions would mean they were slighting their responsibilities. And, too, the salary they were offering — a detail not trifling — was better than twice his current salary. Thoughts of this sort kept running about like clockwork mice in his head, while the murmur of chatter filled the room.

Outside dusk had yielded to black night.

"Look at the time!" someone cried out. "I have to get an early start tomorrow morning, so I'll have to leave."

"Is it really ten o'clock?" exclaimed Faith DeSmedt, glancing at her watch. Then to Bibeau: "Mr. Bibeau, you've been very patient with us. Please understand that we're not experienced trustees. We hope we're doing the right thing, and not asking too much of our finalists. We're taking this search for the right person very seriously. If we get the right person, then he or she'll get the right people all the way down the line, and we'll be offering the kinds of services and doing the kinds of things a good public library should be offering and doing." Then she sat back, happy in the virtuous sensation of duty accomplished.

"I will work on these things in the next few weeks," said Bibeau, emphasizing still further his seriousness. "Where I might need additional facts about the city and the library, I will make assumptions and proceed accordingly." He rose to depart. The secretary said he would drive Bibeau to his motel and take him to the airport the next morning. Bibeau smiled, said thanks, and bid everyone adieu. He and the secretary left.

APPENDIX I

ENTRY FOR WEXLER IN
THE AMERICAN LIBRARY DIRECTORY

P WEXLER PUBLIC LIBRARY, Lester J. V. Halvorsen Memorial Library, 122 Umitilla Road. *Dir* Helen Baskin; *Asst. Dir* Martin Roedder; *Aq* Rosaline Bleecker; *Ch* Eleanor Hatt; *Ref* Gilbert Graham; *YA* Martha Blair; *Tech Serv* Neal Levinsky; *Ref* Lorraine Farran; *Br Coord & Bk-mobile Coord* Gloria Fransson. Staff 59 (prof 15, cler 31)
Founded 1921. Pop served 78,808; Circ 803,572.
Inc $984,020 (incl fed $49,061, state $55,953, city $830,994, other $58,012). Exp Bks $89,957, Per $15,305, Bd $4086, AV $2749; Sal $554,010.
Library Holdings: Bk vols 328,105; Per sub 763, vols bd 4561, micro 301; micro -- Fiche 5591, reels 8148; AV -- Rec, Flm, Fs, Maps, Cht, Art repro. VF 26
Special Collections: Genealogy, Large Print Books; Talking Books, rec, tapes; Hemans Historical Coll; American Culture (American Culture Series); World War II (Fisher Coll); Antique Silver (Budd Coll) Mem of Weymouth Pines Fed Libr Syst
Branches: 4
Argonne, 250 Fowler, *Librn* Kent Poyntz Bk vols 19,909
Butner, 578 Buies, *Librn* Teresa Sherrill Bk vols 35,466
Hiram, 930 Tionesta, *Librn* Susana Wise Bk vols 26,776
Uhrich, 67 Dimmitt, *Librn* Trina Benet Bk vols 6,955
Bookmobiles: 1

APPENDIX II

FACT SHEET FOR WEXLER

Population: 78,808 (latest census). Projection: 5 years 82,000; 10 years 86,000. Recreation: Wexler has 14 city parks of 345 acres, a community center with swimming pool and covered ice-skating rink, 2 golf courses; 16 tennis courts; 2 lighted baseball diamonds; programs for children year round, supervised by the City's Recreation Department; 2 outdoor public pools; football, baseball, basketball, and softball leagues for men, women, and children; bowling, 68 lanes; 6 indoor, 2 outdoor theaters. The Recreation Department sponsors a variety of clubs for radio amateurs, coin and stamp collectors, senior citizens, square dancers, and many others.
School and churches: Public: 18 elementary, 4 junior high, 2 high. Parochial: 4 elementary, 1 high. Wexler Junior College. St. Rita's School of Nursing and Medical Technology. Wexler has 96 churches, 35 denominations. Largest denominations: Roman Catholic, Lutheran, Baptist, Methodist, Presbyterian.
Hospitals: Our Lady of Mercy Hospital, 323 beds. Wexler General Hospital, 278 beds. 16 nursing homes.
Administration: Council-Manager government; Mayor and 6 councilors are elected; city manager heads all departments. Separately elected are the Board of

APPENDIX II (cont'd)

Education, Library Board of Trustees, County Officials; Sanitary District Board of 3 is appointed by the County Court.

Information and Accommodation: Wexler Region Chamber of Commerce, 36 W. Pine St. *Wexler Monitor* (daily and Sunday); *Dairyman's Weekly Review, Wexler Today* (weekly). 4 radio stations and 1 UHF television channel; access to major networks. More than 1,000 rooms in 30-odd hotels and motels.

Culture and Entertainment: Wexler supports a symphony orchestra, Wexler Light Opera Co., Wexler Art League, Janus Players, Summer concerts in Chippiwa Park.

4

WHAT NOW, JEANNE LEFORTE?

At 9:05, Jeanne Leforte (née Nysill) was walking briskly toward the entrance of the central building of the Deuxville (pronounced Dukesville) Public Library, one of the nation's largest urban libraries (Appendix I). Despite the heaviness of the air—the humidity, even at this early time of the day, was as thick and impenetrable as the Spanish moss that clung to the row of ancient trees shading the impressive Corinthian-columned facade of the library—she felt happy, almost light-headed. Why? Last evening her doctor had given her the news she had been eagerly hoping for: she was going to have a baby. She and her husband, John, had wanted a baby for a long time, and this exciting development helped to offset the unfortunate reality of John's predicament: he had been seriously injured several months ago in a car accident, and would be unable to work for some time. Fortunately his company's health insurance plan had covered his medical expenses, but since the mishap was not work related he was not eligible for Workmen's Compensation.

But there was also another reason why she felt happy. This feeling of happiness was based on the belief that her salary would shortly be increased by 15%. Every year at this time, the library (and, in turn, the city) requires performance evaluations for all employees. In the years she had worked at the Deuxville Public, her annual evaluations had been superior in each of the categories on the library personnel office's evaluation form; the comments sections also contained warm words of praise for her and her work. Consequently, she had always received the city's maximum possible raise—the cost of living increment (voted each year by the City Council; it was usually 5%), plus the library's merit increase (a function of the library board of trustees, but usually resolved at 5½ or 6½ % and sometimes even 10%, as this year) based on the performance rating for every year of her tenure as a professional librarian. So, although her husband could not resume work for a while, they would be able to get by on her salary—that is, as long as she got the 15% increase. And in anticipation of it, they had bought a modest home located within 30 minutes driving time from the library.

She was to have her appraisal interview with her supervisor, Marshall Edmonds, at 9:30. It was almost 9:00. She would go to her desk, get her material ready for a meeting at 10:30 of the selection policy and procedures revision committee, which DPL executive director, Lee Derfer, had asked to attend, and have a cup of coffee in the cafeteria before her rendezvous with Edmonds.

Vaguely blissful, but with nothing to occupy her save reflection, she sat in the cafeteria and gave herself up to the physical pleasures of coffee. All was quiescent, languorous, beautiful in the glow of the sunshine slanting into the room through the open window. Again and again she formulated in her fancy, scenes of the future. Her life became grand to her. By a curious chain of thoughts she soon found herself reconstituting in detail her association with the Deuxville Public Library.

Until Lee Derfer, a young, dynamic librarian with a multitude of experiences in all types of library, took over as executive director of the Deuxville Public five years ago, the place was a fascinating, if thoroughly depressing, study in feudal-style administration. Derfer was determined not only to revitalize but to expand library services into heretofore under- and unexplored areas. He instituted staff participation in deciding what changes should take place, to encourage meaningful input on the one hand and to discourage resistance when the changes evolved into policy and procedure on the other. A management team of upper level administrators was created, and the participatory management style pervaded the organization (Appendix II). Derfer built his team by recruiting, nationwide, both experienced librarians with proven records of achievement and those librarians new to the profession who showed good potential. Team members were then given the responsibility of recruiting the staff who would report to them; this was done through an interview/selection committee process to allow for a variety of opinions, with the final choice that of the appropriate administrator.

When Jeanne Nysill had been hired to work as a librarian in the central building's Education Department four years ago, her interview committee was made up of the library personnel assistant executive director, the central library associate executive director, and the head of the Education Department. The interview went smoothly; the committee was impressed by her knowledge of the current library scene, her enthusiasm, and her engaging personality — perfectly suited to public service work — and she was immediately offered a position. Later, she realized that the interview was a *pro forma* procedure, a matter really of placement more than anything else, since she had already been hired by the director when he came to talk with graduating students at her library school several months before. By the time she had returned to school, had finished packing her belongings in her dormitory room, and had made arrangements to have her things shipped from home, she still had more than two weeks in which to return to Deuxville, settle in and find an apartment, and get to know the city.

One afternoon, after she had been on the job a month, she went downtown to apply for life insurance (above and beyond the small policy offered as a benefit of her new job) and met John Leforte, the assistant manager of a branch office of the Amalgamated Life and Casualty Company. Their professional relationship soon blossomed into a personal one, and a year later they became engaged. They were married two months later.

During her second year on the job, word of Leforte's exceptional abilities as an organizer, her thoroughness and attention to detail, and her good working relationships with fellow librarians and support staff in the central library building as a whole as well as in the Education Department, reached the ears of Marshall Edmonds, the Assistant Executive Director of the regional library program for the Deuxville Public Library. Edmonds, himself a former library director and most recently, prior to his position at Deuxville, the head of a midwestern state's library development agency, was brought to DPL by Derfer to help plan for several new regional libraries; it was believed that the regionals would help to bring increased materials and services more rapidly to the neighborhood branches and, more importantly, would relieve some of the ILL pressures on the central collections and staff. Edmonds supervised the planning and construction of two such regional libraries, in the northern and southern parts of the city. A city-instigated, library staff study revealed that the materials, personnel, and maintenance costs of operating the two 100,000 square foot buildings was approaching \$2 million annually and, not surprisingly, the regional building program ground to a screeching halt on the basis of negative cost effectiveness. Fortunately, another assignment awaited Edmonds.

The staff and management team-originated proposal to contract for OCLC services in cataloging (with the thought to future use of the computer-generated tapes to create a COM or online catalog) was unanimously approved by Derfer and the library board of trustees. The decision had far-reaching consequences, for with the plan to utilize OCLC came a complementary strategy to close the Dewey catalog, begin exclusively with LC classification, and reorganize the 20 Dewey-related central building subject departments into five, broad LC-based subject divisions.

As is so frequently the case with central library buildings built in the country's large cities in the early part of the century, Deuxville's main downtown library was beautifully decorated in rare woods and marbles, bronze lighting fixtures and stained glass, but had public spaces cut up into rooms that did not allow convenient access to the collections either by patrons or staff, and certainly did not permit collection growth. Regrouping the collection to accommodate five, broad LC-based subject areas would provide a more logical flow of subject materials for all library users, and would also help to justify expansion needs for the future selling to the board and city council of a new building or an addition.

A stickler for details, sometimes to the point of compulsion, Edmonds was deemed a fortuitous choice to head the monumental reorganization process. As his assistant, Edmonds hand-picked Jeanne Leforte. She was given a leave of absence from her position in the Education Department to take on the special assignment. She did not know at the time that she would never return to that department, or to the larger division that later incorporated it.

There was a feeling of mutual respect between Leforte and her new supervisor from the start. Leforte realized that she had a lot to learn from Edmonds and therefore kept an appropriate student-mentor attitude of deference in most of the crucial decision areas. Edmonds, in turn, lavished her with praise, which was officially documented in the annual personnel evaluations (Appendix III). Consequently, Leforte came to expect — perhaps even take for granted — the periodic boosts of ego and income that the evaluations provided. Her work, in both quantity and substance, was exemplary and superior evaluations were completely deserved.

The reorganization was completed in a little over 24 months, during which time Leforte assumed increasing responsibility (when Edmonds permitted her to do so) and received two excellent evaluations. Concurrent with the emergence of the central building's streamlined subject divisions came two staff retirements: the assistant executive director of technical services and the head of adult materials selection for branches, in the tech services department. The logical choice for the technical services position was Marshall Edmonds, who had several years experience in a similar position before he had become a director and then head of a state library agency. He accepted it happily. An interview committee, consisting of the library personnel officer, Edmonds, and the associate executive director for branches, convened to speak with applicants for the adult materials selection position. Jeanne Leforte had been encouraged to apply for it by Lee Derfer himself. She did so with the understanding that she would be offered the job, with an increase in pay; Edmonds wanted her, too.

Jeanne Leforte did get the position and felt that the working relationship that had been so successful with Edmonds in the immediate past would continue. The management team, through Edmonds, had given her the charge of revamping the policies and procedures for branches to select their adult level materials, and she started to work on this assignment immediately, with a committee of branch librarians and others. It was an exciting opportunity for her to show some real initiative and originality, and she relished it. Edmonds, on the other hand, found that his new position meant he had to work late into the evenings, early in the mornings, and even during weekends; the work load seemed to compound geometrically with each passing day. Having been accustomed to delving into the minutiae of each subordinate's daily operations in his last two positions at DPL, with their small, accommodating numbers of staff, he was suddenly faced with six large divisions with over 150 employees in technical services. Yet, he continued to perpetuate his "one-man show," with all of his division heads reporting their every move to him — moves for which he had had to give permission in the first place. His obsessive concern for detail precluded the delegation of responsibility to others. Very soon tech services division heads, all of whom, except for Leforte, had been in their positions for many years, opted to relinquish a contributing administrative role and adopted instead the comfortable attitude of indifference. For their indifference, they were rewarded with personnel evaluations which reflected an imaginatively fabricated version of the truth, but which did afford the requisite ego boost and commensurate pay increase.

Jeanne Leforte's evaluations continued at their usual high level because she deserved them; and the fact that Edmonds insisted upon involving himself in virtually every aspect of each of his employees' work had long since ceased to trouble her. She was quite used to his management style, and had adapted nicely to it. She had every reason to believe that this year's evaluation would be no different from those of previous years: she would read Edmonds' comments and check the numerical rating, react positively, and utter a few embarrassed words of gratitude. (The evaluation forms were not the kind employees had to sign.) Within two weeks, her paycheck would reflect that her accomplishments of the past year were indeed appreciated.

The appearance of a cafeteria worker to re-fill the salt and pepper shakers tilted her out of her fantasy. She looked at her watch: 9:25. She put her empty cup in the dirty-dish cart, and mounted on the wings of a pure and ingenuous elation the long flight of stairs leading to the offices on the first floor.

Her first hint that all was not well was with the sudden appearance of Consuelo Feng, head of the cataloging division, whose no-nonsense approach to her job was emphasized by the emphatic clicks of her heels along the highly polished terrazzo floors. Leforte could usually identify those footsteps easily; but today then sounded less forceful and deliberate and certainly more rushed than what could normally be expected from the cataloging head. As Feng swept by with an almost inaudible "Good morning, Jeanne" escaping from her lips, Leforte thought she detected the tell-tale indications of crying on her face — the red, swollen eyes, the puffiness. Before she could respond and follow up with a question about her distraught state, Feng escaped to the women's room. "Strange," thought Leforte, "I wonder what happened." Rather than risk being late for her appointment by stopping to find out, she proceeded to Marshall Edmonds' office; she would ask what was bothering her friend at lunch.

Bernice Washington, Edmonds' secretary, jumped nervously as Leforte entered the outer office. "Oh, Jeanne!" she said, turning white, "I have to speak to you."

Leforte glanced at her with interest: "What about, Bernice? What's up?" What with Consuelo Feng in tears and Bernice Washington very pale, and startled, all was incomprehensible.

"Jeanne ... I don't ... I need to talk ...," she spluttered. She could not command herself sufficiently to be able to articulate.

"Bernice!" said Leforte with much curiosity and concern. "Is anything wrong? Are you ill? Is there anything I can do?"

Tears gleamed in Washington's eyes. Astounded and frightened by those shimmering tears, Leforte repeated her questions: "Bernice. Please. Is anything wrong? Can I help?"

Washington hid her face a moment in her hands, and sobbed. Leforte waited in nervous expectation. As the sobbing abated, the secretary's voice regained some steadiness.

"Jeanne," she said feebly. "Mr. Edmonds has become an alcoholic."

Jeanne Leforte experienced precisely the physical discomfort which people feel when an elevator drops unexpectedly. "Oh!" the exclamation escaped her unawares. From her knowledge of him she could not believe it. How could it be that she had not noticed? Well, come to think of it, perhaps she had. But no, she could honestly say that she had seen no change in him. Could this be? Could she not have detected that something in his behavior was awry? Before saying anything, she glanced long into the humid eyes of the woman sitting helplessly in front of her. "Are you sure, Bernice?" she asked, extremely startled by the turn of events.

Washington shot a timid momentary look at her. "Yes," she replied, scarcely audible.

A long silence followed. Then Bernice Washington, having rallied herself, invited Leforte to sit down, which the librarian did, with a weak placatory smile. "I'll let him know you're here in a minute," the secretary said forlornly.

In another moment or so she had regained her self-control, and she managed to tell Jeanne Leforte in a fairly usual tone the whole story.

Said she:

"I'm telling *you*, Jeanne, because I consider you a friend and I respect your judgment. I haven't mentioned this to anyone else. Not Consuelo. Not anyone. I'm hoping you can help me. I don't know what to do. If he had a wife or lived with someone, perhaps I could tell them. But he's alone. He started drinking soon after he took this job. I think the job's too big for him, at least with his style of management. As you know only too well, he's the type who likes to have a finger in every pie, but he can't with so many people reporting to him. As you also know, I've been his secretary since he joined the DPL, so I know him very well. I know he's drinking heavily—he goes through a fifth at work; he keeps the bottle locked in the credenza behind his desk—because he's hung over almost every morning. He also keeps a supply of breath fresheners of various sorts in the credenza, too. He really gulps it down when he works here late at night, which he does most evenings. But the worst is he won't acknowledge he's becoming an alcoholic. He just won't recognize there's a problem. When I mentioned the bottle to him one night when I stayed late, he shrugged it off and said that he just takes a drink or two, and that one or two drinks never did anyone harm. He's able to hide the effects for the most part. I don't think anyone else knows or even suspects. I know Mr. Derfer doesn't suspect anything. He's one of those people who can conceal any signs, but it's affecting his judgment." She paused to wipe the tears from her eyes. Then: "Oh, Jeanne, I need your help, and so does he. You're his favorite person, you know. He likes you better than anyone else."

At this disclosure, a flush flowed from Leforte's cheeks to her neck. She had to make the motion of swallowing. Truth to tell, she liked him too. She was conscious of a strong desire to act wisely, prudently, for the best. She wanted to prove that she was equal to Bernice Washington's confidence in her. She wanted to suggest some course of action splendid and decisive, and was perturbed to find that she could not. She had never before dealt with the problem of alcoholism, and she said so.

Her listener responded that she had not expected Leforte to be able to perceive the perfect solution right then and there, but that together perhaps they could devise something. She recommended: "Jeanne, I must prepare you for your interview with him." She spoke low, like a conspirator. "I must tell you so you won't be too surprised or disappointed."

The young librarian began to discern the significance of what her friend was telling her. Her anxiety increased at a bound. The secretary continued: "He was drunk when he wrote your appraisal one night last week."

At these words Jeanne Leforte gave a little gasp of amazement, and her cheeks paled. The whole mystery stood explained. She experienced a slight feeling of faintness. The secretary was speaking. "I hope I haven't done anything wrong by warning you," she was saying.

"I better go in," Leforte muttered, a wearied, disillusioned expression coming over her pallid features. "I'll see, Bernice, if I can find something for you on what to do when you suspect someone is becoming an alcoholic," she added trying to appear composed.

"You are a true friend, Jeanne," the secretary smiled, relieved. "I knew I could count on you. This is taking a terrible toll on me, too."

Nobody could have guessed from the librarian's placid demeanor that she was in a state of extreme agitation as she moved toward Marshall Edmonds' door. She looked in, and saw her supervisor behind his desk, and she called to him, in a clear voice. "I'm here, Mr. Edmonds."

The man stared at her, as if bewildered. Then he said, "Come in, Jeanne. And close the door, please." She closed it, not knowing what this cautiousness foreshadowed. He was silent for a moment, as if undecided what to say next. His eyes avoided any prolonged encounter with hers. "Sit down please," he bade her. She towed a chair over to his desk.

"When I---" he said in a low voice, and then he began again, "When I filled out your evaluation form last week I wasn't feeling well, Jeanne...."

There was a pause, followed by some remarks on the weather, and then another pause. Leforte studied him surreptitiously. Suddenly she was consumed by a feeling of sadness. Marshall Edmonds seemed pathetic to her, a person more to be pitied than to be scorned.

"Well, Jeanne"—he seemed to be beginning again—"perhaps I should preface your performance evaluation with a brief explanation of what we've done this year, and the changes that were made."

She looked a startled interrogative.

He went on: "I'm sure you're aware that the City of Deuxville decided late last year to eliminate the Civil Service Department, and, in its place, create a City Department of Personnel." He gave a twisted, rather foolish smile, and continued: "Ostensibly, the maneuver was accomplished to curb patronage abuses and make it easier to dismiss deadwood employees in the long run. But one of the things it has done for us, on an immediate basis, is to create a bureaucratic nightmare."

Jeanne Leforte knew of this change in the city's structure but, like most city employees, was cognizant only of its potential benefits and none of the drawbacks. Her agitation subsided suddenly. "Yes," she said calmly.

Sounding as if he had memorized his speech word for word, Edmonds went on: "As a necessary part of this process, the library and other city departments which have their own personnel offices were requested by the new City Department of Personnel to revise their personnel evaluation forms so that information and ratings could be easily transferred from, for example, our own sheet to the city's IBM cards. Our head of acquisitions, Mike Kelly, was involved with the staff committee to design the new form — remember?"

Yes, she remembered that too; but she was not sure what all this had to do with her and her evaluation? She simply nodded, and Edmonds resumed:

"Just prior to our filling out the new forms for this year's evaluation the executive director of the City Department of Personnel spoke to the Library Management Team and explained that evaluations would have to be much more objective, more specific, and less influenced by personalities, friendships, loyalties, etc. than they had been in the past. Supervisors would also be evaluated on the accuracy and fairness of their evaluations of subordinates."

The thought continually arising in her mind was: "Why don't you get to the point, Mr. E.? Why don't you show me what you've said about me?" The words were ready, the sentences framed in her mind. But she was silent.

Edmonds took a manila file folder from his top desk drawer and removed her performance evaluation. With a trembling hand he passed it to her (Appendix IV). The appeal of his eyes was strangely pathetic. He got up, and, putting his hands in the pockets of his trousers, began to walk around the room.

Her eyes traveled quickly over the document, alighting upon the "Comments to the Employee" section on the back. It read:

"Although I have worked closely with and provided direction to Ms. Leforte for three years in a variety of situations, she still requires almost constant monitoring. Her contribution to the reorganization of the central building's subject divisions was noteworthy, but its significance was again compromised by her lack of initiative, which meant that I had to step in frequently when problems arose. She appears to be working well with her committee to revise adult materials selection policy and procedure, but I feel that her often unrealistic suggestions and unwillingness to exert a stronger control over the group will eventually dissipate the effectiveness of the committee's efforts. Ms. Leforte has good potential, so it is particularly disappointing to have to report that she is not now working at a level equivalent to it."

The words sank like a depth-charge into Jeanne Leforte's consciousness. She was mortally pierced. Her brain was in anarchy. She flipped over the document and examined her scored evaluations: all, except for attendance and punctuality, were in the low 70's, the "Fair" range, a devastatingly dramatic plunge from the former heights of her 97 to 99 scores.

She could not speak. The catch was in her throat. She realized the significance of the scores. An average evaluation grade less than the 76 minimum score allowed only for the cost of living increase, 5%, no merit increase at all. A wild thought of leaving the DPL shot through her mind and was gone. After all, with a husband not working, a child on the way, and the responsibility for mortgage payments, she could not afford to be without a job. It was the most astonishing and inauspicious piece of bad luck that had ever happened to her. "Why, Mr. Edmonds?" was the only thing she could induce herself to say.

He was back at his desk now, nervously rearranging his papers. "Jeanne, I wasn't feeling well when I filled it out," he explained, after a long meditative pause. It was plain, from every accent of his voice, that he had done something of which he was terribly ashamed.

She uttered no sound, but her eyes said "Go on."

He continued:

"Please forgive me, Jeanne. But I was not feeling well when I wrote it up. I can't do anything about it because it's already gone to city hall. It has to stand as the official record. I know I was wrong. I was feeling terribly sick when I wrote yours and Consuelo's evaluations. I can't possibly redo them. There would be all sorts of inquiries. Think how bad that would look; my reputation is at stake. I couldn't bear it if Mr. Derfer found out. He doesn't see them. They go directly to the Personnel Department. What would he do to me?" The urgency of his supplication was mirrored in the tense whiteness of his knuckles as he clasped his hands tightly in front of him.

So overset was she by the dramatic surprise of his remarks that she was reduced to staring impotently at him. His face was working and there was a slight haze before his beseeching eyes. With cruel suddenness she was being called upon to cover up for him. But at what cost? That additional 10% translated into a couple of thousand dollars. She was being asked to forego it to save his precious reputation. When she tried to soothe herself with other images — images of John, the baby, the house — she found that they had lost their power.

And then the young librarian, as in a dream, heard from the lips of her supervisor the words, "Jeanne, please let bygones be bygones and put this year's evaluation behind you. I'll try to make it up to you next year." Suddenly, he extracted from his pocket a set of keys and wheeled his chair toward the credenza. But suddenly he stopped and wheeled back. Then he began pushing his hand through his hair, front to back, front to back. She was maintaining a notable silence. "Please say something, Jeanne," he said, when her silence had begun to distress him.

Leforte blew forth a long breath, as if trying to repulse the oppressive heat of the September morning. "I don't know what to say, Mr. Edmonds. I have to think about it." She made the gesture of departing. With a motion of his hand he tried to stay her. "Jeanne, will you not do anything about this, please?" he pleaded. Then he turned pale, nibbled his lips, and she could see tears in his eyes.

"I have a meeting to go to, Mr. Edmonds." She spoke in a voice that showed no emotion. He was rubbing his eyes as she quit his office.

She whirred right by Bernice Washington, without saying a word. When she reached the end of the corridor she discovered that she had gone in the wrong direction. She started to turn back, but realized she did not want to go by Bernice Washington's door. Presently, she found herself in front of a women's washroom. She went in. She looked at her watch, which showed 10:00. She had half an hour before the meeting of her committee. She was moved by a sudden impulse to leave the building and go for a stroll. "Perhaps it will help to clear my thoughts," she reflected. Leaving by a side entrance, she plunged into the street and lost herself amid the crowd.

When she stepped into the meeting room at 10:30, Lee Derfer was already seated. Putting on an acting-for-the-best demeanor, she approached him and extended her hand. "Glad you could make it, Mr. Derfer," she said, making a deliberate effort to appear as if nothing had happened. "We'll get started as soon as everyone arrives."

The executive director shook her hand and smiled graciously. They exchanged inconsequential remarks as one by one the committee members arrived. After everyone was accounted for, she introduced the visitor. As he began to speak, she exhorted herself to pay close attention, not to let herself be so distracted by the earlier event that her mind would be off in some obscure cavern of her soul.

The executive director was saying:

"I asked Jeanne if I could speak with you today so that you might have a little direction in the important work you're doing. I know that Marshall Edmonds has already provided some good advice on the procedural aspects of the committee's charge, and I want to go a bit beyond that to give you a few pointers which will lead you in the directions the management team feels are best suited to the DPL now and in the future. The first thing I want to do is to change the name of the group from the Selection Policy and Procedures Revision Committee to Collection Development Policies and Procedures Committee. The idea is to broaden the perspective and to have you all begin thinking not in terms of revision but in terms of something completely new." Derfer paused. "Any questions or comments so far?"

"I can't seem to see any difference between materials selection and collection development — why the change?" queried Sylvia Grossinger, a branch head.

"Sylvia, I'm glad you asked that question because it will serve as the perfect introduction to that whole subject. I think that materials selection, as significant as the job is in itself, is only part of the larger responsibility of collection development — what many prominent librarians and library science educators consider to be the single element of librarianship which gives it credence as a profession. This is why I started by saying that the committee is doing 'important work.' Much of a library's services influence or are influenced by collection development policies. You all have a very important, crucial task cut out for you. Let me digress for just a moment. Right now the management team is beginning to come to grips with our annual budget process, as it does every year. The city budget director announced that in the next fiscal year the city of Deuxville will adopt a program budget format. One of the ramifications of such a budget is increased accountability of each city department for its individual expenditures and the scrutiny under which all budgeted programs will be held. I think it's a good idea for us to be able to break down the budget into programs of service so that we can plan and evaluate more effectively. However, there was another part of the city budget director's message that was heard for the first time this year and is a harbinger of the future: financial constraints from decreasing tax revenues mean that city departments must do more than present their budget requests. They have to justify them and be prepared to defend them. And, it will be up to this committee to give us the ammunition — the documented evidence — that will support the library's defense of its materials allocations and the personnel expenditures involved in the selection, processing, dissemination, among other things, of those materials."

Observed Ruth Kitano, head of one of the regional libraries:

"I don't want to sound flippant or disrespectful, but I can't imagine us being able to defend or justify anything with the amalgam of grandiose platitudes that make up the present DPL materials selection, or 'collection development' policy, if you will, and I daresay that the same would be true of examples from other libraries of similar size and serving a similar population as DPL!"

"Ruth, that's exactly my point about thinking in terms of something completely new," observed Derfer with benevolent firmness. Then he asked: "How many of you can define the terms 'bibliometrics' or 'operations research (OR)', the latter as it relates to libraries?"

No one on the committee of eight indicated that he or she could do so, and all looked expectantly toward the smiling director.

"I'm really not trying to put anyone on the spot and, frankly, I'm not too surprised and only a little disappointed at your collective ignorance," he commented. "Most of the employment of scientific and statistical methods to study the use of books, periodicals, and other materials, which involve both OR and bibliometrics, has been, for whatever reasons, in academic environments and few studies have been accomplished in the public library—particularly the large urban library setting."

Jeanne Leforte's neck was elongated at the sound of the words "statistical methods." She said:

"The statistical methods course taught at my library school emphasized the 'people' aspect of library use so that relevant data for collection development policy would be gathered primarily from user studies, questionnaires, and community analysis and surveys. Is there more to it than this?"

"Yes, there certainly is, Jeanne," Derfer corroborated her, "and I'd be very proud of all of you if you could come up with the means to draft a model collection development policy for a public library based on some of those other things, such as comprehensive scientific research methodology, rather than, as Ruth succinctly stated a moment ago, 'grandiose platitudes' with liberty and justice for all!"

Kitano burst out laughing to cover her obvious blushing embarrassment, and she was soon encircled with laughter. Derfer waited for the group to quiet down before he continued.

"A number of people have written some fascinating books and articles about OR, bibliometrical studies, measuring and evaluating library effectiveness, etc. Certainly, the kind of 'people oriented' statistical data mentioned by Jeanne should also be used for a present/potential patron analysis framework, but please don't stop there. I'll drop a few hints and clues to arouse your curiosities and to help you start your research. Did you know, for example, that there is a scientific law which can statistically predict usage in subject collections of particular books and periodicals and, by extension, can be used to identify the core of the most active users of the library? Think of the effectiveness of the DPL if that core of most active users could be joined with the subjects for which they have the greatest need! And, are you aware of a mathematical model which helps predict the number of multiple copies of a title which a library needs to purchase to satisfy the demand for it and, using it another way, the ideal loan period for specific types and subjects of books? It's all pretty amazing, isn't it? Perhaps most amazing is the fact that these techniques aren't really 'new' and that librarians have taken so long to acknowledge their value. Budgetary constraints, greater fiscal accountability, and widespread acceptance of the computer have begun to change that attitude, I feel. So, I'd like you all to start thinking about these things and the ripple effect of a library's acquiring materials. How should the materials budget and the personnel allocation which uses it be divided? Our new LIBS 100 circulation system should be a big help with that one. How is the cataloging department, our use of OCLC, etc., impacted by the nature of the materials we select? Should we continue to use the McNaughton rental plan? Are we buying the right formats for most effective use of the collections? More microforms, less hardcopy? What about weeding? Collection development should ideally involve de-acquisitions as an on-going program of equal importance. How should we determine if an item should be stored remotely, rebound, or discarded? How do we ensure that unused or little-used collections will be used, or should we even worry about them? If it's the latter, then how do we justify the space such items are taking on the shelves? Are there items or groups of items which might be moved from open stacks and placed in closed ones? Or vice versa? Is the physical arrangement of the shelving conducive to browsing; is there easy access; a logical flow, or are sections of the same or related subjects on two different floors? Was our recent reorganization of the collection along LC subject lines adequate? There are a lot of questions and no easy answers!"

Leforte and her committee rapidly wrote, in various personal shorthands, the rhetorical questions posed by Derfer. Leforte was first to finish and hence she spoke first. By this time she had resumed the dominion of her soul. The concern associated with the earlier contretemps had been successfully put away.

"Mr. Derfer," she said "I don't think any of us knows how to respond to your questions at the moment and maybe we won't be able to for quite some time; I do know that you've succeeded in conveying to us the importance of the committee's new charge and the challenges and many directions which confront us as we attempt to approach the problem. It will no doubt be an exciting endeavor and we hope to reinforce your confidence in us by doing a really fine job on the collection development policy for the DPL."

The group members nodded their heads in unison, most of them too overwhelmed to think of anything to say.

"Fine, that's just what I was hoping you'd feel," said Derfer. "I don't want to take up any more of your time than necessary so I'll leave you with this final word: Don't be afraid to be innovative for fear of breaking long held traditions or because your proposals might impinge on the functions of library departments which seem to be unrelated to a collection development policy. One of the best things to come out of all this may very well be a new understanding of the interlocking systems of library functions and the need for communication and cooperation both within and between them. Good luck and don't hesitate to ask me or anyone on the management team for advice or assistance!"

Jeanne Leforte felt tired but elated when the session adjourned. She knew that her work as chairperson of this committee would be the kind of meaningful experience that would help her career at DPL and later; perhaps she could even write an article for *LJ* or some other professional publication as a result. She sauntered back to her desk, intending to work, and was a little perturbed to find that she could not work. Her head refused. She sat in her cubicle vaguely staring. How she wished the library staff was unionized. What would John advise her to do? She had much to think about.

APPENDIX I

ENTRY FOR DEUXVILLE PUBLIC LIBRARY IN
THE AMERICAN LIBRARY DIRECTORY

P   DEUXVILLE PUBLIC LIBRARY, 536 North Cyprus Boulevard. *Exec Dir* Lee R. Derfer; *Deputy Exec Dir for Pub Servs* Regina S. Armand; *Dep Exec Dir for Mgt Servs* Sean McDouglas; *Assoc Exec Dir for Central Libr* Robert Callahan; *Assoc Exec Dir for Extension Servs* Margaret Allen; *Asst Exec Dir of Pub Info* Maisie Nelson; *Asst Exec Dir of Develop* Taji J. Theodore; *Asst to the Exec Dir* W. Susumu Kurosawa; *Asst Exec Directors (Pub Servs): Commu Relations & Spec Programs of Serv* Selma Jefferson; *Prog Planning and Eval* Open; *Tech Serv* Marshall Edmonds; *Asst Exec Directors (Mgt Servs): Bldg Programs* Karl Rantoul; *Facilities & Equipment* James P. Robbin; *Finance* R. Patrick Daley, Jr; *Personnel* Lana Seligmann; *Security & Safety* William Finley; *Systems Engineering* Mary W. Persepolis; *Operations Engineering* Arnold Fields; *Asst Directors (Mgt Servs): Finance* Nicholas McWilliams; *Personnel Admin* Kenneth Ptolomy; *Personnel Training* Susan Jenkins; *Operations Engineering* John Urbaczewski; *Public Info Mgrs: Broadcasting* Rhonda Morrow; *Graphic Design* Sarah Jones; *Publicity* Shirley Sass; *Tech Servs: Asst Dir* David Sorvel; *Acq* Michael Kelly; *Cat* Consuelo Feng; *Processing* Juliette Bey; *Redistribution Center* Rachel Tovarich; *Materials Selection: Adult Specialist* Jeanne Leforte; *Youth Specialist* Michele Laughton; *Extension Servs: Coord Systemwide Circ* Richard Petranski; *Chief Northwest District* Open; *Chief Northeast District* Barbara L. Callahan; *Chief Southwest District* Chieko Salazar; *Chief Southeast District* Delano Maxam; *Chief North Regional Library* Ruth Kitano; *Chief South Regional Library* Nettie Pouvoir; *Serv Specialists: Children* Liza Pontoon; *YA* Willa Fox; *Senior Citizens* Jordan Paltz; *Spanish Speaking* Marguerite Ortiz; *Special Programs of Serv Supvr: Blind & Phys Handicpd* Dorna Jeager; *Human Serv Prog* Marnie Grant; *Inst & Correctional Serv Prog* Donald Smythe; *Independent Study Prog* Loretta Conroy; *Coord Interlibrary Coop* Ella Green; *Coord NEH Grant Prog* Stephano Supremi. Staff 2054 (prof 450, nonprof 821, cler 783)
Founded 1895. Pop served 2,985,431; Circ 7,326,890. Inc $45,000,000 (incl fed $10,500,000, state $3,475,000, city $30,925,000, other $100,000). Exp $5,255,000, Bks $4,000,000, Per $900,000, Bd $250,000, Micro $325,000, AV $575,000; Sal $33,695,000
Library Holdings: Bk titles 726,441, vols 7,348,579; Per sub 15,904, vols bd 200,845, micro 214,726; Micro-Fiche 191,805; Av-Rec, A-Tapes, V-Tapes, Flm, Fs, Slides, Maps, Cht
Special Collections: Deuxville Historical records; Civil War artifacts and personal journals; manuscripts of southern writers and poets; Miklós Rózsa Collection of Film Music: recordings, tapes, and musical scores; Deuxville neighborhood histories; photographic archives; autograph catalogs; signed first editions of Samuel Clemens (Mark Twain), Renata Callas, Boris Lugosi, Jordan Field, James Dickey.
Oral history. US, State, UN & Deuxville Doc Dep
Publications: Annual Report; Calendar of Events for the Deuxville Public Library; exhibition catalogs

APPENDIX I (cont'd)

Partic in Southern Library & Information Network; Deuxville Regional Library Councils; OCLC, Inc.

Central Library, 536 North Cyprus Boulevard. *Assoc Exec Dir* Robert Callahan; *Head, Prof Libr* Milton VanDyke; *Head, Programs & Exhibits* Chad Burlick; *Head, AV ctr* Diane Pillifort; *Head, Children's Libr* Lila Olde; *Spec Coll Curator & Archivist* Tremaine Tallahassee

General Information Services Div. Chief Marge Bytes; *Head, Bibliog & ILL Ctr* Marilyn Boric; *Head, Info Ctr* Charlotte Abrams; *Head, Newspapers & Gen Per* Jay Geeson

Business, Science & Technology Div. Chief Ellie J. Charles; *Asst Chief* Roseanne Woods; *Biol Sci* Donald Williamson; *Bus* Roscoe Davis; *Physical Sci* Sonia Paragon; *Tech* George Sylvestri

Fine Arts Div. Chief Melissa Torless; *Asst Chief* Nancy Chumley; *Art* Patrice Wells; *Music* Rosalinde Heller

Literature & Philosophy Div. Chief Herbert Ovaltine; *Asst Chief* Benjamin Herrmann; *Lit* Kelvin Early; *Relig & Philos* Wayne Nascimbene

Social Sciences & Hist Div. Chief Ronald Baum; *Asst Chief* William Graham; *Educ* Alfred Newman; *Hist* Ralph Reese; *Soc Sci* Gene Pectoris

Popular Library. Head Janet Kawasaki; *Foreign Lang* Chul-Ok Lee; *Travel* Simon Bond

Branches: 60; Regional Libraries: 2; Reg. Libr for Blind & Phys. Handicapped: 1

The branches closest to the central library serve the largest populations of minority group members including Afro-American/Black, Hispanic/Spanish surname (of Mexican, Cuban, Puerto Rican, and various Central and South American country backgrounds), Asian American (including Chinese, Japanese, and Filipinos), and new immigrants primarily from Indochina (especially Vietnamese and Cambodians), Korea, Cuba, Haiti, Mexico, and Pakistan. Branches further from the inner city core tend to serve the white majority patrons whose backgrounds include Irish, Italian, Polish, Scandinavian, French Canadian, and German in the main; the city is still very strongly neighborhood and ethnically oriented. A recent influx of Appalachian families has been documented in the central core. Of the four branch districts, the Southeast is predominantly black with all levels of economic and educational attainment; the Southwest is predominantly white working class; the Northwest is primarily white middle class; and the Northeast is the most integrated with all levels of economic and educational attainment (but the highest levels of Deuxville income are here in this district). The North Regional Library serves the two northern branch districts as does the South Regional the southern ones. All districts have an equal number of branches (15) and the district boundary lines are drawn so that each contains inner city as well as outer agencies.

(Appendix II appears on pages 76-77)

APPENDIX II

THE DEUXVILLE PUBLIC LIBRARY ORGANIZATION CHART

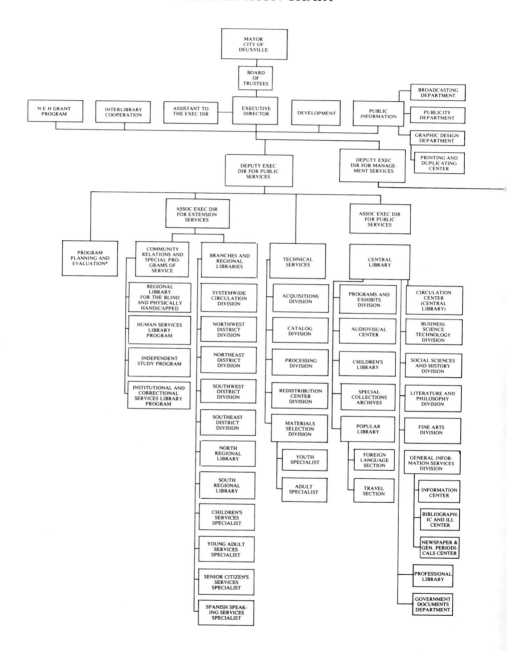

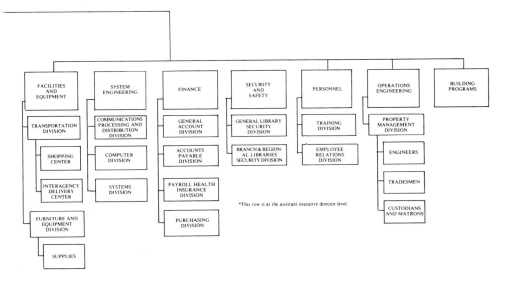

*This row is at the assistant executive director level.

APPENDIX III

PROBATIONARY PERSONNEL EVALUATION
DEUXVILLE PUBLIC LIBRARY

Name___Jeanne Nysill_____Title___Reference Librarian_____

Civil Service Classif.___Librarian I___Department___Education Department

Ratings

(Supervisor:___Paul Krebs, Head, Education Department, Central Library)
              Name   Title

Quality and Quantity of Work	95
Reliability	95
Ability to Work Well with Staff and Public	98
Attendance Record	99
Punctuality Record	99
	Total 486
	Average 97.2

Additional Comments:

Ms. Nysill is an exemplary librarian. She is organized, well groomed, and wonderful with fellow workers and the public. She has shown much initiative in her first six months on the job and always looks for additional work to do once her assignments are completed. I recommend her without reservation for permanent career status at the Deuxville Public Library.

Supervisor's Signature_____PAUL KREBS /s/_____

Form #P-34

APPENDIX III (cont'd)

ANNUAL PERSONNEL EVALUATION

DEUXVILLE PUBLIC LIBRARY

Name___ Jeanne Leforte _____ Title___ Reference Librarian _____

Civil Service Classif.___ Librarian I ___Department___ Education Department

Ratings

(Supervisor:_ Paul Krebs, Head, Education Department, Central Library)_
            Name   Title

Quality and Quantity of Work	97
Reliability	97
Ability to Work Well with Staff and Public	99
Attendance Record	99
Punctuality Record	99
Total	491
Average	98.2

Additional Comments:

After one year on the job, Ms. Leforte continues to perform at the highest levels of competence and efficiency. She seems ready for new challenges; I would hate to lose her from the Education Department but would
not stand in the way of what promises to be a fast rising career.

Supervisor's Signature____ PAUL KREBS/s/ _____

Form #P-33

APPENDIX III (cont'd)

ANNUAL PERSONNEL EVALUATION

<u>DEUXVILLE PUBLIC LIBRARY</u>

Name___Jeanne Leforte_____Title__Coordinator, LC Reorganization Project

Civil Service Classif._Librarian II (Provisional) Dept._Office of M. Edmonds

Ratings

(Supervisor:__Marshall Edmonds, Asst Executive Director (Reorg. Proj))

      Name   Title

Quality and Quantity of Work   97

Reliability   97

Ability to Work Well with Staff and Public   99

Attendance Record   99

Punctuality Record   99

                                              Total___491

                                            Average____98.2

Additional Comments:

It is indeed a pleasure to work with Ms. Leforte on the reorganization
project. She is thorough, thoughtful, and eager to learn. I especially like her ability to work with all levels of library personnel and
her self-direction. I think she will go far at the DPL and in our
profession.

Supervisor's Signature____MARSHALL EDMONDS/s/

                                              Form #P-33

APPENDIX III (cont'd)

ANNUAL PERSONNEL EVALUATION

DEUXVILLE PUBLIC LIBRARY

Name__Jeanne Leforte___Title__Coordinator, LC Reorganization Project__

Civil Service Classif._Librarian II (Provisional)_Dept._Office of M. Edmonds_

Ratings

(Supervisor:__Marshall Edmonds, Asst Executive Director (Reorg. Proj.))
             Name   Title

Quality and Quantity of Work	99
Reliability	99
Ability to Work Well with Staff and Public	99
Attendance Record	99
Punctuality Record	99
Total	495
Average	99

Additional Comments:

Ms. Leforte continues to be the hardest working, most organized
individual in the reorganization project, respected by all who come
into contact with her.

Supervisor's Signature___MARSHALL EDMONDS **/s/**_____

Form #P-33

APPENDIX IV

EMPLOYEE PERFORMANCE EVALUATION

DEUXVILLE PUBLIC LIBRARY

SECTION A

Employee's Last Name	First Name	Middle Initial	Unit
Leforte,	Jeanne	N.	Technical Services

Classification	Working Library Title
Librarian II	Head, Adult Materials Selection

Type of Evaluation

[X] Annual   [ ] Probationary   [ ] Other(Specify)_____

Areas of Responsibility and/or Objectives for Evaluation:

(To be completed by immediate supervisor.)

In charge of materials selection procedures for adult level (above young adult) patrons of central library, regional libraries, and branches. Primarily concerned with popular reading and audiovisual materials but also coordinates selection with central library subject specialists and bibliographers. Compiles, edits, and distributes list of recommended titles to all library agencies; gathers requests from all agencies. Maintains central selection office with appropriate reviewing media and advises librarians about materials suitable for respective agencies. Has been appointed Chairperson, Collection Development Policy and Procedures Committee by the Executive Director.

APPENDIX IV (cont'd)

SECTION B

EVALUATION (To be completed by immediate supervisor.)	Score
1. QUALITY OF WORK Factors to be considered include: Accuracy, communication, neatness, orderliness, organization, thoroughness, initiative.	70
2. QUANTITY OF WORK Consider the amount of work performed in a satisfactory manner and in accordance with established standards.	70
3. DEPENDABILITY Factors to be considered include: employee's ability to complete duties without close supervision; reliability, support of library goals; regards for best interest of institution and those connected with it.	70
4. PERSONAL RELATIONSHIPS Factors to be considered include; adaptability, attitude toward criticism, attitude toward supervision; cooperativeness, relations with fellow workers and relations with the public.	70

5. ATTENDANCE AND PUNCTUALITY		Score		Average
A. Attendance	A	95		of A&B
Absence record during this evaluation	B	95		
period:				95
Number of days excused__5__and unexcused absences__2__				
B. Punctuality				
Factors to be considered in this category's grade in-				

APPENDIX IV (cont'd)

clude late arrivals, early departures, extended
lunch and break periods, taking undue time performing outside errands while on the job. Daily
arrival record during this evaluation period includes ___5___ late arrivals.

SCALE FOR SCORING:		
Outstanding...................90-100		
Excellent.....................86-89	TOTAL OF SCORES:	375
Good..........................76-85	AVERAGE OF THIS TOTAL:	75
Fair..........................70-75		
Unsatisfactory................0-69		

SECTION C

COMMENTS TO EMPLOYEE:

Supervisor should include examples of work expecially well done.
Suggestions as to how work performance could be improved should also
be included.

Although I have worked closely with and provided direction to Ms.
Leforte for three years in a variety of situations, she still requires almost constant monitoring. Her contribution to the reorganization of the central building's subject divisions was noteworthy, but its significance was again compromised by her lack of
initiative, which meant that I had to step in frequently when
problems arose.- She appears to be working well with her committee
to revise adult materials selection policy and procedure, but 1
feel that her often unrealistic suggestions and unwillingness to

APPENDIX IV (cont'd)

exert a stronger control over the group will eventually dissipate the effectiveness of the committee's efforts. Ms. Leforte has good potential so it is particularly disappointing to have to report that she is not now working at a level equivalent to it.

SECTION D

Supervisor's Signature___ MARSHALL EDMONDS/s/_____

5

IS CLEO A TUTELARY MUSE?

Tomas Hernandez drove cautiously in the torrential rain, trying not to swerve on the slick pavement of the turnpike. His small foreign-made car strained with the added burden of an interior packed to capacity with personal belongings and a heavily laden U-Haul trailor attached to the rear. It was difficult for him to appreciate fully all that had happened in the last few months; events had occurred with such decisive rapidity that it was a wonder he felt as confident and excited as he did about the future. He was going to the Midwest, to Rolling Ridge, the corn capitol of the nation, for his second professional job (Appendix I). His mind, alert from the strong coffee he sipped periodically from a large thermos, reconstructed his professional career up to that point.

He had finished his work toward a master's degree in history at a midwestern university, but was unable to find a job in the buyer's market of the time. Discouraged, he returned to his home town, Colony Park, along the eastern seaboard, where director Norbert Crane, immediately offered him a full-time position at the public library; he had worked there, during summer and other vacations and in many capacities, for two years (Appendix II).

One day Crane took Hernandez into his office and fired his imagination about the exciting future and potential for libraries, librarianship, and the CPFPL, and Hernandez's possible contribution to that future. The director encouraged him to go full-time to earn a library degree. After some further discussion Hernandez agreed that it would indeed be a good career choice, so Crane picked up the phone and called the dean of the state university's library school to begin the interview and acceptance process; he also arranged, with full board approval, for the establishment of the Colony Park FPL Tuition Fellowship, which would pay for Hernandez's education. He allowed Hernandez to set his own hours at the library to accommodate his class schedule, and stated that, although CPFPL had awarded him a fellowship, he was under no sense of obligation to work there following graduation. Hernandez soon came to realize that Norbert Crane's philosophy in regard to this situation reflected an unusually enlightened approach, and the ideal was forever etched in his consciousness from the day Crane uttered it: a good librarian working anywhere is a credit and benefit to libraries everywhere. So, unlike most state association or municipal library awarded grants, there was no stipulation of indenture to a state or a library for a number of years if the award was accepted. Hernandez preferred to show his gratitude and loyalty to Crane by staying on as a professional at CPFPL after he had earned his MLS.

In a discussion one morning, Hernandez indicated to Crane the desire to become involved in materials selection, budgeting, and personnel supervision. Because the older man believed in giving employees as much responsibility as they felt ready for, and because he made a practice of trying to find reasons to comply with peoples' requests rather then not to comply, Hernandez was placed in charge of paperback selection and purchasing; he was also appointed supervisor of the summer outreach program so that he could gain experience supervising staff and working in the community. In return, the young librarian took it upon himself to design an entire section of the second floor to be the domain of young adult, and since the library lacked a graphic artist he volunteered to handletter signs and to help with displays and art exhibits—all on his own time. Appreciative of his efforts, Crane purchased a sophisticated offset printing press and other hardware for the production of library booklists, flyers, programs, etc., and gave Hernandez the task of planning the library's public relations activities as well as the design and production of the related materials. To cap it off, when Crane became editor of the state library association magazine he appointed Hernandez production manager. "How considerate of Norbert," Hernandez smiled to himself, "to have allowed my creativity and independence needs those various and constructive outlets for expression." He wondered if—no, hoped that—his new job in Rolling Ridge would allow the same opportunities and challenges.

His thoughts switched to his interview with Roger Balzac, the director of the Rolling Ridge Public Library. It had been scheduled three months before with the full knowledge and consent of Norbert Crane, who encouraged him to move on to advance his career, there being no imminent possibilities for promotion at the CPFPL. "Anyway," the friendly director had said, "you can lose yourself professionally by staying in one place. This will be a good opportunity for you." A decision to take the new job (which had been advertised in *LJ* and the *New York Times*), notice to Crane and the CPFPL, moving arrangements, and other events followed in quick succession. He was hired by Balzac to be the first professional supervisor of the library's outreach services, which included two 40-foot long semi-trailor style bookmobiles and three hospital deposit collections. One of the two branches had been closed several years previously due to a faulty foundation structure; the other was in the process of shutting down at the very time of his interview. The latter branch was in a "disadvantaged" neighborhood, and the vacated building was to be used as a social services center. There were no plans to revive either branch, so the bookmobiles had to fill the vacuum as traveling branches. Circulation in outreach services had been steadily declining, and Balzac said that he hoped Hernandez would be able to reverse the negative curve.

He recalled vividly his initial reaction to meeting Roger Balzac: "What is a man like this doing in a place like this?" Balzac had held jobs in the Northeast, the Mid-Atlantic, Southwest, and West Coast at a variety of medium and large libraries in positions of increasing responsibility. His urbane manner, formidable erudition, and background experience might have led one to conclude that perhaps he was somewhat out of his element there on the prairie. Nothing could have been further from the truth, for Balzac had accomplished miracles since he arrived in Rolling Ridge six years ago.

Shortly after he began as director, he moved the library from a dingy Carnegie mausoleum to a downtown department store that had become vacant. The store was gutted and rebuilt, according to his specifications, into a beautiful, modern facility, decorated in vibrant hues and furnished with the latest Herman Miller offerings. His attention then turned to the improvement of the materials collection and the raising of staff salaries. For his diligence and hard work toward those goals, he was rewarded with a publicly acknowledged local and regional resource of the highest caliber, and with the reputation for the Rolling Ridge PL's having the highest starting professional salaries in the state. His last priority, the others having been successfully met, was the recruitment of a cadre of young professionals whom he felt he could personally train and counsel. No longer a particularly young man himself, at age 45 Balzac intended to retire here, and so had a very personal stake in ensuring his future at the Rolling Ridge PL.

Tomas Hernandez's reveries began to dissolve and his attention shifted to the changed landscape. The rain had ceased. Having entered the next state and a highway off the turnpike, he was amazed by the extraordinary flatness of the land, especially in contrast to the hilly terrain he had grown up with back home. Miles and miles of unobstructed vistas of rich, coffee-brown, almost black soil, broken only by occasional small towns, farms, and grain elevators. Suddenly, the smell struck his nostrils — the pungency of processed corn syrup, as if the car had gone off the road and fallen into the neck of a gigantic Karo bottle. It was not an unpleasant odor, certainly one that he could become used to he decided. The city of Rolling Ridge loomed far in the distance, with the darkness of nothing surrounding it like a protective cloak.

Hernandez soon discovered that Rolling Ridge was not, by any stretch of the imagination, anything like the suburban bedroom community of Colony Park. A manufacturing and processing center, containing almost 100,000 people, it is the headquarters and location of important branch offices for many of the country's industrial giants, especially those companies that deal with farm products and related machinery. As such, it has a large blue collar population of thrifty, hardworking people with a predilection toward conversatism in lifestyle and thought, whose interest in libraries is, by and large, about the same as the sun's interest in them.

And he also soon discovered that Roger Balzac was not anything like Norbert Crane. Balzac not only presented the appearance, but reinforced it with the appropriate manner, of the severe "pater familias" of whom most of the staff was in awe and in fear. As far as Hernandez could determine, no one dared to approach him with suggestions for needed changes in library policy or procedure or, heaven forbid, in his personal management style. This was especially desolating to Hernandez because Norbert Crane had been so exemplary in this regard. The young librarian was not accustomed to seeing scenes of despair unfolding before his eyes with ever increasing frequency: the children's librarian sobbing in frustration, or the head of reference red-faced with mute anger, or the head of technical services mumbling uncontrollably to himself, all as reactions to Balzac. On several occasions he was witness to the sights and sounds of Balzac's own ragged emotionalism, including tantrum-pitched screaming, banging fists on desks, and slamming doors. Senior staff members said that these fevers of truculent behavior had manifested themselves only within the past two or three years. Moods passed over him like wind over a field. He had become unpredictable and inscrutable.

One day, following a particularly unpleasant session, during which Balzac had trampled on Hernandez's ideas for reviving the use of bookmobiles (he had done them all with great success back in Colony Park, but could not get this across to the adamant director), Hernandez decided that if he wished to survive in this restrictive atmosphere his options were clearly the following: don't make waves, do a good job with no fuss of which he could be proud, try to gain Balzac's respect, keep him (Balzac) informed of his activities, and, above all, don't let Balzac bother him. He decided to throw himself into his job, even to the point of learning how to drive the semi-trailers so that he could take them for repairs and inspections when the regular drivers were not available, and even to the point of washing them by hand every Sunday (there were no car washes in the city large enough to accommodate them).

Since Balzac discountenanced virtually every idea Hernandez and children's librarian, Kate Lespran, had the courage to suggest, they decided one day to take it upon themselves without his knowledge to go out and solicit funds from some of the large corn processors and farm equipment manufactures for a public relations campaign they had in mind for a children's program. "Perhaps if we do it this way," Hernandez had reasoned, "and show him our success after the fact, we'll reach a point where we can do things *with* his approval." "It's worth a try, I suppose," Lespran had replied, doubtfully. On their third call, they got a donation of $1,000.00. They were beside themselves with joy, and, like two children going to their father proudly to display good report cards, they hurried back to tell Balzac.

They found him in his habitually cluttered office, buried beneath stacks of paperwork. Hernandez paused at his door for a moment and took in those details of the director's appearance that showed above the desk. His bodily frame, verging on obesity, appeared to have fallen into disrepair, as though he had ceased to be interested in it. There was a small bald spot on the crown of his head, and his chin was covered with a short graying beard. There were many wrinkles in the hollows between his eyes and his cheeks; and the eyes were sad; they were very sad.

"Yes, what is it?" asked the director absently, as Hernandez rapped at his door.

"Sorry, Mr. Balzac," offered Hernandez diffidently. "Your secretary wasn't at her desk, so we thought we'd tell you the good news ourselves."

"Oh? Yes. What is it?" Balzac asked, economizing time by doing some figuring on his calculator the while.

"Kate and I visited some of the local businesses to ask for donations to help with a special program we've been planning," stated Hernandez, with a peculiar mixture of reluctance and eagerness.

"And we've been very successful at it, too!" Lespran adventured. "We got a check for $1,000.00."

The two produced the check, smiles of pride and happiness spreading over their faces.

"Humph!" grunted the director, accepting the check with a preoccupied air. "I'm surprised that your contributor didn't complain about not being approached by the director or one of the Friends. I'm not sure you should be doing this. Raising money is my job." There was a note of finality in Balzac's voice that clearly signalled their time was up, and he was impatient to get back to his desk.

"Well, we just wanted to tell you what we've been up to," Hernandez defended himself, as Lespran tugged on his sleeve to get him to leave. She could see signs of an emotional crisis. Roger Balzac mumbled inarticulately, and buried himself in his papers. The two deflated employees exchanged looks and slipped quietly out of the room. Balzac retained the check.

At Hernandez's desk, Hernandez described the encounter as futile and ludicrous, and concluded that it tallied entirely with Lespran's expectation of it. Balzac had succeeded in transforming the news into an offense.

"I can't take it any more, Tom," said Lespran, in a trembling and wrathful voice. "I can't take it! The man's gone bananas."

Tom Hernandez knew that there had been a "running feud" between Lespran and Balzac during the last year or so, but he had never seen the children's librarian so upset. She was one great bleeding resentment.

"Try not to let him get under your skin, Kate," he tried to comfort her. "If you realize that this is his way, and that probably nothing can change him, then life will be easier for you."

"I suppose you're right. But why, I ask you, can he not be supportive, even once in a while? Is that asking too much? His way is always the right way—the only way. I'm getting tired of it, really, and my bringing these problems home to my husband every night is not at all helpful, you know what I mean?" She lowered her voice. "You know, Tom, if I ever find another job—and I'm already looking—there will be some fireworks around here before I leave, I can guarantee you that!"

Her young companion was exceedingly perturbed by this tidbit of news; he knew that Kate Lespran was not one to make empty threats. After a few additional pronouncements on Balzac's testiness, the children's librarian went back to work.

Dozens of times the Lesprans had had Tom Hernandez and a few other library friends over for dinner and the evening. About a month after their miscarried attempt to demonstrate success and then inform Balzac later of what they had done, the Lesprans had the group over again. After a typically huge meal, Kate announced to the slightly tipsy assembly that she had found another job.

The first to congratulate her were the head of reference, James Emerson Jones III and his wife Margaret. Said he: "I'm so happy for you, Kate! But I also have an announcement: I'll be leaving Rolling Ridge, too! I got another job!"

Kate Lespran and her husband and Jones and his wife all laughed merrily, while Hernandez and the fourth member of the group, head of technical services Ralph Pershing, sat glumly by.

"How could you do this to us?" Hernandez and Pershing said, almost simultaneously. "We'll be left to face Balzac alone."

Tom Hernandez tried not to show how sad he felt about his friends' leaving, and managed to keep up a cheerful facade until the party broke up.

The next few weeks were pure hell for Roger Balzac. Ever true to her word, Kate Lespran found an appropriate vehicle for her revenge: the local press. It all began when Balzac and Pershing had an altercation (their's was another of the "running feuds" in the library), and Pershing was fired. The library board, in public meeting, asked Balzac why so many of the young professionals, all fairly recent hirees, were leaving at the same time. A reporter for the city paper decided to call Lespran to get her side of the story, since her complaints to many of the mothers of her patrons about Balzac had rallied a considerable force to her defense during her tenure, and they had told the paper to ask Lespran her reasons for resignation.

In a painfully detailed letter to the editor, and articles headlined "Children's Librarian Charges City Library Director with Harrassment and Incompetence" and "Librarians Quit Because of Director," Lespran allowed vent for her fury. Before the furor had time to quiet down, the board of trustees, in special session, decided to hand Balzac an official reprimand with the warning that if more staff resigned and the cause of resignation could even be remotely connected to his management style or personality, he would be asked to resign himself.

The morning that the Lesprans left for the West Coast where Kate's new job was—the Jones' had merely stolen away as inconspicuously as possible—Hernandez returned to his apartment and found a letter from the director of personnel for the Mitford Public Library one of the nation's largest urban systems, serving 2,000,000 residents and located in the same state, north of Rolling Ridge. It read:

Dear Mr. Hernandez:

A very good friend of mine, Norbert Crane, has recommended you for a newly created position with our library system. As you probably know, the city of Mitford has several large populations of Spanish speaking and other minority residents and we are in need of a good librarian, preferably of Hispanic background, to coordinate the library's service efforts to those important communities. I should tell you that Mr. Crane thinks very highly of you and your abilities, and I trust his judgment without qualification. He says you would be the right person for this job, and I am therefore very eager to meet you to tell you more about it.

There is only one problem: the library's budget requires that, if you are interested in the position and are able to move to Mitford, you start working within two weeks of the date of this letter. I fully realize that this is a difficult decision to make, especially since professional courtesy in the library world ideally promotes the theory that a one month notice be given before resignation. However, I feel that this is a once in a lifetime opportunity which you cannot afford to pass up, and I'm sure Roger Balzac would not hesitate to let you go to further a promising career.

Please telephone me collect at your earliest convenience so that we can discuss your future, hopefully with the Mitford Public Library.

Sincerely,

/s/ ALINE ALCINDOR,
Director of Personnel

The letter sent Tomas Hernandez into a frenzy of conflicting reactions: ecstatic jubilation and ego-tripping, wild speculation and outrageous fantasy, compounded by confusion and indirection. What should he do? Surely this was something he would want to share with local friends; he could not, unfortunately, because they had all left the city by then. Tom Hernandez never felt so alone in his entire life. He spent a miserable Sunday talking long distance to family and friends in the East. Their advice, typically, was for him to do what he thought best. Norbert Crane, with whom he had been corresponding since he left Colony Park and in whom he had been confiding his unhappiness, advised him to take the Mitford job. At his mentor's prompting, he resolved to find out more about the Mitford Public Library position. He also resolved to talk with Cleo Passantino, the head of RRPL readers' services, a young librarian who had been at the library for three years and with whom he had had little contact. Perhaps Passantino, whose job put her into almost daily contact with the director, had found a way to cope with his unusual management style (or lack of it). After all, thought Hernandez, she *had* lasted three whole years in the place!

Monday Hernandez called Aline Alcindor and was told that the position at the Mitford P.L. was one that, in addition to its own possibilities for creativity and challenge, could eventually lead to a middle management level job in the library's special programs of service division. He would have to start at a beginning step in the Librarian I civil service salary schedule, however, so that permanent employment status would be assured. (The option, Alcindor confided, was to come in as a "non-career, temporary" appointment at a higher salary but with no civil service protection, which she felt would be an unwise decision.) By city-administered examination and promotion, his current salary range would be equalled and surpassed within a year to a year and a half. With Mitford's higher cost of living, Hernandez realized that he would have to think carefully about the ramifications of taking a salary cut, temporary though it might be. And, how would that look on his resume?

Hernandez spotted Cleo Passantino as she was putting on her coat to go home for lunch. "Cleo," he began, "I know we haven't ever been very close and I guess it's because I and my three recently departed colleagues always considered you to be part of the RRPL 'establishment' so to speak." Passantino put on a concerned expression. Hernandez continued. "I'd like your advice on a couple of things and, frankly, I need to talk to someone and you're the most likely candidate. How about our going out for lunch—my treat?"

"That sounds fine, Tom," smiled Passantino guardedly. "You always seemed so involved with your circle of friends and they with each other that I somehow felt I would be intruding if I ever wanted to join in."

"I never even considered your feelings or whether you and your husband would have liked to join us on our social get-togethers. I'm very, very sorry, ashamed, and embarrassed," confessed Hernandez, with polite sincerity.

"Don't let it bother you and I won't let it affect me," said Passantino, with an enchanting smile. "Now, what's on your mind?"

By then they had walked to a small restaurant, and had told the waitress that they wanted the hamburger plate and coffee.

"You seem to know how to get along so well with Mr. Balzac—what's your secret of success?" asked Hernandez.

The readers' services librarian was not at a loss for words. "Well, I hope this doesn't sound like an off-the-wall remark but have you ever heard of or read anything about the so called mid-life crisis?"

Coincidentally, Hernandez had been planning to read Gail Sheehy's *Passages* and other books on life stages and aging, including Daniel Levinson's Yale study, to help prepare his own father (and his family) for an impending retirement, and he mentioned this to Passantino.

"Good, then you have some idea as to what I'm getting at. I'm convinced that this is precisely what's affecting Roger. You know, he was an entirely different person when I first began here three years ago. He could never have been considered an ideal boss—really, have you ever worked for one?" (Hernandez conjured up Norbert Crane but kept his mouth shut) "—but he came pretty close back then. Concerned, thoughtful, supportive, humorous—all those traits lacking from the present boss were available in abundance. Now he's seldom happy, never satisfied, temperamental, stubborn; his behavior at times can be charitably characterized as erratic—guess I needn't tell *you* about such things. It seems like he's itching for a change but doesn't know exactly the direction or directions to pursue in order to accomplish the change." (Hmmmm, thought Hernandez, we all feel that way, especially me right now!) "When he was younger he really turned RRPL around, from a backwater, two-bit operation to the respected institution it is today. Maybe there are no more challenges here for him and he's getting restless, which is complicated by the realization that he's no longer a young man. Notice the way he drives himself and the staff. He'll get an ulcer or a heart attack if he doesn't watch out. His behavior fits the pattern perfectly for a man his age. You'll see that when you delve into the literature."

"This is all very well, Cleo," said Hernandez, "but it's not showing me how you deal with it."

"Okay, Tom, so the first thing you do is recognize that the problem exists and then you do your best, as you say, to deal with it. You talk with the guy; you support him even if he doesn't support you; you put up with his didactic approach because the man's got experience and intelligence and you might learn something. Maybe it's the frustrated library school professor in him crying to come out—whatever it is, give him a chance to show you what he knows. You try to steer him toward other pursuits, other goals, especially in the ALA if he persists in being library-oriented. His perspectives need widening since Rolling Ridge can seem confining at times. And did you know that he left his wife of 20 years and is living alone? Some day you may go through the same thing and I'll bet you'd appreciate having a colleague, even a younger one, with whom you could communicate. Wouldn't you agree?" Passantino looked at Hernandez expectantly.

"But is it really worth the time and effort? To be blunt about it—is it our responsibility to try to help in a situation like this?" Hernandez countered.

"Listen, my husband's a teacher in the city school system, Tom. We both have a stake in our futures in Rolling Ridge and so I have no choice, if I want to continue at the library. That's bringing it down to a realistic viewpoint on the one hand. On the other, don't you think that people should do things just because it is the humane course of action? Forget about responsibilities in a job-related sense. What is our responsibility to a fellow human being, who in this case happens to be a respected library director who is also our boss? So many books and articles are churned out about the top administrator's responsibilities toward staff; rare or non-existant are those which discuss the responsibilities and relationships which should also go in the other direction! Hey, I'm tired of this soap box—how's your hamburger?"

"Pretty good, although I tend to like mine rarer," laughed Hernandez. Then he said: "The mid-life crisis is something I'd never considered in his case."

"Well, there's something else you might want to consider too," said Passantino, curling her lips amicably.

"What's that?" inquired Hernandez, curious.

"Well, it's a technique for dealing with a superior you might never have heard of before. I've found it very effective."

Hernandez eyes her slyly. "Come on, Svengali, let me in on the secret. What is it? Do you have old Roger hypnotized or something?"

"You're closer than you might think," replied the grinning Passantino, "but it's not that! Look, let's get back to the library. I have something in my desk that will make your eyes pop!"

"This I've got to see!"

Back at her desk, Cleo Passantino produced a long sheet of graph paper with a sawtooth squiggle traced down the center of it.

"One of the things I've learned," she explained calmly, "is that human beings have individual cyclic patterns of behavior, emotional tone, stuff like that. I made it a point to contact Balzac at least twice a day—as I can do easily on my job—and I graphed his mood, roughly, each time I saw him. After a couple of months, I had his overall behavior pretty well pegged. See?"

Tom Hernandez was thunderstruck. "That's the damnedest thing I ever saw or heard of!" Cleo Passantino was proving that there were novelties under the sun.

"It's called biorhythms," continued the young woman, gratified by his show of interest. "The technique doesn't suggest that people are exactly regular in the patterns they make, but there's a fair consistency. I've graphed myself, and I find that I have a twenty-one-day cycle of emotional ups and downs. If I have a tough problem to deal with, I try to hit it on the upswing."

Tom Hernandez was the very mirror of amazement.

Cleo Passantino gave a little laugh. "This line," she went on, tracing with her finger the ups and downs, "is a graphic representation of Roger Balzac's moods. See there's a definite pattern of about 16 days between his highs and his lows, but also there's an overlapping line at about 27 days, when he's really high!"

You could have pushed the young man over with a feather. "Does it really work?" he chaffed her.

"I always hit him on the top of his highs when I want something," the imperturbable Passantino answered. "And I almost always get what I want!"

Tom Hernandez dropped back in his chair. "I'm going to look into this and the business of mid-life crisis," he said, amused at such a confession. "They can't do any harm. And I need all the help I can get!"

"Don't forget, Tom," said she, "nobody ever claimed these are exact sciences, but there's something to them. I find that they help me, at any rate, to understand people better. I find I can be more understanding and respectful of them because I have a pretty good idea of what they're experiencing and going through, and I have an idea what to expect from them next. This sort of stuff has certainly made me understand myself better. And another thing I've found effective. Instead of making a list of his defects, I've made a list of his strengths, and concentrated on those."

"Cleo!" he said, rising. "How can I thank you? I really appreciate your sharing these thoughts with me. I'm not going to rule any of them out. Thanks a million!"

As they were thus talking, Roger Balzac's secretary rushed up to Hernandez.

"Mr. Balzac would like to see you, Tom," she said in hushed tones, adding rapidly, "Don't worry, I think it's good news!"

He excused himself to Passantino, who winked at him in a peculiar way, and proceeded immediately to the director's office. He reflected along the way on the conversation with the head of readers' services, and smiled when he concluded that Balzac's biorhythm chart must have been peaking at that very moment—or so he hoped.

"Hello, Tom!" said the director, greeting him enthusiastically, as he rounded his desk to shake hands, which he did with unrestrained ardor. "Come in and have a seat. I have quite a surprise for you!" Roger Balzac was genuinely happy, and Hernandez imagined that the peak of the biorhythm squiggle was going right off the chart.

The director went on, his excitement straining impatiently in the leash: "Tom, I received notice in today's mail that our library has been given a $75,000 award to fund a really impressive public relations campaign which could be used as a model for other medium-sized libraries. We'll be able to purchase equipment we've been wanting for ages: an electronic offset printer; collators and folding machines and other graphic production-related paraphernalia; video, film, and photographic equipment — you name it. Also, artist's materials and supplies, software for the equipment we purchase, and other things. The company sponsoring the award wants to find out how much can be done in terms of effective public relations and publicity using only local library talent. This was all Cleo's idea."

It was obvious that Balzac's enthusiasm for the grant lifted his spirits up from their normal sagging state. His manner was more animated, but not in the usual petulant sense: he even seemed years younger. And he could be enthusiastic — there's a strength! Hernandez was beginning to revise his views.

"Congratulations, Mr. Balzac!" exclaimed Hernandez, quickening to the fascinating possibilities of the announcement. "That's wonderful news. I'm really proud of you and Cleo! The staff will be very pleased to hear it. This is quite an accomplishment for our library — and, especially, a long overdue recognition of the kind of institution you direct and the priorities you set for it." Hernandez surprised himself that the words came out so easily. This was not meant to be a piece of puffery designed to provide an ego boost for Balzac: the convivial atmosphere was contagious and he spoke with complete sincerity.

"Thank you, Tom, thank you," said Balzac, perceptibly reddening. "Yes, I think everyone has a right to be pleased."

Then suddenly he extinguished his smile and arranged his countenance so that his listener should suppose him to be profoundly disturbed. ("Oh, no!" Hernandez's unspoken thoughts ran. "It was too good to be true. He's slipping back into a churlish mood.")

"Tom?" the director said, averting his eyes.

"Yes" (very slowly).

"I want to ask you to be coordinator of the experimental PR campaign, naturally with a salary increase. I know you would do a splendid job." This with a tremendous air of intimacy.

Tomas Hernandez did not know what to answer. He had been thinking of leaving. Beneath his courteous exterior he hid a sudden spasm of profound agitation. He was bowled over. The idea was exquisite but full of terror. He was pleased, flattered, astonished. But was he up to it? Indeed, he was so startled by the unexpected request that he could not reply. He blew his nose to hide his confusion.

But Balzac had anticipated that he would have been surprised. When he spoke, he spoke with a most understanding inflection. "Tom," he began, catching the other's eye, and holding it firmly. "You may not realize, at your age and in this stage of your career, that what is known as the 'old boy/old girl' network is still pretty strong in the profession, and, well, it has come to my attention that you might be thinking of leaving us to work in Mitford, as head of their minority outreach service program. I hope you'll think very seriously about all the advantages and disadvantages — career-wise and personally — of both positions in their respective environments before you make up your mind. I would like you to stay with us, obviously, but the choice must be yours and yours alone."

The young librarian sat uncomfortably in the visitor's chair, surprised that Roger Balzac knew of his offer and even more surprised that he would confront him with it. Should he, Tom Hernandez, have mentioned that he was thinking of leaving? He felt momentarily sheepish. But there was no trace of sinisterness in Balzac's manner. Astonishing, though, how news traveled in the library field!

"I'll need your answer right away, Tom," the director was saying pleasantly. There was in his voice a note of dependence upon him, of appeal to him.

Hernandez was flattered. His self-respect returned to him rapidly. He had been feeling like a cipher, a nonentity. This he knew happens to employees who are not given a word of encouragement, some recognition. But were Balzac's motives entirely pure? He could ill afford another resignation. Here was an opportunity to wreak vengeance upon him for his treatment of Kate Lespran and Ralph Pershing and James Emerson Jones III. But it might be a pyrrhic victory. And is there nothing to be said on the other side? Is a feud ever all one-sided? No one ever did hear Roger Balzac's side. And then there's Cleo Passantino. She had survived. She had counseled kindness and understanding (coupled with a little divination!), and got on with him swimmingly. These thoughts and many more like them flitted to and fro ceaselessly over the troubled surface of his mind. He had to decide. There was something inexpressibly poignant about the sight of the once powerful Roger Balzac sitting quiescently like a victim in a noose across the desk from him, knowing his job and possibly his future was in jeopardy; it touched young Hernandez's imagination. He had yet to immerse himself in the writings of the mid-life crisis researchers, but from the skimming he had given them he knew that something like a chemical agent was working in Balzac's defenseless mind, and that the hapless fellow was trying not to succumb to it. The younger librarian had a horror of sentimentality, but he could not arrest the softening of his heart. With a sudden uncontrollable outburst of feeling which staggered while it satisfied him, he put out his hand. "I'll stay, Mr. Balzac," he announced, "and I'll do the job."

"That's wonderful, Tom!" said the director with a deep sigh. They clasped hands with a perfect understanding.

APPENDIX I

ENTRY FOR ROLLING RIDGE PUBLIC LIBRARY IN THE AMERICAN LIBRARY DIRECTORY

P   ROLLING RIDGE PUBLIC LIBRARY, 425 S Daniels Pkwy,
Dir Roger Balzac, *ILL & Ref* James E. Jones; *Ad* Cleo Passantino; *Ch* Kate Lespran; *YA & Media* Open; *Outreach* Tomas Hernandez; *Tech Serv* Ralph Pershing; *Acq* Kathy Spring; *Cat* John Balabar; Staff: 45 (prof 18; cler 27)
Founded 1865. Pop served 99,054; Circ 553,537
Inc $1,739,020 (inc. fed $56,921). Exp Bks $85,651, Per $14,160, Bd $7,500, Micro $3,500, AV $15,965; Sal $783,000 (prof $190,572, nonprof $150,806, cler $441,622)
Library Holdings: Bk titles 95,573, vols 224,879; Micro-Fiche 25,818, reels 8,221; Av-Rec 5,260, A-Tapes 655, Flm 352, Maps, Art repro 300. VF 220
Special Collections: US Doc Dep
Bookmobiles: 2

APPENDIX II

ENTRY FOR COLONY PARK FREE PUBLIC LIBRARY IN THE AMERICAN LIBRARY DIRECTORY

P   COLONY PARK FREE PUBLIC LIBRARY, 70 S Park Avenue, *Dir* Norbert Crane; *Asst Dir* Opal G. Wells; *Head, Info Servs* Lorrie Sune; *Head, Tech Serv* Betty Truex; *Ch* Melba Gortner; *YA* Cheryl Martell; *AV* Jane Vargas; Staff: 38 (prof 14; cler 24)
Founded 1890. Pop served 44,500; Circ 355,913
Inc $800,000 (incl state $50,000, city $750,000). Exp Bks $150,000, Per $15,000, Bd $5,000, Micro $3,000, AV $10,000; Sal $500,000 (prof $200,000, cler $300,000)
Library Holdings: Bk titles 175,833, vols 298,115; Per sub 947; Micro-Fiche 5,509, reels 6,823; AV-Rec 10,000, A-Tapes 276, V-Tapes 153, Flm 406, Fl 646, Slides 4,906, Ov tr, Maps, Art repro 193. VF 127
Special Collections: Art & music; folk arts; Colony Park history; state history; ethnic studies; feminism; bus & mgt
Branches: 1
Clairview Avenue, 986 Clairview Avenue, Lbrn Helen Furth
Bk vols 50,000

APPENDIX III

ENTRY FOR ROLLING RIDGE IN EDITOR & PUBLISHER MARKET GUIDE

ROLLING RIDGE

1—LOCATION: Richland County (SMSA). E&P Map K-5, County Seat. 250 mi. S from Mitford. Agricultural area; Corn Processing Center; Manufacturing.

2—TRANSPORTATION: Railroads — Norwood and Southern; A&N; Carterville Central; Carterville Terminal System.
Motor Freight Carriers — 52
Intercity Bus Lines — Corona Transit; Continental Greyhouse.
Airlines — Ozalleny.

3—POPULATION:
Corp. City Most recent cen. 99,054.
Primary Mkt. Area — ABC:
    Most recent cen 450,783
County/SMSA Most recent cen. 150,742.

4—HOUSEHOLDS:
Most recent census City 34,978; County/SMSA 44,899
Primary Mkt. Area — ABC:
    Most recent cen 145,032

APPENDIX III (cont'd)

5 – BANKS:	Number	Deposits
Commercial Banks	10	$700,536,406
Sav. & Loan Assns.	5	$350,543,980

6 – PASSENGER AUTOS: County 75,425

7 – ELECTRIC METERS: Residence 40,364

8 – GAS METERS: Residence 37,022

9 – PRINCIPAL INDUSTRIES (CZ): Industry, No. of Wage Earners – Graders, Tractors 6,002; Corn Processing 5343; Air Conditioners-Carburetors 1,750; Gas & Water Systems 1,103; Castings & Fittings 1,462; Window Glass 590; Tires 3,568 Av. Wkly Wage, all industry $285.

10 – CLIMATE: Min. & Max. Temp. – Spring 27-93; Summer 43-94; Fall 1-81; Winter 1-73. First killing frost, Oct. 27. Last killing frost, April 27.

11 – TAP WATER: Alkaline, soft, fluoridated.

12 – RETAILING: Principal Shopping Center – 9 blocks on Cornell Street, 9 on North Main Street; 4 on East Main, East Plains; East Waller; S Daniels Pkwy.

Nearby Shopping Centers

Name of Shopping Center	No. of Stores	Principal Store and/or Supermarket
Burtell Village	25	Wollworth's, A&D
Colony	23	Thrift Drugs
Fargate Plaza	30	Kriegels, Wofgreen, Golden's
Norview Mall	15	N.A.
Southland	10	Thrift Drugs
Elms	8	N.A.
North Shore	8	A&D

Principal Shopping Days: Mon., Fri., Sat.
Stores Open Evenings: Dept. – Mon., Fri. Food until 9 and Midnight.

13 – RETAIL OUTLETS: Department Stores – Miller Bros. 3; Carter, Pierson, Skoll; J. C. Nickell; Montgomery Wells; Sears Rareback; Golden's; Golden's Home Center.
Variety Stores – Wollworth 2; Kriegel 1; Ben Franks 4.
Discount Stores – Cousin Fritz; J-Mart 2; Turnwheel.
Chain Drug Stores (CZ): Wofgreen 2; Thrift 2; SupeRol 1; Ercoe's 2; Ruth Jones 3; Royalcraft 2; Wilbey 1; Oshkosh 2.
Chain Food Supermarkets: Eyers 3; A&D 3; Krolleys 3; Togler 4; Buyrite 1; Robin's 2; Lloyd's 2.
Other Chain Stores – Keath Furn; Carter's, Xenon (Jewelry); Songer Co.; Firestop; Goodmonth 2; Goodranch (Tires, appliances); Hickert (Paint and

APPENDIX III (cont'd)

Wallpaper); Pittsfield Plate Glass (Glass, Paint, & Wallpaper); Sherman-Wilson (Paint & Wallpaper); Fannie Hill, Dutch May (Candies); Bollers, Kenneys, Waltersons (Shoes); Radio House; Team Electrics; Playbuck; Remnant Shack.

14 — NEWSPAPERS: Tribune (m) 40,976; Bugler (e) 31,001; comb (m&e) 71,977; (S(67,322.
Local Contact for Advertising and Merchandising Data: Ronald Krebbs, Adv. Mgr. or Willard Stielow, Nat. Adv. Mgr., Tribune & Bugler.
National Representative: Burnham/Newspaper Sales.

APPENDIX IV

ENTRIES FOR ROLLING RIDGE IN
BROADCASTING/CABLE YEARBOOK

Rolling Ridge. General Electronics Cablevision. 2435 E. Waller Street. Tom Ford, mgr; Bob Crine, chief tech.
  Serves Rolling Ridge, Richland County. Top 100 TV market.
  Subscribers: 25,078; homes passed 32,760; total homes in franchised area: 32,760. Started 1/70. Length 430 mi. Charges: instal $25; $10/mo. Franchise fee 8%.
  Channel usage: total ch capacity 40; TV chs 7; pay cable 1; automated 3; access 2; other origination programming 1; technically unavailable 1; available unused 25. Allband FM.
  TV Stations: WALD Rolling Ridge (17-1, ABC); WCRE Lancaster (3-3, CBS); WTOP Lancaster (15-5, NBC); WBMT Tremont (20-10, NBC); WRI-TV McCormick (9-9, Ind, cc); KICJ-TV St. Lauds (11-11, Ind, cc); WONN-TV Kilgore (12-8, ETV). Microwave: American Video, Inc.
  ■Pay cable: one ch (HBO); 10,000 subscribers.
  Origination — automated: ch 13 (weather, 170 hrs); ch 2 (public service 170 hrs); ch 13 (news, 170 hrs). Other origination: ch 4 (film, studio, tape, 40 hrs). Adv. accepted; annual volume $30,000.
  Ownership: General Electronics Cablevision.

Rolling Ridge

WXZ (AM) — Format: MOR.

WFCC (FM) — Format: Modern country; Spec prog: Farm 10 hrs wkly.

WMMT (FM) — Format: Prog jazz.; Spec prog: Class 10 hrs, jazz 10 hrs wkly.

WCRN (AM) — Format: MOR, Contemporary; Spec prog: Farm 20 hrs wkly.

WCRN (FM) — Format: Contemp, MOR.

ORGANIZING

6

MY DOOR IS ALWAYS OPEN

Malcolm Stanhope put a check mark beside the last item on his list of topics to be discussed with the principal. The two had spent almost an hour in an informal discussion of various matters that came within his jurisdiction as head of the library media center at John Brown Junior High School in Los Pasos. It was a grand day, one of those dazzling spectacular blue and gold days of early fall.

"Well, I guess that's it, Mrs. Rood," Stanhope said, with a feeling of satisfaction. He inserted his pencil in his shirt pocket with the rapid gesture of habit, and got up. "Thank you for spending this time with me and answering my questions."

Henrietta Rood nodded and smiled appreciatively. "I make a practice of getting together with department heads for relaxed unpressured talks like this about once a month," she said, "so we'll be doing it again—many times! I'll give you a call toward the middle of October, about a week before our next meeting, so you'll have time to think of anything you'd like to talk over with me. If you don't have anything specific, we'll just chatter away and let things develop!" Her face broke into a warm friendly smile.

"That sounds great," Stanhope declared, with unconscious eagerness.

"Now, whenever you want to see me about anything between these get-togethers," she resumed, "don't hesitate to drop by—anytime. My door is always open."

The media specialist thanked her again and started toward the door.

"Oh, by the way, Malcolm," she called after him. "Did you see the results of that opinionnaire your predecessor administered just before the end of school last May?" And then, not pausing, "I *knew* there was something I was forgetting to ask you."

Stanhope frowned his incomprehension, and began to comb his memory for some clue as to what she was speaking of. "No," he replied hesitantly, moving closer to her desk.

Seeing his confusion, Rood explained that she thought he might have come across Hamilton Brody's study as he was going through his desk or his file cabinet. She reached over and picked up a manila folder and handed him the contents (Appendix I). Stanhope accepted it, and slipped into the chair again. After scanning the pages with the facile rapidity of an expert reader, he confirmed his ignorance of it. The principal nodded understandingly, and asked for the document back. She thumbed the pages slowly, explaining that the study had been conducted to try to ascertain student attitudes toward the media center, why they used it, which facilities they used, and to see if they had suggestions for bettering it.

Stanhope hitched his chair closer to her desk, his face serious in concentration, and asked what had been done with the study.

The principal laughed. "Nothing! Ham — he initiated it by the way — was to have come up with a plan for improving facilities and services based on the results by the end of October. But ..., well, he's a couple of thousand miles away!" Then, leaning back in her chair and with an impish smile playing about her mouth, she said: "You know I can't quite get used to the idea of him giving up *his* job to follow his wife. You know the story, don't you?"

Stanhope said he understood that Brody's wife had become a state librarian somewhere on the east coast, and that he had resigned to accompany her.

Rood bubbled over in another laugh. "Right!" she said. "I can't quite get used to the idea of a man following a women to a new job. When I was a young woman it was always the other way around! If Mr. Rood — God rest his soul — had ever been transferred, I would most assuredly have gone with him. But not the other way around!"

"Times have changed," her listener said.

"Yes," she sighed, "and I guess we have to change with them." Then she shook her head repeatedly.

"You said Mr. Brody planned to do something about the survey this fall," Stanhope said, gently interrupting the flow of her thoughts.

"Oh, yes, they only learned about her appointment at the end of June. She started her new job August 1st." She paused, and thought a moment. "We were lucky you happened to be sitting in your dean's office when I called about the position, and that you could come over for an interview right away."

"It worked out beautifully for me," said Stanhope, in eager assent. "She was looking over my resume when you called." Then, changing the subject, "I wonder, Mrs. Rood, if I could make a copy of the report in case I can't find one in the media center."

Rood passed it to him with the remark that she would like him to do what Brody was to have done: give her a plan for developing the center based on the results. Stanhope turned at once to the recommendation page. "I notice," he said, "that Mr. Brody — Ham — suggested more material and staff."

"Yes," acknowledged Rood. "He was also to compare us to the most recent ALA standards, by the way, to see where we fall short. I'd like you to do that, too."

"Uh, huh," Stanhope nodded. "And if I feel that I should add items like typewriters — I mention them because they're singled out for special attention — I should just go ahead and put them in my report to you?"

"Exactly. And include prices. But also, imagine that you have a magic wand. What would you like to see happen in the media center if you were to wave it?" She smiled.

Stanhope returned her smile. "Speaking of prices, Mrs. Rood, how much money do I have to work with this year?" He had neglected to ask about the administration of the LMC budget during his interview. The question was innocently and diplomatically couched.

Henrietta Rood was gentle but authoritative when she gave answer. "I guess this didn't come up in your interview, but that's my area. I look after the budget. Department heads submit to me what they feel they need or want, and I decide whether they can have it. The budget is confidential. Only I and the assistant principal see it."

Stanhope experienced a hanging moment of uneasiness. His eyes questioned hers. "I don't know how much I have to work with then?" he said, moving his neck as though his collar was not comfortable. As soon as he had uttered the words he suspected that he had said something decisive and irretrievable.

"That's true. I consider the budget to be an administrative function, and my responsibility. I'll let you know if you're spending too much!" She said this firmly and yet endearingly, and met his eyes with her eyes. There was nothing malevolent in her response or in her look; she simply stated it as if it was the most natural thing in the world, not in the least abnormal.

Malcolm Stanhope sealed back a protest. There was the sound of a commotion in the corridor; the principal excused herself to go and investigate it.

This gave Stanhope a chance to withdraw into the inner compartment of his mind. He sat still, full in the eye of the sun, and meditated. His meditations took—for him—an unusual tern. He began for the first time to question Henrietta Rood's behavior. Hitherto her behavior had been unexampled. But just as a person with a vague discomfort dimly fears cancer, so he dimly feared that there might be something to watch for in the way she handled people. Steady, my friend! he enjoined himself. Don't get carried away! Henrietta Rood was preeminently a comfortable woman, with a certain elegance and a graciousness of heart that expressed itself in her face. Her attitude enabled him, and everyone else on the staff from what he could gather in the brief time he had been there, to establish a pleasant familiarity with her. She paid everyone the compliment of respecting what is subtle and unique in each of them. In conversing with her you hadn't got to tread lightly and warily, lest at any moment you might rupture the relationship, and tumble into eternal disgrace. You could talk to her about anything—except the budget. She brandishes a "Hands Off" sign whenever that topic is brought up. Perhaps, he questioned himself, this is the way every principal operates, and there is nothing untoward in it. He didn't know, but he would find out. He would also find out what sort of budgets they prepared when and if they prepared their own. Yes, he was glad that he had veered from the edge of possible conflict, and had not let his sense of hurt pride get out of hand. Life at John Brown Junior High seemed to approach the Utopian. A vast satisfaction had filled him as he went about his work, and he wanted to keep it that way. Anyway, experience had taught him that a subordinate who attempts to subdue a superordinate is almost always lost; the superordinate has too many advantages in such a contest.

By the time she returned he was fully composed. Thinking the matter out in the calmness of solitude restored his balance. He would live with her code on the budget—for now anyway! There would be other opportunities to broach the subject. He would put it into abeyance.

"Sometimes the kids get a little unruly!" she announced in that easy familiar style of hers as she sat down. "But everything's under control! Now, where were we?"

"You were saying that I should go ahead and make plans based on the survey results," he reminded her cheerfully.

Rood nodded in response. In addition to identifying how service could be better she would like him to design a questionnaire for teachers, to see how well their needs are being met.

Stanhope drew from his pocket his pencil and from his folder a note-pad, and began to write. He superscribed the date—"9/16." Then on the next line:

"#1. Develop plan for improving services based on opinionnaire results."

"#2. Design questionnaire to be distributed to teachers."

Rood waited while he wrote. "I'll help you with the teacher questionnaire," she offered. "I helped Ham design the student one." She paused, then: "Let me know what you think of it. I think it was quite good. I don't know how he selected his samples though."

Stanhope wrote:

"#3. Evaluate student opinionnaire." After this one he made two exclamation marks—"!!"

He spoke: "One thing did occur to me. Did you consider making a correlation between student achievement and the questionnaire results?"

"I'm not entirely sure what you mean."

"Did you think of tabulating the results by how the students did academically? I'm wondering if poorer students feel differently about the media center than better ones."

"I suppose it would have been interesting information to have, but no, we don't have a mixed ability response. I'm not sure how you'd get it, anyway."

She stretched out her arm and read her watch. "I have another appointment in a few minutes, Malcolm. So I'll have to----"

She stopped: he had started to write again:

"#4. Compare media center to national standards."

"I didn't mean to interrupt you, Mrs. Rood," he explained, smiling. "I just remembered another item to look into!"

She smiled back. "By the way, feel free to redesign the layout of the LMC in any way you think will make it more efficient (Appendix II). If you feel a more propitious arrangement is called for, show it to me when you present your report. You have to stay within the permanent walls, however. You can move anything inside."

Stanhope wrote:

"#5. Redesign layout, if advisable. Stay within area. Everything else is movable."

"I think that's about it, isn't it, Malcolm?" she said, rubbing her hands with a roundabout motion. He had been told that the action denoted the termination of the chat. He smiled and rose, "I'll get this to you by the end of October, Mrs. Rood."

"Fine," she said. They said good-bye, and he left. On his way out he made a copy of the document on the machine in the secretary's office.

Located in an isolated section of the Southwest, Los Pasos sits under the brassy sun on a wide plain below a low range of hills. It is the only market and supply center for the farmers of the region for hundreds of miles around. Thus it lives quite independently. The most recent census counted 28,604 people in the city, of whom 4,478 are nonwhite. The nonwhite total includes 2,035 blacks, 1,962 Mexican Americans, 298 Indians, 104 Chinese, and 79 Japanese. Of the total population, 4,218 are enrolled in the public school system—506 at the high school, 648 at the junior high, and 3,028 at the eight elementary schools. Of the 684 students at the junior high 248 are in grade 7, 232 in grade 8, and 204 in grade 9.

John Brown Junior High School was erected in 1898, and both the east and west wings were added in 1949. Counting the media center (which everyone persists in calling the library), there are 26 classrooms, 2 shops (one for auto repair and one for woodworking), a basement gymnasium, and a flat-floor auditorium. There are also specially equipped rooms for music, art, consumer education and other phases of homemaking; science and biology rooms occupy the top floor of the almost century-old center section. The student/teacher ratio at John Brown is 21 to 1.

The media center is located on the second floor of the original structure (it has three floors), along with the teachers' room, the music and art rooms, and the auditorium; the principal's and administrative offices are on the first floor. Malcolm Stanhope—he is almost invariably referred to as the librarian—is the only full-time employee in the media center; he is assisted by student aides. The LMC's complete collection is as follows:

Books: 8,738 volumes
Reference Books: 439 volumes
Periodicals: 77 titles
Newspapers: 6 titles
Filmstrips (sound and silent): 407 items
Slides and Transparencies: 60 items
16mm and Super 8mm Sound Films: 18 titles
Graphics (pictures, maps, and prints): 580 items
Recordings (disc): 408 items
Recordings (tape): 32 items
Cassettes: 64 items
Books for Faculty: 54 volumes
Professional Periodicals: 7 titles

The school also has access to the collection at the high school, some seven miles away, on interlibrary loan. As with John Brown, this facility has a staff of one professional media specialist. There are no other library facilities in the immediate area, except for a woefully inadequate public library. The high school's collection follows:

Books: 9,556 volumes
Periodicals: 64 titles
Newspapers: 8 titles
Filmstrips (sound and silent): 418 items
Slides and Transparencies: 94 items
16mm and Super 8mm Sound Films: 83 items
Super 8mm Films, Silent: 54 items
Recordings (disc): 488 items
Recordings (tape): 53 items
Cassettes: 103 items
Books for Faculty: 63 volumes
Professional Periodicals: 9 titles
Specimens: 50 items

Henrietta Rood is about 60 years old. A native of the state but not of Los Pasos, she possesses in addition to a bachelor's degree in English, a master's in education. She has been principal at John Brown a little over 11 years.

Malcolm Stanhope, also a native of the state, entered the library field at the age of 30, after having been a computer salesman for eight years. He worked part-time at the circulation desk in an academic library while pursuing his library degree, which he obtained in the spring of this year. This is his first professional job.

At the end of his busy day with the media center empty, Stanhope settled down in his chair for a quiet minute or two to consider the list of items he had drawn up during his discussion with the principal, and what his recommendations would be. He wondered momentarily if he should approach the other four department heads to see if he could get them to join him in an effort to gain some control over their budgets.... Perhaps he was exaggerating a molehill into a mountain....

APPENDIX I

June 18

TO: Henrietta Rood, Principal, John Brown Junior High School
FROM: Hamilton Brody, Media Specialist

Enclosed please find a report of the results of the student opinionnaire administered in May at my instigation.

As you will recall, the survey was intended to find out how well the media center is meeting the needs of students. Specifically, it attempted to secure answers to the following questions: the students' attitude toward the media center; the reasons students use the media center; what faacilities they use most; and what suggestions they have for improving services.

The opinionnaire was given to randomly selected students (roughly 15%) from all three grades. There were 676 students in the school in May—246 in grade 7, 228 in grade 8, and 202 in grade 9. In grade 7, 36 students were questioned; in grade 8, 34; and in grade 9, 30. It was hoped that the survey would also uncover any distinctive differences between opinions by grade levels.

Directions for the opinionnaire were explained by me; I personally visited home rooms at the start of the day. Students were to leave the forms unsigned. The opinionnaire consisted of ten questions (a copy is appended to this report). Students had a choice of four responses from "Much of the time" to "Not at all." There was space at the bottom of the form to respond to the following two questions: "What do you like most about the media center?" And "In your opinion how can the media center be improved?" Most students chose not to answer these questions, unfortunately.

P.S. Unfortunately, the custodian mistook the completed forms and my worksheets for trash one night, and disposed of them. I'm glad he did it after I had completed my summary!

TABLE I

RESPONSE OF SEVENTH GRADE STUDENTS TO
MEDIA CENTER OPINIONNAIRE

	MUCH		SOME		LITTLE		NOT AT ALL	
	No.	%	No.	%	No.	%	No.	%
1. When you are in the media center, how much of your time is spent reading library books and magazines?	9	25.0	14	38.9	10	27.8	3	8.3
2. When you are in the media center, how much difficulty do you have finding necessary material?	3	8.3	12	33.3	13	36.1	8	22.2
3. How much of your independent study time do you spend in the media center?	9	25.0	14	38.9	10	27.8	3	8.3
4. Do you ask the media specialist for help if problems arise concerning materials?	3	8.3	5	13.9	15	41.7	13	36.1
5. How much do you use the media center for research?	8	22.2	10	27.8	10	27.8	8	22.2
6. Do you use records, tapes, and filmstrips in the media center?	2	5.6	6	16.7	4	11.1	24	66.7
7. How much time do you spend doing homework in the media center?	1	2.8	4	11.1	7	19.4	24	66.7
8. When you are in the media center, how much of your time is spent using reference books?	1	2.8	6	16.7	6	16.7	23	63.9
9. Do you feel your media center time is used wisely?	13	36.1	16	44.4	3	8.3	4	11.1
10. Do you feel the media specialist knows you as an individual and can give you individual help?	2	5.6	4	11.1	5	13.9	25	69.4

Total number responding: 36

ANALYSIS OF TABLE I

Almost two-thirds (63.9%) of seventh graders said they spent their time reading books and magazines in the media center. Fifty-eight percent (58.3%) claimed to have little difficulty in locating materials. Almost two-thirds (63.9%) said they spent their independent study time in the media center, but over seventy-seven percent (77.8%) said they were reluctant to ask the media specialist for help when problems arose concerning library materials. An equal number (50%) said they used the media center for research as those who said they did not (50%). Over seventy-seven percent (77.8%) responded that they did not use records, tapes, and filmstrips in the media center, with eighty-six percent (86.1%) saying that they spent little time doing homework in the media center. Over eighty percent (80.6%) did not use reference books; an equal number (80.5%) claimed that they used their time wisely while in the media center. Over eighty-three percent (83.3%) felt that they were practically unknown to the media specialist.

TABLE II

RESPONSE OF EIGHTH GRADE STUDENTS TO MEDIA CENTER OPINIONNAIRE

	MUCH		SOME		LITTLE		NOT AT ALL	
	No.	%	No.	%	No.	%	No.	%
1. When you are in the media center, how much of your time is spent reading library books and magazines?	10	29.4	16	47.0	7	20.5	1	2.9
2. When you are in the media center, how much difficulty do you have finding necessary material?	2	5.9	13	38.2	13	38.2	6	17.6
3. How much of your independent study time do you spend in the media center?	8	23.5	15	44.1	9	26.4	2	5.9
4. Do you ask the media specialist for help if problems arise concerning materials?	5	14.7	8	23.5	15	44.1	6	17.6
5. How much do you use the media center for research?	9	26.4	11	32.4	13	38.2	1	2.9
6. Do you use records, tapes, and filmstrips in the media center?	3	8.8	6	17.6	6	17.6	19	55.9
7. How much time do you spend doing homework in the media center?	3	8.8	7	20.5	11	32.4	13	38.2
8. When you are in the media center, how much of your time is spent using reference books?	2	5.9	7	20.5	9	26.4	16	47.0
9. Do you feel your media center time is used wisely?	11	32.4	14	41.1	5	14.7	4	11.7
10. Do you feel the media specialist knows you as an individual and can give you individual help?	3	8.8	6	17.6	7	20.5	18	52.9

Total number responding: 34

ANALYSIS OF TABLE II

Over seventy-six percent (76.4%) of eighth grade students spent their time reading books and magazines in the media center. Almost the same percent as the seventh graders (55.8%) said they had little difficulty locating material. Two-thirds (67.6%) spent their independent study time in the media center, but sixty-one percent (61.7%) said they did not ask the media specialist for help when problems arose. A higher percent than the seventh graders (58.8%) identified that they used the media center for research. As with the seventh graders though, over seventy-three percent (73.5%) did not spend their time doing homework in the media center, and seventy-three percent (73.4%) did not use reference materials. Seventy-three percent (73.5%) claimed they spent their time wisely when they were in the media center. An equal number (73.4%) felt the media specialist did not know them as individuals and could not give them individual help.

A comparison between the seventh and eighth grade students shows there is no appreciable difference in their responses, except that fewer eighth graders said they were reluctant to ask the media specialist for help when problems arose concerning library materials. Fewer, too, felt the media specialist did not know them.

TABLE III

RESPONSE OF NINTH GRADE STUDENTS TO
MEDIA CENTER OPINIONNAIRE

	MUCH		SOME		LITTLE		NOT AT ALL	
	No.	%	No.	%	No.	%	No.	%
1. When you are in the media center, how much of your time is spent reading library books and magazines?	11	36.7	12	40.0	6	20.0	1	3.3
2. When you are in the media center, how much difficulty do you have finding necessary material?	1	3.3	5	16.7	10	33.3	14	46.7
3. How much of your independent study time do you spend in the media center?	8	26.7	14	46.7	5	16.7	3	10.0
4. Do you ask the media specialist for help if problems arise concerning materials?	7	23.3	12	40.0	8	26.7	3	10.0
5. How much do you use the media center for research?	6	20.0	14	46.7	8	26.7	2	6.7
6. Do you use records, tapes, and filmstrips in the media center?	2	6.7	6	20.0	7	23.3	15	50.0
7. How much time do you spend doing homework in the media center?	2	6.7	3	10.0	12	40.0	13	43.3
8. When you are in the media center, how much of your time is spent using reference books?	4	13.3	6	20.0	8	26.7	12	40.0
9. Do you feel your media center time is used wisely?	12	40.0	13	43.3	4	13.3	1	3.3
10. Do you feel the media specialist knows you as an individual and can give you individual help?	3	10.0	7	23.3	12	40.0	8	26.7

Total number responding: 30

ANALYSIS OF TABLE III

Seventy-six percent (76.7%) of ninth graders responded that they spent much or some of their time reading media center books and magazines when they were in the media center. Eighty percent (80%) had little or no difficulty locating materials. Seventy-three percent (73.4%) said they spent much or some of their independent study time in the media center, and two-thirds (63.3%) responded that they asked the media specialist for help when problems arose concerning materials. Two-thirds (66.7%) used the media center for research, but as with the seventh and eighth graders seventy-three percent (73.3%) did not make use of the media center's records, tapes, and filmstrips. Eighty-three percent (83.3%) did not spend much time doing homework in the media center, but two-thirds (66.7%) made little or no use of reference books. Eighty-three percent (83.3%) felt their time was wisely used when they visited the media center. Two-thirds (66.7%) claimed that the media specialist did not know them as individuals or could give them help.

The ninth grade students appeared to be fairly well oriented to media center use, since eighty percent of them had little or no difficulty locating necessary materials, and two-thirds of them sought the help of the media specialist whenever problems arose concerning the use of materials.

TABLE IV

COMPOSITE OF RESPONSES OF SEVENTH, EIGHTH, AND NINTH GRADE STUDENTS

	MUCH		SOME		LITTLE		NOT AT ALL	
	No.	%	No.	%	No.	%	No.	%
1. When you are in the media center, how much of your time is spent reading library books and magazines?	30	30.0	42	42.0	23	23.0	5	5.0
2. When you are in the media center, how much difficulty do you have finding necessary material?	6	6.0	30	30.0	36	36.0	28	28.0
3. How much of your independent study time do you spend in the media center?	25	25.0	43	43.0	24	24.0	8	8.0
4. Do you ask the media specialist for help if problems arise concerning materials?	15	15.0	25	25.0	38	38.0	22	22.0
5. How much do you use the media center for research?	23	23.0	35	35.0	31	31.0	11	11.0
6. Do you use records, tapes, and filmstrips in the media center?	7	7.0	18	18.0	17	17.0	58	58.0
7. How much time do you spend doing homework in the media center?	6	6.0	14	14.0	30	30.0	50	50.0
8. When you are in the media center, how much of your time is spent using reference books?	7	7.0	19	19.0	23	23.0	51	51.0
9. Do you feel your media center time is used wisely?	36	36.0	43	43.0	12	12.0	9	9.0
10. Do you feel the media specialist knows you as an individual and can give you individual help?	8	8.0	17	17.0	24	24.0	51	51.0

Total number responding: 100

ANALYSIS OF TABLE IV

It would appear that the majority of students (75%) did not feel the media specialist knew them or could give them individual help. The majority (79%) also felt their time was wisely used when they visited the media center. "Wise use" seemed to mean reading books and magazines—72% said that was what they did. A further 58% said they used the media center "much" or "some" for research, and 80% that they did not do homework when they visited the media center. Sixty-eight percent said they spent much or some of their independent study time in the media center. More (64%) seemed not to have difficulty finding necessary material than less (36%). It would appear, too, that more (60%) than less (40%) did not ask the media specialist for help if they did have problems concerning materials. The majority (75%) did not use records, tapes, and filmstrips, or reference materials (74%).

It would appear that ninth graders are better oriented to the media center than eighth and seventh graders. It would appear, too, that more ninth graders feel the media specialist knew them as individuals and could give them individual help.

TABLE V

SUGGESTIONS LISTED BY STUDENTS ON OPINIONNAIRE

What do you like most about the media center?

	7th Grade	8th Grade	9th Grade	Total
Magazines	6	4	4	14
Books	2	3	6	11
Tapes	2	2	5	9
Comfortable chairs	1	2	1	4
Quiet atmosphere	1	1	2	4

In your opinion, how can the media center be improved?

	7th Grade	8th Grade	9th Grade	Total
More seats	13	12	9	34
More books	11	14	16	31
More quiet	5	5	6	16
More people to help us	4	4	6	14
More foreign language books	3	7	3	13
Typewriters	0	2	3	5
More magazines and newspapers	1	2	1	4
Friendlier librarian	0	1	2	3
Background music	0	2	1	3

As can be seen, a maximum of thirty-four students made suggestions for improvement. The responses ranged from increased seating capacity to background music.

TABLE V (cont'd)

Recommendations

1. That more money is needed to begin to bring the media center up to the standards for materials, including such items as typewriters.

2. That additional staff be hired so that more professional attention and services can be given to students.

3. That we begin at once to establish some goals and objectives for the media center.

SAMPLE OPINIONNAIRE

The media specialist is interested in knowing your opinions about the media center. Please circle the word which most accurately describes your opinion about each question:

	MUCH of the time	SOME of the time	LITTLE of the time	NOT AT ALL
1. When you are in the media center, how much of your time is spent reading library books and magazines?	MUCH	SOME	LITTLE	NOT AT ALL
2. When you are in the media center, how much difficulty do you have finding necessary material?	MUCH	SOME	LITTLE	NOT AT ALL
3. How much of your independent study time do you spend in the media center?	MUCH	SOME	LITTLE	NOT AT ALL
4. Do you ask the media specialist for help if problems arise concerning materials?	MUCH	SOME	LITTLE	NOT AT ALL
5. How much do you use the media center for research?	MUCH	SOME	LITTLE	NOT AT ALL
6. Do you use records, tapes, and filmstrips in the media center?	MUCH	SOME	LITTLE	NOT AT ALL
7. How much time do you spend doing homework in the media center?	MUCH	SOME	LITTLE	NOT AT ALL
8. When you are in the media center, how much of your time is spent using reference books?	MUCH	SOME	LITTLE	NOT AT ALL
9. Do you feel your media center time is used wisely?	MUCH	SOME	LITTLE	NOT AT ALL
10. Do you feel the media specialist knows you as an individual and can give you individual help?	MUCH	SOME	LITTLE	NOT AT ALL

What do you like most of all about the media center?

In your opinion, how can the media center be improved?

MEDIA CENTER PLAN

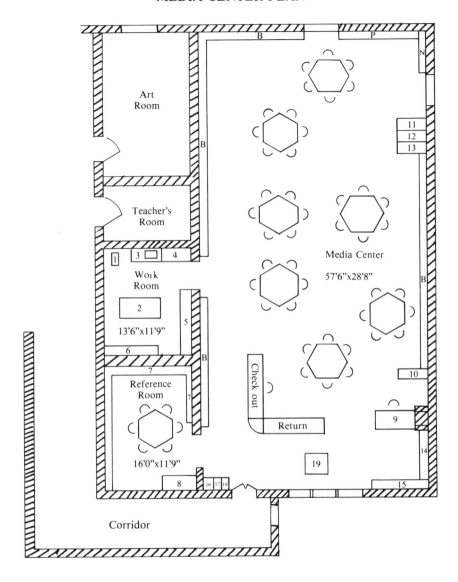

Legend

1. Book cart
2. Work desk
3. Sink
4. Counter
5. Workroom shelves
6. Faculty books and periodicals
7. Reference books
8. Films and filmstrips
9. Media Specialist's desk
10. Office file cabinet
11. Picture, print, and map file cabinet
12. Pamphlet file cabinet
13. Slides and transparencies file
14. Recordings (disc)
15. Recordings (tape) and cassettes
16. Overhead projector
17. 16mm movie projector
18. 8mm movie projector
19. Card catalog

B   Bookshelves
P   Periodical rack
N   Newspaper rack

7

THE LIFE OF STAFF

Junctionville began modestly. When George Washington was born, it was no more than a tiny crossroads settlement of 37 families. But the fertility of the muck and silt topsoil soon made it a profitable farming community, and its location on a navigable river gave it a place in the flow of people and commerce. By the time the Constitution was ratified, it boasted a population óf 4,000. Its first real economic stirrings occurred, however, in the early 1800s, when a cotton mill and a carriage-making plant began operations. Encouraged by these developments, successive waves of cheap labor immigrated from Europe. The town grew at an unprecedented pace, and when the first shot was fired at Ft. Sumter it was home for 30,000. Factories and mills sprang up, and with them row upon row of tight boxlike workers' houses. Junctionville established itself early as an ordinary work-a-day manufacturing city, a city without glitter or charm. Rapid growth coupled with an emphasis on industrial production meant that niceties would have to wait: there were textiles to be made and buggies to be turned out. The bulk of the town's residents had little time for culture, for the theater, for the erudite lecture. By the turn of the century the population had reached its highwater mark — 75,000.

When the market for shining victorias and handy runabouts was climaxed by the building of "horseless carriages," and tax benefits and lower wages lured mill owners south, thousands emigrated westward. Those who remained were forced to find other sources of income. By some extra stamina or heritage of endurance they contrived to exist by becoming peddlars. Scores of them set out on foot to seek a market in outlying districts for the small industries that had supplied their local needs. Wherever they went they discovered demands for new articles, which they ingeniously devised tools to manufacture. Within a few years, sections of their abandoned mills and factories were partitioned into small shops manufacturing hundreds of diversified products: paper containers, overalls, wire products, icepicks, furniture, building supplies, soap, buttons, wallpaper, kitchenware, shirts, cosmetics, carpets, paint — the list goes on. But these items do not spell prosperity. The population waxed again slightly, then waned again, until it finally stabilized around its present 55,000.

Today, Junctionville does not depend upon any one class of manufactured goods for its existence. Its overall appearance bespeaks its industrial history. It has a time-worn and frayed look. Many old buildings are trembling into ruin. But urban renewal is on the scene. To be sure, it still has its congeries of mills and fatories, its grimy huddle of frame dwellings and congested tenements, its stark, jagged skyline, but its old face is gradually changing. The central business district has been considerably rejuvenated. Lawyers, doctors, and other professional workers have followed the example of the merchants and established themselves in the first floors of old buildings. The vista of main street shows in addition to the jumble and squeeze of shops, a 12-story skyscraper, several impressive banks, and a few elderly housing units. Substantial improvements in access and off-street parking have been made, and shopping centers now stud the landscape. The broad tree-lined streets with large Victorian homes surrounded by ample greenery on what were once the outskirts of town – the gracious and expansive habitations of the wealthy mill and factory owners – gradually yield to a miscellany of recent bungalows, modest cottages, and modern apartment buildings.

Like any large city, Junctionville is a community of great ethnic and sociometric variety, and like them its races and nationalities are slowly losing their individuality in the inescapable process of Americanization. The city was at ethnic peace – until recently. The influx of large numbers of Spanish-speaking people has brought to the surface feelings of antagonism on the part of many established residents, who feel threatened by the "encroachment" of "have-nots" into their neighborhoods.

Junctionville is a consolidated town and city with council-manager government and, until ten years ago, non-partisan elections. Counties play no political role in the state; towns and cities provide nearly all local government services. The councilor with the most votes becomes mayor, a position that confers little beyond title and gavel. The mayor, like other councilors, is unsalaried and has virtually no administrative or appointive powers. The city has returned a majority for every Democratic presidential candidate since 1916, when Woodrow Wilson took 65% of the city's vote against the redoubtable Charles Evans Hughes. It has voted Democratic in every gubernatorial election since 1918. Its socioeconomic status, as measured by such characteristics as family size, level of education, age, income, and occupation, is heavily lower class.

This is changing slightly though as increasing numbers of middle-class families are moving back to the city after an exodus a decade or two ago. This class – educated, articulate, forward-looking – spends its career in the bureaucratic ranks of big, efficiently managed corporations and, not surprisingly, looks for the same style of leadership in its local government. It is impatient with Junctionville for its failure to move ahead as fast as it would like and is bothered by the city's drabness and general lack of "class and culture."

A semi-cosmopolitan group, it has brought with it increased service demands, including a school system that will get its children into good colleges. It has found its voice in the city manager of eight years – Reginald H. Groome. At 36, with a master's degree in public administration, and "from away" (as newcomers are described by native-born Junctionvillers), Groome has been convinced of the need to expand the city's commercial, industrial, and recreational facilities, and has attempted to make at least a modest advance in local cultural offerings. He has recruited a well-trained cadre of professional local government officials, most of whom are also "from away" and all of whom are committed to making Junctionville a dynamic and progressive place to live. Under the city charter the manager picks department heads (with the exception of the schools and public library, both of which have boards), and the staff is selected with the assistance of a personnel office. In his efforts to broaden the tax base, Groome has been actively courting industry – with some moderate success. In the past five years, 15 firms have opened plants or offices.

Pitted against Groome and the "progressives" are the mayor and the "standpatters." Many long-term residents feel that Junctionville should be governed the way it was before Groome appeared – by "good old boys" who had worked their way up, who eschewed issues, and who faithfully rewarded their cronies. The politicians they most admire practice the organic politics of O'Connor's Frank Skeffington. Until Groome appeared, city officials were chosen not so much for their ability to administer the affairs of their offices as for who they knew; hence, old-style machine politics with its accompanying corruption found a congenial atmosphere in which to operate. And also until Groome appeared, newcomers were a nullity as an active political force, exerting little influence in city affairs.

The "standpatters" have seen power shift away from themselves to the newcomers and other lifelong "progressive" Junctionvillers, who were muted under previous administrations. This has made them sometimes stubborn beyond reason, to the detriment of the community. Reg Groome has accomplished his revitalization program against odds that would have overwhelmed a weaker and less determined person. Those who oppose him have no ideological objections to industrial growth or commercial expansion, but they do when it comes to the schools and the public library. Three of the five councilors, one of whom is the mayor, thwart him at virtually every turn in his efforts on behalf of these institutions.

Groome was successful—over their protestations—five years ago in gaining voter approval for a $2.5 million bond issue to finance the construction of a new public library building. This structure with its liberal display of glass against a framework of steel and concrete has been acclaimed one of the most imaginatively designed and functional in the state. But not only was the building unacceptable to the standpatters—it was totally out of keeping with the style of the other public buildings—it was a "frivolous" expenditure to boot. As far as they were concerned there was nothing wrong with the old building; furthermore, libraries simply are not as essential to the life of the community as better police protection, improved fire-fighting and public works equipment, increased street lighting, and the like. Junctionville is not a "Cadillac" town, they asseverated. Their concept of education is static rather than dynamic. Typically, they feel the schools have become too "gimmicky" and have gotten away from "basics." When last year the superintendent of schools requested a third assistant, they were especially indignant. "He's building himself a small empire," one protested bitterly. The superintendent withdrew his request at the urging of the city manager, who suggested he defer it until a more apposite time; they agreed to expend their energies on a new auditorium for the high school, which had a better chance of being approved. The superintendent and school board members make it a practice to trust Groome's judgment when it comes to budget appropriations, having long since learned that he has a sort of "sixth sense" when it comes to the politics of the possible.

Reg Groome seems to be exactly what the doctor ordered for Junctionville. The mere fact that he has survived against his "moss-backed" opponents attests to his abilities as an executive and his skills as a diplomat. Like any good politician he keenly understands the importance of a public image, and knows that one cannot be popular with everyone and still be a forward-looking manager. People find him a hard person to say no to. His supporters call him a "smoothie," while his critics generally portray him as a "glib con man"—perspective is everything. But even his critics give him top marks as an energetic, bright, and well-organized person—reluctantly to be sure. His voracious appetite for detail and numbers is coupled with astounding powers of recall. He is a stickler for detail and can tear apart a budget or a balance sheet faster than anyone. As an administrator, he pushes authority as far down the hierarchy as possible and has little patience for foot-dragging and ignorance. He himself learned early to make decisions and to pursue them hard. His demands and requests are always reasonable.

Like most other older core cities, there are many urgent problems confronting the manager and council of Junctionville: inadequate water and sewage facilities, limited public transportation, polluted air, excessive power costs, crime. These make heavy demands on the precious tax dollar. Even with Groome's efforts to ease tax burden pressures on individual property owners through industrial development, the tax rate is very steep. While Groome and the progressives have over the years had their differences with the mayor and the standpatters — to put it mildly — one thing they are in firm agreement about is that taxes have been pushed as far as they can be. The standpatters argue, and the progressives agree, that the tax line must be held in the interest of attracting industry. Both factions realize that new expenditures must not be undertaken if they mean increasing taxes; they are thus in the position of having to choose between demands for higher services and demands to minimize tax increases. They have agreed this year to concentrate on minimizing expenditures.

Consequently, each department is being carefully scrutinized to determine whether it is being operated with maximum efficiency. In his effort to make Junctionville "an attractive city to live in and a nice place to raise children" (as it is vaunted in a promotional brochure), Groome has been conspicuously supportive of the public library, both in terms of encouraging use and financially, since he views it as one way of broadening the city's cultural life. Thus, when he approached the trustees and the library director at their February meeting with a request that they compare Junctionville's library with libraries in other communities of comparable size to Junctionville to see how it measures up, the trustees were happy to oblige. Specifically, the manager stated that he was interested in seeing how the library compared in regard to a) circulation per capita, b) expenditures per capita, c) ratio of staff to population, and d) percent of income spent on salaries. He added that he would welcome learning of, and seeing demonstrated where possible, other ways librarians have of measuring library effectiveness. He reminded the assemblage that the mayor and a few others considered the library budget and the number of professional staff to be grossly inflated, and that he hoped to show that Junctionville was "getting its money's worth" from its library. "I'd love to be able to get them off my back," he remonstrated with a deep sigh.

In the course of roaming back and forth over a number of topics the library director of a year, Maude Poitevant Watman, a smile playing about her mouth and pausing as if to gather herself up for a leap, asked the manager whether he thought there was a chance they could soon fill the assistant director's position, which had been vacant for six months. (The assistant had left to take a directorship.) About that time, the manager and council as one of their austerity measures had issued a moratorium on all hiring except for "absolutely essential services" — Groome insisted on the word "absolutely" — which they described as police, fire, and sanitation. (The manager himself has been without a public information officer for three months.) Without an assistant library director other staff members, including the director, have had to absorb the assistant's duties. A wonderful grin spread over the manager's face and to everyone's surprise he responded that he "would be willing to go to bat for a replacement of some sort," but he wasn't sure an assistant director was what was needed. He proposed a business manager. Several members of the group raised polite brows and implored him to go on.

The substance of the manager's comments were: After having studied the organization chart (Appendix I) and the job descriptions for the various positions (Appendix II), the position of assistant director in a public library the size of Junctionville's presents several problems, both for the position holder and the director. Either assistants have full responsibility in a line capacity for the entire operation, with every department head reporting to them (and through them every member of the staff); or they are assigned staff positions with no one reporting to them, except perhaps a secretary or a clerk; or some of the staff reports to the assistant and some to the director—the line people reporting to the assistant and the staff to the director in the case of Junctionville.

Under the first arrangement (full responsibility in a line capacity), the director has only one person reporting directly to him or her—a one-over-one relationship. (The secretary is excluded from consideration here.) This means that strictly speaking all communications and directions must go through the assistant. The director is obligated to clear virtually everything involving the staff through the assistant; to fail to do so is to risk impairing relations, for even in casual discussions between the director and department heads ideas may come up which are suddenly translated into plans for action or procedural changes. The participants in the discussion may neglect to inform the assistant about what has transpired, thus leaving him or her out of the decision-making process and consequently in the dark about what is going on. Both participants in the discussion must decide who will inform the assistant, thereby adding an additional burden—that of having to add yet another thing to an already crowded calendar of things to remember. With this set-up, the director is blocked from his or her subordinates and can quickly lose touch with what is going on; either the assistant or the director is superfluous.

The trustees and the director reflected carefully on what the manager was saying, but no one made a comment. The manager resumed. Under the second arrangement (staff position), the assistant's position frequently degenerates into a "catch-all" position, with the assistant ending up with a number of miscellaneous odd-jobs (sometimes "keep-busy" type jobs, well below his or her capabilities) and no real authority—not a very appetizing thought for anyone who wishes to play a key role in the operations of the library.

At this point the chairwoman inquired if this explains why there seems to be such discontent among assistant directors of public libraries. She reported that she sat with a group of assistants at a recent regional library association meeting banquet, and that to a person they had complained about their positions—for many of the reasons the manager had given. Another remarked that there had been considerable turnover among assistants at the Junctionville library in the 10 years he had been on the board, there having been five in that period of time. One, the most recent, had become a director of another public library; two had left the library field altogether; and two had changed to other types of libraries—one became a high school media-specialist and the other the head of circulation in an academic library. A third trustee said that they couldn't draw any conclusions from these limited experiences, and wondered if any studies had been conducted on dissatisfaction among assistant public library directors. Watman stated that she was not aware of any, but that she, too, as an assistant in another public library had felt the same frustrations. She said the arrangement she had operated under was similar to that of Junctionville's in that part of the staff reported to her and part to the director. She admitted it was not ideal.

The manager proceeded to explain how he saw this third arrangement. The problem with it, he said, is that some support service staff members not at the same grade step as the assistant, and frequently below department head grade steps, report directly to the director. The line people who perform library work per se (reference, technical services, acquisitions, etc.) are one step removed from the director. This would be equitable if staff members who perform support services (displays, publicity, etc.) were also one step removed — that is, if there were several assistants and they reported to one of them.

In the case of Junctionville, he went on, the only people who report directly to the director (in addition to the assistant) are the administrative secretary, the community services librarian, and the exhibits librarian. The heads of the various departments (adult services, children's, audio-visual, circulation, and technical services) report to the assistant. What is needed in Junctionville, he asserted, is for the director to broaden her span of control by eliminating the position of assistant director — that is, by reducing the number of reporting levels. The more people through whom a communication passes, he said, the more its meaning tends to be delayed, diffused, distorted, and lost. The closer the director is to the work being done, the better for all concerned. He said he felt, therefore, that a "business manager" is required who would consolidate and be responsible for the "business" related activities that are currently being performed by several staff members. By having business activities removed, these staff members would be able to concentrate on their proper work — that of providing library service to the citizens of Junctionville. He proposed that a full-time position — it could be called "Library Business Manager" or "Assistant to the Director for Business Management" or some other title — be established. He also proposed that the person report directly to the director. The director would thus have nine people reporting to her — a manageable number by anyone's standard.

At this point one of the trustees, scratching his head, raised the question of the qualifications of such a person. Another asked whether the job had a future for anyone with ambition. The manager treated the questions respectfully, pointing out that public school systems employ business managers who usually report to the superintendent (or an assistant) and who don't expect to become principals or superintendents. He suggested the same arrangement could obtain in the case of the public library. "You wouldn't hire a professionally trained librarian for the job," he said in the tone of one presenting a challenge; "he or she should possess a bachelor's degree or its equivalent in business or public administration."

That said, Groome glanced at his watch and announced that he had another meeting to go to. "I'd like you to look into this possibility," he said, rising. "I can probably get the council and the finance committee to endorse the idea — and the position." Then he delivered the clincher. "Let's be realistic about this. There are those in town — and we all know who they are — who feel there are too many professionals on the staff. The person occupying this position would not be a professional librarian. It boils down to this position or none."

His listeners looked around at each other and acknowledged the verity of his statement by nodding assents. "Mind you," the manager appended, "I'm suggesting this as a permanent arrangement, not as a stop-gap measure. I think it makes eminent sense, for the reasons I've outlined." He started toward the door. Watman said there were questions as to who the branch, bookmobile, and custodial staff would report to, and who would serve as director in her absence. Groome stopped in the doorway and responded that these were matters she would have to work out. He suggested she write a job description for the position and re-write those of the existing positions, culling from them "business type" activities and making changes in responsibility where necessary. He said she would also have to draw up a new organization chart — it would be up to her to determine the grade step for the new position — and invited her to make a list of questions, should any arise. Then he added, with a knowing and indulgent smile, "When you're looking at the organization chart and job descriptions, Maude, you might want to consider reclassifying some positions. It seems to me that some positions are over-classified and some under-classified. Also, I think the job descriptions leave a bit to be desired. Let me know what you think when you present all this to me. We may not be able to do anything right away, but it'll be something to plan for." Watman concurred with him on the grade steps, and indicated her willingness to pursue the other matters that had been discussed.

The chairwoman thanked the manager for attending the meeting and sharing his thoughts with them. He smiled again, waved goodbye, and departed. After a brief review of Groome's proposals, a trustee moved that Watman proceed with the requests. The seconder of the motion appended that she would like the librarian to have her report ready for the March meeting, if possible. Watman made a sign in the affirmative. The amendment was acceptable to the mover, and the motion passed unanimously. Watman wondered how the profession would react to the idea of a business manager instead of assistant, opining that some would not appreciate seeing professional positions eliminated. They talked about this for a little while, then moved on to another item of business.

The Junctionville Board of Library Trustees is composed of five persons appointed by the city manager for staggered terms of five years. At the present, it consists of: a housewife, who is serving as chairwoman, a stockbroker, a retired head of the health department, an owner of a hardware store, and an attorney. Like their school counterparts, they have tried to cooperate with Groome in every way possible, recognizing and appreciating his efforts on behalf of the library.

The Junctionville Public Library operates from a 60,000 square-foot main building, a branch, and a bookmobile. The main building is open 72 hours a week and the branch and bookmobile 40 hours. (The previous building had 16,450 square feet and was open 60 hours; the branch and bookmobile were open 40 hours each, as now.) Last year, the library circulated 508,396 items and answered 24,000 reference questions. Over 12,000 people watched 310 films shown in the library, while more than 265,000 viewed films borrowed from the library for showing in the community. In various meeting rooms in the library, 1,378 meetings were held, which were free and open to the public. The library extends its traditional services to those homebound due to illness or handicaps through its Community Services Librarian. (Appendix III shows the *American Library Directory* entry for Junctionville.)

APPENDIX I

ORGANIZATION CHART

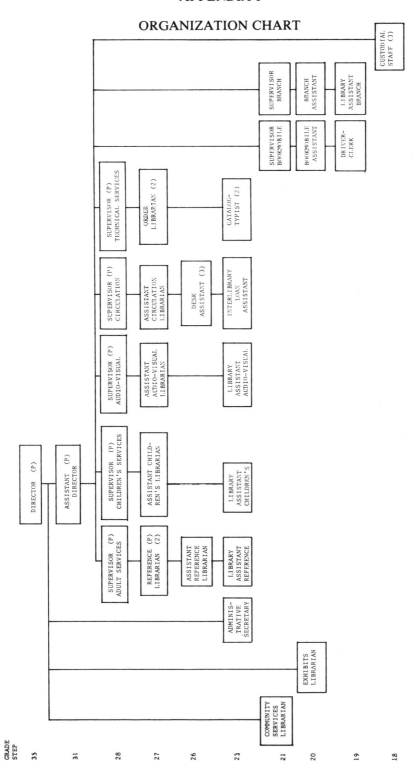

P – Denotes professional librarian holding master's degree in librarianship

Total staff – 36

APPENDIX II

JOB DESCRIPTIONS

LIBRARY DIRECTOR (GRADE STEP 35)

General Statement of Duties: Performs administrative and professional library work in the direction and supervision of the public library; does related work as required.

Distinguishing Features of the Class: An employee in this class is responsible for the direction and administration of all activities of the library system according to the policies and rules of the Board of Library Trustees, the ordinances of the city and laws of the state. Within these general policies and available resources the Director plans, directs and executes a program of varied library services related to the community needs.

Examples of Work:
Plans, organizes and administers programs and procedures governing library service; plans and executes programs that will stimulate effective use of library resources and acts as consultant and advisor to groups participating in educational programs.

Maintains public relations by addressing community groups, preparing reports, press releases and in other ways makes the library and its services known to the community; cooperates and consults with officials of other public and educational agencies on common library problems.

Interprets objectives, plans and organizes new activities and coordinates activities; oversees the selection of materials that will stimulate and satisfy the different reading and educational interests of the community.

Reviews and approves accessions of books, periodicals and other materials; drafts and presents policy recommendations to the Board of Trustees for adoption.

Makes recommendations to the Board regarding appointments, promotions and other personnel matters.

Renders professional library opinion in the planning of library buildings and facilities.

Draws up and submits annual budget to Board of Library Trustees; administers the budget as approved by the Board of Library Trustees.

Maintains up-to-date figures of trustee and special funds.

Plans, drafts and administers standard procedures for branch library operations and for other services.

Plans, organizes and conducts training for new staff members; arranges special training activities and programs; prepares work programs, budget estimates and other regular and special reports.

Serves as chairperson of the Material Selection Committee.

APPENDIX II (cont'd)

Assigns, schedules and reviews work of subordinates; administers personnel performance evaluation program.

Maintains employee discipline and morale; consults and advises department heads on difficult problems, improvements and expansion of services.

Sees that the buildings, grounds, and equipment are kept in good condition.

Relieves staff assistants and librarians in their absence; reads professional literature and keeps abreast of new developments in the library field.

Required Knowledge, Skills and Abilities: Comprehensive knowledge of professional library science and administration; ability to interpret community interests and needs and to plan appropriate library services; ability to meet the public and to maintain their confidence; ability to speak and write effectively; broad knowledge of library materials and methods, maintenance and building problems; broad knowledge of public affairs.

Acceptable Experience and Training: Extensive experience in professional library work and graduation from an accredited library school.

ASSISTANT LIBRARY DIRECTOR (GRADE STEP 31)

General Statement of Duties: Provides administrative and professional assistance to the Director in the direction and supervision of the library, its branches, and bookmobiles; does related work as required.

Distinguishing Features of the Class: An employee in this class is responsible for planning, organizing, directing, and coordinating all activities of the library under the general direction of the Director. Supervision is exercised over all subordinate line library personnel.

Examples of Work:
Acts for the Director in his or her absence.

Conducts preliminary personnel interviewing, making recommendations.

Assigns, supervises and evaluates work of all personnel in all branches and departments of the library system.

Acts as immediate supervisor to the custodial staff.

Participates in meetings of the Board of Library Trustees and other boards and committees.

Acts as vice-chairperson of the Materials Selection Committee.

Interprets objectives of the library to the staff; plans and organizes new activities and services.

Conducts staff conferences and meetings and in-service training.

Maintains employee morale and discipline.

APPENDIX II (cont'd)

Prepares work programs, preliminary budget estimates, regular and special reports.

Distributes book, materials, and supplies budgets to each department; maintains control over expenditures.

Prepares staff studies such as personnel turnover, work volume, and time studies; prepares studies of use of the library and profiles of library users — habits, hours, days, needs, etc.

Participates in recruiting and selection of sub-professionals, clerks and custodians.

Is responsible for the operation and maintenance of library buildings and vehicles; prepares contracts and arranges for equipment maintenance.

Cooperates and consults with officials of other public and educational agencies on common problems.

Handles book and magazine bids; determines records and forms required.

Participates in the activities of professional and related associations.

Keeps abreast of current trends and new professional techniques.

General assignments are received from and work is reviewed by the Director through conferences.

Assists in developing detailed procedures and in maintaining standards.

Required Knowledge, Skills and Abilities: Thorough knowledge of professional library science procedures; ability to supervise, direct and lead personnel; ability to speak and write effectively; ability to meet the public; enthusiasm; resourcefulness; tact; initiative; good judgment; ability to interpret community interests and needs to aid in planning appropriate library services.

Acceptable Experience and Training: Considerable experience in professional library work and possession of a master of library science degree issued by an accredited library school.

SUPERVISOR OF ADULT SERVICES (GRADE STEP 28)

General Statement of Duties: Performs professional and supervisory tasks in the library; does related work as required.

Distinguishing Features of the Class: Employees in this class are responsible for directing a group in a major area of library activity such as Adult Services, Service to Children, Technical Processing, and Branch and Bookmobile Library Services. Supervision may be exercised over the work of librarians, library assistants, library pages, student assistants, and part-time adults. The work is performed under the general direction of the Assistant Library Director.

APPENDIX II (cont'd)

Examples of Work:
Directs a major professional service area involving the supervision of adult services throughout the entire library system, including the branch library and the bookmobile services.

Supervises staff and coordinates activities of the department. Assists staff on difficult reference questions requiring deeper experience and knowledge of subject matter as opposed, for example, to information-type questions.

Plans and guides adult programming such as film series, discussion groups, etc.

Develops in-service training programs for both professional and non-professional staff of own department and reviews and evaluates their performance.

Compiles bibliographies and annotated lists and assigns material for review or evaluation.

Directs selection of reference materials and participates in development of collection for young adults and adults in the library system as a whole.

Prepares necessary reports.

Maintains relations with public and parochial schools, colleges and adult education agencies in the community to help them derive the full benefit of services offered by this department of the library.

Attends professional meetings and participates in activities.

Keeps abreast of current trends and new professional techniques.

Interviews prospective personnel and makes recommendations.

Required Knowledge, Skills and Abilities: Broad background and knowledge of bibliographic sources. Ability to lead and direct staff. Ability to interpret community interests and needs. Ability to develop systems and methods to get maximum use out of library materials. Ability to meet and deal with people effectively. Some knowledge of reader interest level. Ability to establish and maintain effective working, advisory and consulting relationships with community groups. Good knowledge of publisher and dealer practices and methods of library supply resources; ability to speak and write effectively; pleasing personality; friendliness; enthusiasm; resourcefulness; initiative; tact; good judgment.

Acceptable Experience and Training: College graduate plus graduate degree in library science. Extensive professional library experience; administrative experience.

SUPERVISOR OF CHILDREN'S SERVICES (GRADE STEP 28)

General Statement of Duties: Performs professional and supervisory tasks in the library; does related work as required.

APPENDIX II (cont'd)

Distinguishing Features of the Class: Employees in this class are responsible for directing a group in a major area of library activity such as Adult Service, Service to Children, Technical Processing, and Branch and Bookmobile Libraries. Supervision may be exercised over the work of librarians, library assistants, library pages, student assistants, and part-time adults. The work is performed under the general direction of the Assistant Library Director.

Examples of Work:
Directs a major professional service area, involving the supervision of children's services throughout the entire library system, including the branch library and the bookmobile services to children.

Plans and guides all children's programming, which includes the Summer Reading Club, story hours, etc.

Answers reference questions.

Assists students, teachers, and parents in selecting materials.

Compiles lists of materials.

Directs selection of children's books and materials and maintenance of the collection.

Prepares reports.

Speaks to community groups regarding children's literature, reading problems, etc.

Maintains relations with public and parochial schools to help them get the full benefit of services offered by this department of the library.

Plans programs for parents.

Leads Junior Great Books discussion groups.

Plans schedules, assigns duties, and instructs and supervises departmental staff, arranging in-service training as needed. Attends professional meetings and participates in activities.

Required Knowledge, Skills and Abilities: Substantial knowledge of professional library science and administration; good knowledge of children's literature and reader interest levels; good knowledge of resources; ability to develop work programs and plan and supervise the work of others; ability to speak and write effectively; pleasing personality; friendliness; enthusiasm; resourcefulness; initiative; tact; good judgment.

Acceptable Experience and Training: Some professional library experience, preferably in children's services, and possession of a master of library science degree from an accredited library school.

APPENDIX II (cont'd)

SUPERVISOR OF AUDIO-VISUAL SERVICES (GRADE STEP 28)

General Statement of Duties: Performs professional tasks in the library; does related work as required.

Distinguishing Features of the Class: Employees in this class are responsible for directing a group in a major area of library activity such as Adult Services, Service to Children, Technical Processing, and Branch and Bookmobile libraries. Supervision may be exercised over the work of librarians, library assistants, library pages, student assistants, and part-time adults. The work is performed under the general direction of the Assistant Library Director.

Examples of Work:
Directs a major professional service area, involving the supervision of audio-visual services throughout the entire library system, including the branch library and the bookmobile services.

Supervises staff and coordinates activities in the department.

Schedules staff and directs overall policies of the department.

Assists with departmental budget preparation and appropriates line-item expenditures.

Programs film and live events for library and associated civic organizations.

Maintains and develops subject collection in art, architecture, dance, music, and photography.

Maintains and develops record, art print, sculpture, film (8mm and 16mm), filmstrip, slide, periodical, videotape, audiocassette, and photography collections.

Maintains, circulates, and purchases all hardware necessary for items listed above.

Compiles bibliographies and annotated lists and assigns material for review or evaluation.

Required Knowledge, Skills and Abilities: Broad background and knowledge of audio-visual materials. Ability to lead and direct staff. Ability to interpret needs of the community. Good knowledge of publisher and dealer practices and methods of supply resources. Ability to speak and write effectively; pleasing personality; friendliness; enthusiasm; resourcefulness; tact; good judgment.

Acceptable Experience and Training: College graduate plus graduate degree in library science from an accredited library school. Professional experience and/or background in the arts.

APPENDIX II (cont'd)

SUPERVISOR OF CIRCULATION SERVICES (GRADE STEP 28)

General Statement of Duties: Performs professional and supervisory tasks in the library; does related work as required.

Distinguishing Features of the Class: Employees in this class are responsible for directing a group in a major area of library activity such as Adult Service, Service for Children, Technical Processing, and Branch and Bookmobile Library Services. Supervision may be exercised over the work of librarians, library assistants, library pages, student assistants, and part-time adults. The work is performed under the general direction of the Assistant Library Director.

Examples of Work:
Is responsible for the circulation procedures that protect a huge investment and enables borrowers to locate material wanted. A library collection is for use, and without circulation rules and procedures service suffers — e.g., a book not in the right place on the shelves is lost to the reader because it cannot be found.

Must train staff, composed of well-informed non-professionals and pages, to take care of the readers coming into the library to their satisfaction. The circulation staff must be friendly and helpful in representing the library to the reader. Schedules a staff for a 72-hour work week to cover the following duties:
Registration of borrowers.
Checking out books and other materials.
Maintaining circulation records.
Checking in items returned to the library.
Collecting special materials. This means examining closely certain items such as records, picture books, and the like each time they are borrowed and returned for their protection.
Sending overdue notices.
Collecting fines.
Handling reserve books.
Checking in magazines and getting them ready for circulation.
Paging and getting books from the shelves upon request.
Collecting statistics as a guide to future planning.
Interlibrary loan requests and staffing the teletype.
Telephone operators.
Shelving and filing, which involves returning books to the shelves.
Shelf reading, which must be done regularly to maintain order. This is especially important with our open stacks.
Improving shelf appearance to take care of over-crowding, books needing mending or binding.
Shifting books to new areas, which may involve measuring, estimating future needs, adjusting shelf heights, correcting shelf labels, and reshelving.
Taking inventory.
Reading room maintenance.
Catalog assistance.

APPENDIX II (cont'd)

Supervising inventory of all resources in the collection.
Accounting for all money received at the circulation desk.

Handles minor complaints and arguments.

Designs forms for records.

Required Knowledge, Skills and Abilities: Broad reading background; ability to lead and direct staff; ability to interpret community interests and needs; ability to develop systems and methods to get maximum use out of library materials; ability to meet and deal with people effectively; some knowledge of reader interest level.

Acceptable Experience and Training: College graduate plus graduate degree in library science; extensive professional library experience; administrative experience.

SUPERVISOR OF TECHNICAL SERVICES (GRADE STEP 28)

General Statement of Duties: Performs professional and supervisory tasks in the library; does related work as required.

Distinguishing Features of the Class: Employees in this class are responsible for directing a group in a major area of library activity such as Adult Service, Service to Children, Technical Processing, and Branch and Bookmobile Libraries. Supervision may be exercised over the work of librarians, library assistants, library pages, student assistants, and part-time adults. The work is performed under the general direction of the Assistant Library Director.

Examples of Work:
Catalogs materials, which include books, magazines, art and sculpture reproductions, films, slides, filmstrips.

Supervises the preparation of materials for binding.

Supervises mending of books and the preparation of books and materials for circulation such as covering, pasting in pockets, etc.

Conducts in-service training for department staff.

Transacts financial dealings with jobbers; keeps financial accounts of standing orders.

Supervises ordering of books and other materials and the checking in of same when received.

Checks all invoices, computes discounts, distributes costs, etc.

Revises and checks all operations, including the filing of catalog cards.

Prepares work schedules.

Prepares statistical reports; keeps records.

APPENDIX II (cont'd)

Evaluates gift books for inclusion in the collection; writes necessary correspondence.

Prepares subject bibliographies.

Participates in professional organizations and their activities.

Required Knowledge, Skills and Abilities: Good knowledge of professional library science and administration; good knowledge of publisher and dealer practices and methods of library supply resources; ability to develop work programs and plan and supervise the work of others; ability to speak and write effectively; good judgment.

Acceptable Experience and Training: Some professional library experience and possession of a master of library science degree issued by an accredited library school.

REFERENCE LIBRARIAN (GRADE STEP 27)

General Statement of Duties: Performs professional tasks in the library; does related work as required.

Distinguishing Features of the Class: This is the beginning class of professional library work calling for the application of the principles of library science to assignments. However, no specialization or previous library experience is required. Routine library problems are solved independently. More experienced librarians are available for assistance on difficult problems or situations. Immediate supervision may be exercised over the work of assistants.

Examples of Work:
Scheduled to answer reference questions received via telephone or on referral from the circulation department. These are in-depth questions often requiring considerable research. Constantly checks reference collection to keep it up-to-date. Recommends purchases.

Answers requests by mail from all over the country for local information.

Is a member of the Material Selection Committee that meets weekly.

Reviews books, checks subject bibliographies for books to fill gaps in the collection in special subject areas.

Recommends books for adults and students that are suitable to age, knowledge, and taste of the reader.

Constantly weeds the collection and finds replacements. This involves evaluating worn and out-of-date material.

Supervises the reference staff and pages assigned to the department.

Prepares articles on new material received by the library.

Writes book reviews.

Prepares booklists and annotated bibliographies.

APPENDIX II (cont'd)

Required Knowledge, Skills and Abilities: Good knowledge of professional library science and administration; good knowledge of reader interest levels; extensive knowledge of bibliographic and reference tools; ability to speak and write effectively; pleasing personality; friendliness; enthusiasm; resourcefulness; initiative; tact; good judgment; persistency; good memory; imagination; accuracy; thoroughness.

Acceptable Experience and Training: Professional library experience and possession of a master of library science degree issued by an accredited library school.

ASSISTANT CHILDREN'S LIBRARIAN (GRADE STEP 27)

General Statement of Duties: Performs semi-professional tasks in the library; does related work as required.

Distinguishing Features of the Class: This is a semi-professional class of library work, calling for the application of course procedures of library science to assignments.

Examples of Work:
Instructs youngsters in the use of the library, the card catalog, and basic reference books.

Answers reference questions.

Assists students, teachers and parents in selecting materials.

Compiles book lists.

Conducts children's story hours at various age levels.

Participates in selection of children's books and materials and maintenance of the collection.

Prepares reports and keeps records.

Assists in training library assistants and pages.

Files catalog cards.

Must assist the supervisor of Children's Services in all phases of running the department with the additional and expanded programming made possible by the move to larger quarters—story hours, puppet theatre, parents' programs, films, Junior Great Books.

Required Knowledge, Skills and Abilities: Some knowledge of library principles, methods, techniques and procedures. Familiarity with bibliographic and reference tools.

Acceptable Experience and Training: College graduate with course work in library science; experience in library work and children's literature desirable.

APPENDIX II (cont'd)

ASSISTANT AUDIO-VISUAL LIBRARIAN (GRADE STEP 27)

General Statement of Duties: Performs a variety of preprofessional duties in the library; does related work as required.

Distinguishing Features of the Class: This work is on the preprofessional level in the library field. Although much of the work is clerical in nature, it involves the application of standard library routines. An employee in this class must have an interest in literature and a capacity to acquire a working knowledge of library techniques. Work is subject to the direct supervision of a professional librarian. Immediate supervision may be executed over the work of library assistants, library pages and student assistants. An employee in this class is expected to acquire degree or non-degree training in library work to prepare him/herself for increasing responsibilities.

Examples of Work:
Assists Supervisor of Audio-Visual Services in maintaining that department and in booking audio-visual materials for use both in and out of the library.

Maintains register of film users.

Prepares statistical reports and keeps records of equipment and materials.

Orders through immediate supervisor replacement parts for equipment—8mm and 16mm projectors, slide projectors, filmstrip projectors, record players.

Sets up equipment and library programs.

Inspects each film when returned. These vary in length from 50 feet to 2,000 feet. Every foot must be inspected before being issued to another borrower, both for the protection of the film and to ensure the borrower of a successful program. Makes minor repairs to films as needed, replaces broken leaders.

Ships films to a laboratory for perma-filming (a protective coating to increase the life of the film) and cleaning as needed.

Assists in maintaining files of film catalogs, free film listings, catalogs of films available from other governmental agencies.

Attends preview sessions at which films being considered for purchase must be evaluated.

Assists in reference and readers' services in this department in the absence of the department head to provide adequate service during the 72-hour work week.

Required Knowledge, Skills and Abilities: Must have a mechanical sense and ability to diagnose equipment problems in this department and take proper action, such as replacing an exciter lamp in a projector. Must have a working knowledge of the book collection as well as the audio-visual materials available. Ability to get along well with others; proficiency in typing; ability to keep records and make reports; pleasing personality.

Acceptable Experience and Training: College graduate with some experience, or any equivalent combination of experience and training.

APPENDIX II (cont'd)

ASSISTANT CIRCULATION LIBRARIAN (GRADE STEP 27)

General Statement of Duties: Performs a variety of preprofessional duties in the library; does related work as required.

Distinguishing Features of the Class: This work is on the preprofessional level in the library field. Although much of the work is clerical in nature, the work involves the application of standard library routines. An employee in this class must have an interest in literature and a capacity to acquire a working knowledge of library techniques. Work is subject to the direct supervision of a professional librarian. Immediate supervision may be executed over the work of library assistants, library pages, and student assistants. An employee in this class is expected to acquire degree or non-degree training in library work to prepare himself for increasing responsibilities.

Examples of Work:
Keeps library assistants and pages working according to supervisor's scheduling when supervisor is not on duty.

Reads shelves.

Assists in training library assistants and pages.

Assists borrowers in using the card catalog.

Answers questions pertaining to directories.

In charge of Circulation Department in absence of supervisor.

Required Knowledge, Skills and Abilities: Knowledge of library routines and procedures; good working knowledge of and interest in literature; ability to get along well with others; ability to type, file and keep records.

Acceptable Experience and Training: College graduate or any equivalent combination of experience and training providing the required knowledge, skills and abilities; some experience.

ORDER LIBRARIAN (GRADE STEP 27)

General Statement of Duties: Performs routine subprofessional duties in the library; does related work as required.

Distinguishing Features of the Class: This work is of the beginning subprofessional level in the library field, requiring interest in and capacity to acquire a working knowledge of library techniques. The work is performed under the immediate supervision of a professional librarian who outlines routines to be observed and who is available for consultation on special problems that arise. An employee in this class is expected to acquire degree or non-degree training in library work to prepare him/herself for increasing responsibilities.

APPENDIX II (cont'd)

Examples of Work:
Research (searching) and checking of book orders received from book selection committee. This involves checking files to avoid duplication of books and searching for Library of Congress catalog card numbers for ordering purposes.

Orders books, records, and other materials.

Types and sorts order slips.

Orders Library of Congress and Wilson catalog cards.

Checks in orders against order slips and invoices when received.

Follows up on Continuation Orders — books that are published more or less regularly are on standing order to be shipped as published.

Filing of order slips and catalog cards when received before books arrive.

Writes letters for direct orders and follow-ups.

Checks in bindery books.

Checks bibliographies against the card catalog for library holdings.

Required Knowledge, Skills and Abilities: Some knowledge of and an interest in books; ability to get along well with others; ability to keep records; willingness to learn professional library techniques; aptitude for library work; ability to type with reasonable speed and accuracy.

Acceptable Experience and Training: Completion of a standard high school course and two years of college or university training or acceptable library experience approved by the Board of Library Trustees upon recommendation of the Library Director; preferably graduation from a college or university of recognized standing; or any equivalent combination of experience and training which provides the required knowledge, skills, and abilities.

ASSISTANT REFERENCE LIBRARIAN (GRADE STEP 26)

General Statement of Duties: Performs semi-professional tasks in the library; does related work as required.

Distinguishing Features of the Class: This is a semi-professional class of library work, calling for the application of course procedures of library science to assignments.

Examples of Work:
Answers general reference questions.

Helps patrons in the use of reference materials.

Assists readers in selection of library materials.

Participates in selection of books and building the collection in one or more subject areas such as science, technology, etc.

APPENDIX II (cont'd)

Assists in supervision of library assistants and pages assigned to the Reference Department in the absence of the Reference Librarian.

Works an alternate or complementary schedule with the Reference Librarian in covering the 72 hours per week that the library is open so that library users will be assured of professional help whenever it is needed.

Maintains and collects files of pamphlets. Many pamphlets contain the most up-to-date material on a subject such as drugs, planned parenthood.

Required Knowledge, Skills and Abilities: Knowledge of the principles and practices of professional library work. Ability to meet and deal with people effectively. Broad reading background and familiarity with bibliographic and reference tools. Must be able to work without immediate supervision.

Acceptable Experience and Training: College graduate with course work leading to a master's degree from an accredited library school.

DESK ASSISTANT (GRADE STEP 26)

General Statement of Duties: Performs routine subprofessional duties in the library; does related work as required.

Distinguishing Features of the Class: This work is of the beginning subprofessional level in the library field; requiring interest in and capacity to acquire a working knowledge of library techniques; the work is performed under the immediate supervision of professional librarians or library assistants of a higher grade who outline routines to be observed and who are available for consultation on special problems that arise.

Examples of Work:
Assists in registering new borrowers.

Works at the circulation desk checking materials in and out.

Notes changes of addresses, names, and telephone numbers in registration book.

Shelves books and assists in keeping order in the stacks.

Reads shelves and removes books requiring attention.

Answers routine telephone and patron questions.

Takes reserves for materials and searches for these materials.

Files first, second, and third overdue notices in their respective locations in the circulation file.

Types overdue notices on a four-page form, mailing the first notice and subsequent notices according to a certain time schedule. With the third notice a copy of the law concerning library property is enclosed. Failing to return books after this notice the patron receives a letter from the city solicitor with the

APPENDIX II (cont'd)

replacement cost of the materials noted. When notices are not delivered by the post office, all leads are checked to try to retrieve the missing material. Mends materials when necessary.

Required Knowledge, Skills and Abilities: Some knowledge of and interest in library materials; ability to get along well with public; ability to keep records and make reports; willingness to learn; ability to type with reasonable speed and accuracy; pleasing personality.

Acceptable Experience and Training: Completion of a standard high school course and two years of college or university training or acceptable library experience approved by the Board of Library Trustees upon recommendation of the Library Director; or any equivalent combination of experience and training which provides the required knowledge, skills, and abilities.

ADMINISTRATIVE SECRETARY (GRADE STEP 23)

General Statement of Duties: Performs difficult stenographic and clerical tasks; does related work as required.

Distinguishing Features of the Class: This is high level clerical work usually involving responsible secretarial duties performed for a major department head. Considerable judgment is required in establishing or adapting work procedures to new situations and in performing varied clerical and minor administrative services to conserve the time of a superior. The work is reviewed upon completion but frequently no check is made of data compiled or records prepared. Supervision is sometimes exercised over clerical assistants engaged in the performance of routine functions.

Examples of Work:
Takes and transcribes difficult dictation involving technical, legal, financial, or engineering terminology.

Signs supervisor's name to correspondence, inter-office memos, requisitions, and related documents.

Prepares replies to correspondence from brief dictated notes or on own initiative.

Performs administrative assistant duties including preparing relatively simple specifications, reviewing budget requests for completeness and proper form, and reviewing expenditures and accounts.

Calculates time sheet information and wages for library personnel.

Maintains personnel records.

Establishes and maintains cross-reference files and establishes file categories.

Types complex statistical and accounting reports requiring a number of separate tabulations.

APPENDIX II (cont'd)

Responsible for ordering, storage, and distribution of library supplies and equipment.

Screens visitors, telephone calls, and incoming mail, personally answering those inquiries which in the employee's judgment do not require the supervisor's attention.

Does bookkeeping and maintains financial records which are involved in purchasing, book order work, binding, etc.

Coordinates business activities with city departments.

Ensures that department budgets do not become overdrawn.

Prepares requisitions, vouchers, budgets, and other data.

Searches files and a variety of source material to serve as background for reports dictated by supervisors.

Reviews outgoing mail prepared by other clerks for form, accuracy, and adherence to office policy.

Keeps accurate bookkeeping records.

Required Knowledge, Skills and Abilities: Thorough knowledge of office terminology, procedures, and equipment and of business arithmetic and English; some knowledge of elementary bookkeeping; ability to take and transcribe dictation at a high rate of speed; ability to follow complex oral and written directions; ability to get along well with others; demonstrated ability to maintain complex clerical records and prepare reports from such records; ability to make decisions in accordance with laws, ordinances, regulations, and established procedures where errors could easily result in additional costs to the city government; ability to make relatively complex mathematical computations rapidly and accurately; ability to plan and supervise work of others; good judgment; tact and courtesy.

Acceptable Experience and Training: Considerable progressively responsible experience in clerical work which shall have involved taking and transcribing dictation and completion of a standard high school course with business school training which provides the required knowledge, skills, and abilities.

LIBRARY ASSISTANT REFERENCE (GRADE STEP 23)

General Statement of Duties: Performs routine subprofessional duties in the library; does related work as required.

Distinguishing Features of the Class: This work is of the beginning subprofessional level in the library field; requiring interest in and capacity to acquire a working knowledge of library techniques. The work is performed under the immediate supervision of professional librarians or library assistants of a higher grade who outline routines to be observed and who are available for

APPENDIX II (cont'd)

consultation on special problems that arise. An employee in this class is expected to acquire degree or non-degree training in library work to prepare him/herself for greater responsibilities.

Examples of Work:
Assists readers in locating books.

Helps patrons with the card catalog, the guide to periodicals.

Checks and distributes incoming periodical mail.

Records receipt of and displays newspapers, magazines, pamphlets, college catalogs; posts bulletin board notices; etc.

Prepares magazines (other than current) for circulation, which requires reinforcement, typing of card and pocket, and pasting.

Shelves magazines and keeps them in order both in open racks and closed stacks.

Prepares Rolodex card for patron's use showing the library's holdings of each magazine and keeps the file up-to-date.

Records addresses of publishers, subscription prices, single copy prices (in case of lost issues) for visual file information.

Sends for sample copies of magazines being considered for purchase by the selection committee.

Writes to claim issues not received.

Orders replacements for lost magazines.

Prepares volumes of magazines to be sent to the bindery.

Maintains the current file of college catalogs.

Annually reviews holdings and discards out-dated issues according to library policy.

Required Knowledge, Skills and Abilities: Some knowledge of and an interest in books; ability to get along well with others; ability to keep records and make reports; willingness to learn professional library techniques; aptitude for library work; pleasing personality.

Acceptable Experience and Training: Completion of a standard high school course and two years of college or university training or acceptable library experience approved by the Board of Library Trustees upon recommendation by the Library Director; preferably graduation from a college or university of recognized standing; or any equivalent combination of experience and training which provides the required knowledge, skills, and abilities.

LIBRARY ASSISTANT CHILDREN'S (GRADE STEP 23)

General Statement of Duties: Performs routine subprofessional duties in the library; does related work as required.

Distinguishing Features of the Class: This work is of the beginning subprofessional level in the library field, requiring interest in and capacity to acquire a working knowledge of library techniques. The work is performed under the immediate supervision of professional librarians or library assistants of a higher grade who outline routines to be observed and who are available for consultation on special problems that arise. An employee in this class is expected to acquire degree or non-degree training in library work to prepare him/herself for increasing responsibilities.

Examples of Work:
Helps children and other patrons to find books.

Helps in answering routine questions.

May conduct story hours or other children's programs under the immediate supervision of the Assistant Children's Librarian.

Assists in maintaining picture and pamphlet files.

Processes magazines for circulation.

Looks at new books as they are added to the collection.

Performs clerical tasks for supervisor.

Answers telephone.

Registers children for Summer Reading Club, story hours, etc.

Assists in library instruction for various children's groups such as Girl Scouts, grade school classes, kindergartens, etc.

Shelves books and reads shelves.

Required Knowledge, Skills and Abilities: Some knowledge of and an interest in children's books and materials; willingness to learn public library techniques; ability to keep records accurately; ability to type with reasonable speed and accuracy; ability to meet and serve the public.

Acceptable Experience and Training: Completion of high school course and two years of college or university training or commensurate library experience acceptable by approval of the Board of Library Trustees upon recommendation of the Library Director.

LIBRARY ASSISTANT AUDIO-VISUAL (GRADE STEP 23)

General Statement of Duties: Performs professional tasks in the library; does related work as required.

Distinguishing Features of the Class: This is a subprofessional position involving a mixture of clerical and professional duties and skills. Resourcefulness, ingenuity, flexibility, and tact are necessary qualifications for successfully working with the public. Additionally, some subject knowledge and a willingness to work with audio-visual equipment is expected. Library assistants are expected

APPENDIX II (cont'd)

to learn and become fully competent in the daily operations of the department and should be prepared to become involved in any departmental activity. They are directly responsible to the department supervisor, who may assign specific duties as well as routine functions. Library assistants are encouraged to seek and acquire further library training on either the degree or the non-degree level.

Examples of Work:
Understand, use, and maintain circulation system for nonprint materials and audio-visual equipment.

Assist patrons in any reasonable way; help in locating information or materials.

Answer reference questions when possible or assist the librarian in such work.

Become familiar with the book and nonprint collections.

Filing and shelving of books, records, films, and periodicals within the department.

Shelf reading to maintain the integrity and usefulness of the collections.

Booking of audio-visual materials for use in and out of the library.

Maintenance of records and statistical reports.

Inspection, cleaning, and maintenance of film collections.

Preview and evaluate films and other materials being considered for purchase.

Operate audio-visual equipment, such as film, filmstrip, and slide projectors, record players, tape recorders and videotape equipment. Function as projectionist.

Cleaning, servicing, and minor repair of audio-visual equipment.

Library assistants are encouraged to think creatively and to propose and develop special programs on their own within the departmental framework.

Perform any and all tasks assigned by the departmental supervisor.

Help to educate the public in the use of all departmental equipment and materials.

Required Knowledge, Skills and Abilities: College graduate with some experience or any equivalent combination of experience and training. Candidates should be familiar with libraries and should be able to learn rapidly library routines. Subject knowledge and mechanical sense are strong assets. Must be able to work well with others and interact positively with the general public. Must be flexible and able to cope with situations as they arise.

Acceptable Experience and Training: Completion of a standard high school course and two years of college or university training or acceptable library experience approved by the Board of Library Trustees upon recommendation of the Director.

APPENDIX II (cont'd)

INTERLIBRARY LOAN ASSISTANT (GRADE STEP 23)

General Statement of Duties: Performs subprofessional tasks in the library; does related work as required.

Distinguishing Features of the Class: This work is of the beginning subprofessional level in the library field, requiring interest in and capacity to acquire a working knowledge of library techniques. The work is performed under the immediate supervision of professional librarians or library assistants of a higher grade who outline routines to be observed and who are available for consultation on special problems that arise. An employee in this class is expected to acquire degree or non-degree training in library work to prepare him/herself for greater responsibilities.

Examples of Work:
Processes interlibrary loans.

Does searching and verifying in catalogs to determine if requests are property entered.

Charges and discharges materials.

Secures books and other materials from shelves for outside requests.

Wraps and ties packages.

Completes printed forms and form letters.

Maintains records and files of borrower's requests.

Required Knowledge, Skills and Abilities: Some knowledge of and an interest in books; aptitude for library work; proficiency in letter writing, typing, and filing.

Acceptable Experience and Training: Completion of a standard high school course and two years of college or university training or acceptable library experience approved by the Board of Library Trustees upon recommendation of the Director; or any equivalent combination of experience and training which provides the required knowledge, skills, and abilities.

CATALOG-TYPIST (GRADE STEP 23)

General Statement of Duties: Performs routine subprofessional duties in the library; does related work as required.

Distinguishing Features of the Class: This work is of the beginning subprofessional level in the library field, requiring interest in and capacity to acquire a working knowledge of library techniques. The work is performed under the immediate supervision of professional librarians or library assistants of a higher grade who outline routines to be observed and who are available for consultation on special problems that arise. An employee in this class is expected

APPENDIX II (cont'd)

to acquire degree or non-degree training in library work to prepare him/herself for increasing responsibilities.

Examples of Work:
Searches and processes all adult, young adult, and children's fiction.

Types all catalog cards for fiction and adult non-fiction books and children's books, including book card, pocket, and label for each book that circulates; also all cards relating to reference books.

Types new cards and pockets for books that have to be mended and all books returned from the bindery.

Pulls all cards from the main catalog relating to books that are lost or destroyed.

Replaces worn out cards in the catalog with new ones.

Re-catalogs old books (of value) from circulating to reference.

Files cards in the main catalog.

Files shelf list cards after books have been checked and placed on shelf for covering and pasting.

Required Knowledge, Skills and Abilities: Some knowledge of and an interest in books; ability to get along well with others; aptitude for library work; proficiency in typing and filing.

Acceptable Experience and Training: Completion of a standard high school course and two years of college or university training or acceptable library experience approved by the Board of Library Trustees upon recommendation of the Director; preferably graduation from a college or university of recognized standing; or any equivalent combination of experience and training which provides the required knowledge, skills, and abilities.

COMMUNITY SERVICES LIBRARIAN (GRADE STEP 21)

General Statement of Duties: Performs a variety of preprofessional duties in and out of the library; does related work as required.

Distinguishing Features of the Class: This work is on the preprofessional level in the library field. Although much of the work is clerical in nature, the work involves the application of standard library routines. An employee in this class must have an interest in literature and a capacity to acquire a working knowledge of library techniques. Work is subject to the direct supervision of the Director. An employee in this class is expected to acquire degree or non-degree training in library work to prepare him/herself for increasing responsibilities.

Examples of Work:
Develops and strengthens lines of communication between the library and the community.

APPENDIX II (cont'd)

Meets with parent and neighborhood groups and enlists and encourages their participation in library activities.

Establishes communication with community organizations, religious institutions, and private agencies and helps plan programs with them using library materials such as books, films and slides, book talks, etc.

Helps interpret library goals to community groups and organizations.

Keeps a log of visits, calls, and conferences.

Helps arrange library space and time for meetings, orientation, etc.

Must be thoroughly familiar with all library services and policies and work closely with the Children's Librarian.

Assists Librarian and Adult Services Librarian, as well as those in the branch and bookmobile, in programming.

Assists with community programs both during and after library hours.

Work is performed with considerable independence in accordance with library policies, subject to close review by supervisor of plans, problems, progress, and results.

Required Knowledge, Skills and Abilities: A good basic knowledge of library procedures and goals. The ability to understand and identify with the community. A background of participation in community groups; ability to work with people.

Acceptable Experience and Training: Some experience and a college degree or any equivalent combination of experience and training which provides the required knowledge, skills, and abilities.

SUPERVISOR-BOOKMOBILE (GRADE STEP 21)

General Statement of Duties: Performs a variety of preprofessional duties in the bookmobile; does related work as required.

Distinguishing Features of the Class: This work is on the preprofessional level in the library field. Although much of the work is clerical in nature, the work involves the application of standard library routines. An employee in this class must have an interest in literature and a capacity to acquire a working knowledge of library techniques. Work is subject to the direct supervision of the Assistant Library Director. Immediate supervision is executed over the work of library assistants and a driver-clerk. An employee in this class is expected to acquire degree or non-degree training in library work to prepare him/herself for increasing responsibilities.

Examples of Work:
Supervises circulation and loan activities of the Bookmobile under the direction

APPENDIX II (cont'd)

of the Assistant Director and coordinates with the Supervisor of Adult Services and the Supervisor of Children's Services.

Evaluates Bookmobile stops and makes recommendations of changes in the schedule.

Investigates possible new stops as location, number of potential users in the vicinity, parking spots, approaches, etc., are concerned.

Prepares statistics and reports.

Recommends books for the collection.

Trains and supervises library assistants and schedules their work.

Responsible for the book collection and rotation on the Bookmobile shelves.

Assists borrowers in selection of materials and answers such questions as time and resources allow.

Takes reserves on books not on board at the time, which must be borrowed from the main library collection for the next visit.

Supervises the Summer Reading Club.

Required Knowledge, Skills and Abilities: Good working knowledge of and interest in literature; ability to get along well with others; ability to keep records and make reports; willingness to learn professional library techniques; aptitude for library work; proficiency in typing; pleasing personality.

Acceptable Experience and Training: College graduate with some experience or any equivalent combination of experience and training which provides the required knowledge, skills, and abilities; some course work in public library techniques.

SUPERVISOR-BRANCH (GRADE STEP 21)

General Statement of Duties: Performs a variety of preprofessional duties in the branch; does related work as required.

Distinguishing Features of the Class: This work is on the preprofessional level in the library field. Although much of the work is clerical in nature, the work involves the application of standard library routines. An employee in this class must have an interest in literature and a capacity to acquire a working knowledge of library techniques. Work is subject to the direct supervision of the Assistant Library Director. Immediate supervision may be executed over the work of library assistants, library pages, and student assistants. An employee in this class is expected to acquire degree or non-degree training in library work to prepare him/herself for increasing responsibilities.

Examples of Work:
Supervises circulation and loan activities in the branch library under the

APPENDIX II (cont'd)

immediate direction of the Assistant Director and coordinates with the Supervisor of Adult Services and the Supervisor of Children's Services. Works with the Community Services Librarian on programming and use of facilities.

Recommends books and other materials for the branch collection.

Trains and supervises non-professional personnel — a library assistant, pages, and a janitor who divides his or her time between the main building and the branch; schedules their work.

Responsible for the maintenance of the building and the book collection.

Prepares statistics and reports.

Files catalog cards.

Must be able to arrange books according to reader interests.

Must keep abreast of the needs of the people in the area in which the library is located and keep the library materials geared to popular and timely subjects.

Supervises use of listening stations for phonograph records.

Arranges special exhibits with the cooperation of the Exhibits Librarian.

Supervises a reading room containing newspapers, popular magazines, and current fiction.

Conduct story hours and film programs with assistance from the supervising department heads.

Required Knowledge, Skills and Abilities: Good working knowledge of and interest in literature; ability to get along well with others; ability to keep records and make reports; willingness to learn professional library techniques; aptitude for library work; proficiency in typing and filing; pleasing personality.

Acceptable Experience and Training: College graduate with some experience or any equivalent combination of experience and training which provides the required knowledge, skills, and abilities; some course work in public library techniques.

EXHIBITS LIBRARIAN (GRADE STEP 20)

General Statement of Duties: Performs a variety of preprofessional duties in and out of the library; does related work as required.

Distinguishing Features of the Class: This work is on the preprofessional level in the library field. Although much of the work is clerical in nature, it involves the application of standard library routines. An employee in this class must have an interest in literature and a capacity to acquire a working knowledge of library techniques. Work is subject to the direct supervision of the Director. An employee in this class is expected to acquire degree or non-degree training in library work to prepare him/herself for increasing responsibilities.

APPENDIX II (cont'd)

Examples of Work:
This person is responsible for the execution of displays and exhibits throughout the library and its extensions as well as special exhibits outside of the library. This requires conferences with department heads and other librarians with regard to materials, scope, etc., in accordance with overall library goals and programs.

Responsible for display areas in the entry, the hanging cubes, kiosks in the children's area, art and artifact exhibits, browsing area, special exhibits in the multi-purpose room.

Schedules and coordinates all exhibits making sure that they are timely and relevant — e.g., ecology, Washington's Birthday, United Nations Day, Spring — all designed to widen reader's use of library materials, make them aware of the library's many services, create interest in different subjects.

Distributes exhibit and promotional materials outside of the library such as setting up windows in banks and store fronts for National Library Week, Children's Book Week, and a continuing campaign for advertising library services.

Works with the community services librarian in providing materials relating to holidays for churches, sidewalk displays where the library goes to the people, various institutes as part of promoting Junctionville as a better place in which to work and live.

Designs covers and layouts of booklists, brochures, posters, etc.

Required Knowledge, Skills and Abilities: Must have some knowledge of library principles, methods, techniques and procedures. Must have a knowledge of and interest in books. Must have considerable creative ability and artistic talent and be able to work in various media. Some clerical skill.

Acceptable Experience and Training: At least two years of college with course work in public library techniques or any equivalent combination of experience and training which provides the required knowledge, skills, and abilities.

BOOKMOBILE ASSISTANT (GRADE STEP 20)

General Statement of Duties: Performs routine subprofessional duties in a public library; does related work as required.

Distinguishing Features of the Class: This work is of the beginning subprofessional level in the library field, requiring interest in and capacity to acquire a working knowledge of library techniques. The work is performed under the immediate supervision of professional librarians or library assistants of a higher grade who outline routines to be observed and who are available for consultation on special problems that might arise. An employee in this class is expected to acquire degree or non-degree training in library work to prepare him/herself for increasing responsibilities.

APPENDIX II (cont'd)

Examples of Work:
Drives Bookmobile to and from each stop during the absence of the Bookmobile Driver.

Receives and checks in books while on the road, making any minor repairs as time allows.

Sorts books belonging to other departments when returned to the Bookmobile.

Collects fines as necessary.

Shelves books and assists readers in selection of reading material.

Helps in replenishing supply of books before starting out each day.

Prepares overdue notices.

Mends books and maintains records.

Compiles daily circulation count.

Takes requests from both adults and children for books not on the Bookmobile.

Assists in general reference work as time and resources allow.

Required Knowledge, Skills and Abilities: Some knowledge of and an interest in books; ability to get along well with others; ability to keep records; willingness to learn professional library techniques; aptitude for library work; ability to type with reasonable speed and accuracy; pleasing personality; good physical condition.

Additional Requirement: Possession of a commercial driver's license issued by the state.

Acceptable Experience and Training: Completion of a standard high school course and two years of college or university training or acceptable library experience approved by the Board of Library Trustees upon recommendation by the Chief Librarian; preferably graduation from a college or university of recognized standing; or any equivalent combination of experience and training which provides the required knowledge, skills, and abilities.

BRANCH ASSISTANT (GRADE STEP 20)

General Statement of Duties: Performs routine subprofessional duties in the branch; does related work as required.

Distinguishing Features of the Class: This is a subprofessional position involving a mixture of clerical and subprofessional duties and skills, requiring interest in and capacity to acquire a working knowledge of library techniques. The work is performed under the immediate supervision of the branch librarian. An employee in this class is expected to acquire degree or non-degree training in library work to prepare him/herself for increasing responsibilities.

APPENDIX II (cont'd)

Examples of Work:
Helps patrons find books and materials.

Helps patrons with the card catalog and answers routine questions.

Registers new borrowers.

Assists branch librarian with story hours and film programs.

Maintains collection.

Prepares reports and keeps records.

Works at circulation desk, checking material in and out.

Takes reserves for material and searches for these materials.

Required Knowledge, Skills and Abilities: Good working knowledge of and interest in literature; ability to get along with others; ability to keep records and make reports; proficiency in typing; pleasing personality.

Acceptable Training and Experience: A high school diploma with knowledge of filing and record keeping; library experience is desirable but not required.

DRIVER CLERK (GRADE STEP 19)

General Statement of Duties: Operates the Bookmobile and performs routine clerical tasks in connection with the Bookmobile service; does related work as required.

Distinguishing Features of the Class: This position involves responsibility for the safe and efficient operation of the Bookmobile. In addition to the driving responsibility, the Driver Clerk is called upon to assist a professional librarian in servicing the public. The work is performed under the immediate supervision of a professional librarian.

Examples of Work:
Drives Bookmobile to and from each stop.

Loads and unloads the Bookmobile with books selected by the supervisory librarian.

Checks in books being returned at the various stops and shelves them as time allows.

Checks out books, takes applications for new cards, lost cards and changes of address.

Takes reference requests.

Assists patrons in locating special materials, explaining Bookmobile procedures as requested.

APPENDIX II (cont'd)

Before proceeding to the next stop, stamps a supply of cards with the current due date.

Keeps the charging machine cleaned and serviced.

Responsible for preventive maintenance and servicing of the Bookmobile.

Responsible for keeping the inside of the Bookmobile clean.

Required Knowledge, Skills and Abilities: Good knowledge of the operation of trucks and buses in a safe and efficient manner; good knowledge of the city's streets and state and local driving laws and regulations; ability to understand and follow oral and written instructions; ability to make routine computations; ability to get along with others; good judgment.

Additional Requirement: Possession of a commercial driver's license issued by the state.

Acceptable Experience and Training: Preferably some experience as a bus driver or a truck driver and completion of a standard high school course and preferably some clerical or library clerical experience; or any equivalent combination of experience and training which provides the required knowledge, skills, and abilities.

LIBRARY ASSISTANT-BRANCH (GRADE STEP 19)

General Statement of Duties: Performs routine subprofessional duties in the branch; does related work as required.

Distinguishing Features of the Class: This work is of the beginning subprofessional level in the library field; it requires an interest in and capacity to acquire a working knowledge of library techniques. The work is performed under the immediate supervision of a professional librarian or a library assistant of a higher grade, who outline routines to be observed and who are available for consultation on special problems that arise.

Examples of Work:
Assists in registering new borrowers.

Works at circulation desk charging materials in and out.

Inspects materials when returned, mending when needed.

Reads shelves.

Files overdue notices in the manner of the desk assistant.

Answers the telephone and distributes incoming mail.

Shelves new material.

Performs clerical tasks for supervisors.

APPENDIX II (cont'd)

Required Knowledge, Skills and Abilities: Some knowledge of and interest in library materials; ability to get along with public; ability to keep records and make reports; willingness to learn; pleasing personality.

Acceptable Experience and Training: A high school diploma with knowledge of filing and record keeping; library experience helpful but not required.

CUSTODIAN (GRADE STEP 18)

General Statement of Duties: Performs routine building cleaning tasks; does related work as required.

Distinguishing Features of the Class: This is manual work requiring efficient performance of simple building cleaning and maintenance duties. All Custodians report directly to the Assistant Library Director but also work under general supervision on routine recurring assignments, receiving specific instructions on each new or unusual assignment. The work is occasionally reviewed by inspection.

Examples of Work:
Opens and closes library according to schedule; remains to lock up after scheduled meetings after library hours.

Sweeps, mops, polishes, vacuums floors as required.

Keeps walks clean; cleans snow and spreads salt and sand in winter.

Cleans lavatories; wash basins, drinking fountains, and empties wastebaskets daily.

Sets up chairs and tables in multi-purpose room and other areas as needed.

Performs simple painting tasks.

Washes windows and polishes furniture.

Dusts woodwork, furniture and other articles.

Collects paper and rubbish, packs and sets it out for pickup.

Mows lawns, cultivates trees and shrubs, and other grounds tasks.

Makes minor repairs to buildings, equipment, and furniture.

Raises and lowers the flag each working day and on holidays in accordance with the flag code.

Delivers packages and messages.

Empties book return box each morning.

Checks heating system periodically.

Performs related building cleaning tasks.

APPENDIX II (cont'd)

Maintains a checklist of supplies used — bulbs, paper towels, cleanser, fertilizer, etc. — and provides supervisor with requisition for needed items.

The above tasks apply to the Bookmobile, as well.

Must cover the entire library schedule.

Required Knowledge, Skills and Abilities: Some knowledge of building cleaning practices, supplies, and equipment and ability to use them economically and efficiently; ability to understand and follow simple oral and written directions; thoroughness; dependability; good physical condition.

Acceptable Experience and Training: High school diploma or equivalent combination of experience and training; preferably some building cleaning and maintenance experience.

APPENDIX III

ENTRY FOR JUNCTIONVILLE IN
AMERICAN LIBRARY DIRECTORY

P   JUNCTIONVILLE PUBLIC LIBRARY, 1 E Lafayette. Founded 1836. Pop served 55,000; Circ 508,396. *Dir* Maude Poitevant Watman; *Asst Dir* Richard Jones; *ILL* Lee Owens; *Tech Servs* Leo Lowery; *Ref* Angeline Krell & Barton Cullerton; *Commun Servs* Annetta Quick; *Bkmobile Coordr* Bonnie Lonberg. Staff 36 (9 prof, cler 27) Inc $580,312 (city funded). Exp 146,239, Bks 58,495, Per 8335 Bd 4680 Micro 2050 AV 8455; Sal $434,073 (prof 173,630, cler 260,443) Bk vols 161,864; Per sub 579; vols bd 1350; micro 1828. Micro Hldgs: Fiche 500, Reels 1328. AV: Rec. A-Tapes, V-Tapes, Flm, Fs, Slides, Maps, Cht, Art repro. VF 40
Special subjects: Art-archi, bus, music, rel
Special collections: History of Junctionville, Junctionville Oral History
Branches: 1
Castle Heights, 34 Broad St. Librn Heather Champe Bk vols 29,832
Bookmobiles: 1

8

MAE GETS A JOB

Voris University is located on three campuses at Hackley, a modern industrial city in the land of the buttes and the sagebrush plains. The uptown campus, comprising some 90 acres, is at the heart of the urban area of 55,000 population. Six miles to the south lie the 325-acre Greendale campus and the 220-acre University Medical Center.

VU is both a land-grant institution and a comprehensive major research university in the state. Its distinctive mission within the system of higher education is to serve as a center for graduate education, professional education and training, research, extension, public services, and continuing education. It is organized into 16 colleges, schools, and divisions, which include 89 academic departments, located in 120 buildings (including residential facilities). These academic units offer 157 different programs, leading to degrees at either the bachelor's, master's, or doctoral level.

Academic year enrollment on all campuses is about 24,000. Summer enrollment generally exceeds 5,000, while various extension programs throughout the state enroll approximately 4,000 students. Full-time faculty number about 1,700, with over half having the doctorate; employees of the institution total approximately 5,000. VU has a total budget in excess of $200 million for the present fiscal year. As part of the state-supported system of higher education, it is governed by the state Board of Regents; there is also a law advisory board.

The university has a single library system whose director, Elsbeth Bajalović, reports to the provost, and has the rank of professor. Her age is 35. The system consists of the three major units and several working collections, which are housed in those departments that have demonstrated a need for them. There are six assistant directors: four at the uptown campus (administration, public services, collection development, and technical services), one at the Greendale campus (called director of the Greendale campus and assistant director of the University Libraries), and one at the Medical Center (called director of the Medical Center library and assistant director of the University Libraries) (Appendix I). The assistant directors report to Bajalović and hold faculty rank. The directors at the Greendale campus (i.e., the graduate school) and the Medical Center have assistant directors.

Mae Noel-Pardon joined the uptown campus library staff two years ago, right out of library school, as a reference librarian. Having devoted herself to medical librarianship in her elective course work, she hoped when she received her degree to put her knowledge to work at a university medical school, preferably (before long, she trusted) as a director. Upon accepting the job, she made it known that she would appreciate being considered for a position at the Medical Center library when one became available.

Little did she expect then that two years later, at the age of 30, she would be sitting in Bajalović's office and hearing the director say, with the joy of the bringer of glad tidings: "How would you like to be acting director of the Medical Center library?"

Her amazement was apparent as she blurted out, "I'd love it!"

A broad grin came over the other woman's face. "Splendid!" she said, with an air of settling the business. "Now let me tell you something about the job."

Noel-Pardon jumped her chair closer. Bajalović commenced by stating that she assumed Noel-Pardon had heard that Faye Weir (the Medical Center library director for the past three years) had suffered a nervous breakdown and would be on leave of absence for at least six months. Weir had requested when she returned to be transferred to a smaller departmental library, but a decision had not yet been made on her request—although she had done a fine job at the Medical Center, and although the staff (with the exception of the assistant director) had accepted her well. Noel-Pardon expressed sympathy for Weir, saying she had heard about it "via the grapevine." Bajalović then said she and the assistant director for public services felt Noel-Pardon was an unusually capable person. In her last appraisal they had observed how she blended many attractive personal qualities with intelligence, energy, and determination, and that they had identified her as someone to be considered for early promotion. The young appointee swelled with pride. "I've been very happy here," she remarked. She could think of nothing else to say.

The director resumed. Her assistants enjoy considerable freedom of action, she said, and she does not exercise close supervision over them. It is her policy to let each person run his or her department, and she encourages individual initiative in making decisions. She is there for consultation, but other than that Noel-Pardon would be free to administer the library as she saw fit. She pointed out that the budget for the Medical Center library was appropriated from the Medical Center, and that the Medical Center library director also reports to the dean of the medical school, who reports directly to the president. By personal choice, the dean stays out of the selection of library personnel. As the person in charge, then, Noel-Pardon would be responsible for every activity of the library—supervising fiscal matters, making policy decisions, selecting and organizing materials, providing services, directing the staff, and so forth. The operation of its services requires 18 people. Seven are professional employees, and the others are clerical workers; there is the usual complement of student assistants (Appendix II).

Bajalović observed with a warm smile that she had been doing most of the talking and invited Noel-Pardon to ask questions or make comments.

"When do I start?" the younger woman inquired eagerly.

"In one week—on Monday, the 19th."

That was fine. Bajalović then said that rather than for her to attempt to cover the things *she* thought the acting director should know about she would prefer Noel-Pardon to accumulate a list of questions she would like answers to once she had been on the job a week or two. Noel-Pardon thought this a strange way to operate, but said she understood.

A question occurred to her right away. "Would it be bold of me to ask," she said hesitantly, "why if the Medical Center library is virtually an autonomous unit—I am right in assuming the staff there does it's own selection of materials, its own cataloging, everything, am I not?—"

"Yes," interpolated the other.

"—Well, wouldn't it be better if it was a *completely* autonomous library? Many medical school libraries are only affiliated with their medical schools. As I see it the library has physical and operational autonomy, but not administrative autonomy."

There was no immediate reply from the director. "You don't waste any time making suggestions, do you?" said she, at length, musingly. "It's the old centralization versus decentralization question. I tell you what, look into the pros and cons of the idea. I'll consider them. I must admit that I have very little to do with the medical library, and it might not be a bad idea. Perhaps some form of coordinated decentralization is the answer, but anyway we'd have to sell it to the administration. Send me a memo in the form of a recommendation. Be sure to include ideas on how to sell it. This is all *very* preliminary, of course."

Noel-Pardon nodded and remarked that she would do some work on it in the next week.

"By the way," Bajalović appended, very quickly, "you won't be able to have any overlap time with Faye. She left last Friday. The assistant is in charge this week. I'll call him and tell him about your appointment."

Which, too, was fine. Thereupon Noel-Pardon said:

"This may sound strange, but in a way I think it's a good idea not to have any overlap time with one's predecessor. He or she can transmit all kinds of prejudices about staff members to the successor and these can be some sort of self-fulfilling prophecy."

"I'm not sure I know what you mean." Bajalović was interested.

"Well, if I'm told beforehand that so-and-so is not too bright, and not to expect too much from him or her, I might approach that person differently than I would if I hadn't been told anything. What I mean is, I can't then start with a clean slate toward everybody. I might find myself looking for signs to confirm somebody else's notion and in some mysterious way help to retard the person at his or her present level."

Bajalović entreated her to go on.

"Well," recommenced the young librarian, buoyed up by the director's interest, "I believe that everybody is a good employee until they prove differently to *me*—not to some other person. If I make the assumption that they're top-notch, I'll transmit that confidence to them and they'll live up to my expectations. But if I'm warned about them beforehand, I can't approach them completely without prejudice."

"I see," remarked the director thoughtfully. "Is there any evidence to support your claim?"

"I think this is what Douglas McGregor is saying in his book *The Human Side of Enterprise.* You see, it can work the other way, too. The predecessor can have his or her favorites, and I can be pre-conditioned to expect more from them—the so-called "halo" effect. People react differently with different people. There's no reason to suppose that if *I* have a bad relationship with someone, another person will, too."

"Yes, but don't you think that a new person should be warned about a potential problem? If they're forewarned they might take special pains to try to ensure that a relationship works. They might give extra attention to the person and his or her special needs."

"Maybe," Noel-Pardon agreed, but without conviction.

"I think a person would be derelict in his or her duty not to forewarn someone about a problem," the director suggested tactfully. Then: "For instance,

I'd feel negligent if I didn't tell you that you might have trouble with Craig Duff (the assistant director at the Medical Center library). Now if you'd prefer me not to, I won't," she added, after a calm inspection of her new assistant.

Noel-Pardon looked her fairly in the face and smiled guardedly. "You'll have to tell me now! Remember, what I said is just a theory!"

Craig T. Duff, aged 57 and a tenured professional librarian at the associate professor rank, had worked at the Medical Center library for 29 years, of which 16 were as assistant director. He did not expect or want promotion, and in all probability would not leave his present job until retirement. He was said to be "100% loyal" to the library and perfectly satisfied with his position. He has good relations with the faculty and students, but not the staff (none of whom were interested in taking over from Faye Weir).

There were two main problems with Duff. First, he is dogmatic and autocratic, given to intimidating staff members and involving himself in the pettiest of details. His subordinates — everyone reports through him to the director of the Medical Center library — suffer from the quickness and depth of his fury when he disapproves of something. He's frequently abusive of them, doling out severe tongue-lashings for perceived shortcomings. Second, he has not been responsive to instructions from any director — especially a younger one, and *especially* a woman, whom he views with a mixture of sexist attitudes and resigned acceptance.

Noel-Pardon seemed puzzled, taken back. "How come he's been kept on? And how come the staff stays?"

"I thought you'd ask that!" Bajalović said with a responsive smile. "Well, he has tenure, of course." Her eyes had a 'far away' look, as she added, "He's a complex paradoxical man. He sets difficult goals for himself and his staff. He looks for perfection in everybody, and he gets upset when he doesn't see it."

The young librarian nodded comprehension. The elder woman proceeded: "As far as the staff is concerned, some people will tolerate a lot of abuse before they do anything. I rarely see them, and when I do they never discuss him. Frankly, I don't go looking for problems. What I know comes from his supervisors. But I have heard good comments — excellent comments — about him from the faculty of the Medical School. I don't know if he's been reported to the Staff Association, which as you know only organizes social activities anyway. From my standpoint, things are going along nicely at that library."

"It looks like I've got my work cut out for me!" Noel-Pardon exclaimed stoutly. She was cheerful, but it was the cheerfulness of determined effort.

Elsbeth Bajalović then explained why *she* had told Noel-Pardon about the job rather than the latter's immediate boss — the assistant director for public services. She said it was her practice to announce promotions, and since Noel-Pardon would be reporting to her ("unless the library becomes a separate entity, of course!") she wanted to have the opportunity to talk with her. They discussed a number of other matters, including salary, which was most satisfactory. Finally, they parted with Noel-Pardon saying that she would present her preliminary thoughts on decentralization at the earliest opportunity. She would also keep her informed on how things were going with Craig Duff, and would make a list of questions — many of which she would attempt to find answers to where possible.

During her first week on the new job, Mae Noel-Pardon met several faculty members and had a short chat with the dean of the medical school, who confirmed that he had nothing to do with the library other than to help establish the budget. As far as he was concerned, the Medical Center library director reported to the director of the university libraries — except when it came to fiscal matters. She also familiarized herself with the library, and had individual "get-acquainted" discussions with every member of the staff, none of whom she had met previously, although she had talked to a few, including Duff, by phone in the course of answering reference questions. No one complained about Duff to her, and she decided not to probe for discontents. She did observe, however, that his conduct was pretty well as it had been described: he was a hard-driving taskmaster and thoroughly autocratic. But he did not seem to resent her — at least that she could detect. Their contacts were cordial and business-like. Maybe the reports about him were greatly exaggerated, she began to suspect, or perhaps her philosophy of expecting the best from people was working.

Her feeling of well-being was soon rudely shattered. One day, during her second week, when she was talking with him about the upcoming conference of the Association of College and Research Libraries, being held in another state 300 miles away, she suggested with innocence that it might be a good idea to have the head of the cataloging department attend. A representative of the Library of Congress would be there to outline some new cataloging decisions.

Duff regarded her with astonishment. "I have always attended those conferences," he snorted. "If there's anything the staff should know, I tell them."

Noel-Pardon had been ready to smile. But the smile was put to sudden death. "I didn't know that you always went," she affirmed. "I thought it might be a good idea if the person who is directly involved — "

"I can't adjust my style to every new person who comes in here, you know," he blurted out, in a tone dictatorial and almost savage. "The dean only allocates enough money in the budget to send one person to that conference, and it's always been me. The director of this library has had his — I suppose I should say, or *her* — way paid to the ALA annual convention and I've had mine paid to this one. There isn't money to send anyone else to conferences. You'll find that out. And even if there was I don't think the staff should go."

As he was thus speaking, he had edged closer to the door.

"I'd like to talk to you more about this," pursued Noel-Pardon, with all the casualness that she could assume.

His reply was unconciliating. "I have work to do," he said. "I don't think there's anything more to say. I'm not going to change my mind." And, as if by way of indicating that he had thrown down the gauntlet, he added, "I can be unpleasant. I warn you."

With that, he turned on his heel and hastened away.

Mae Noel-Pardon got up and went over to the window. A custodian was hosing down the walkway. How she envied him his uncomplicated existence. She wondered what she should do right now — whether to chase after Duff and order him to come back or wait and see him later, after she had regained her composure. He's clearly a Theory X manager, she said to herself, thinking of McGregor. Then, her thoughts reverted to Elsbeth Bajalović. Would she support her if she took firm action with Duff? And what would that action be? How does one go about terminating a tenured member of the staff? If Duff, with his stern authoritarianism, is Theory X, is Bajalović, with her casual, laissez-faire approach, Theory Y? Her mind was an arena of perplexing questions. Why is he behaving so obnoxiously? Are women bosses having trouble with men subordinates? Has anyone investigated this and compiled a list of recommendations? Does Duff have psychological problems? How do you tell a subordinate he or she might need to see a psychiatrist? Maybe I could give him some books to read. Is there anything to bibliotherapy? How about a T-group or an encounter group? Would that do any good? Can I force him to attend? Where would the money come from to pay for it? How about taking an MBO approach? She stood meditative as the sun descended. She must act. "What should I do?"

APPENDIX I

VORIS UNIVERSITY ORGANIZATION CHART – TOP ECHELON

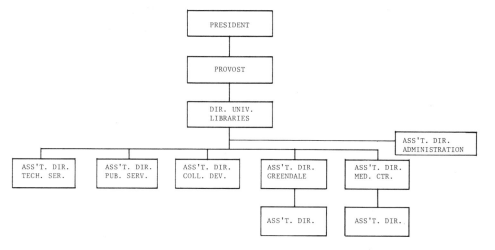

APPENDIX II

VORIS UNIVERSITY ORGANIZATION CHART – MEDICAL CENTER LIBRARY

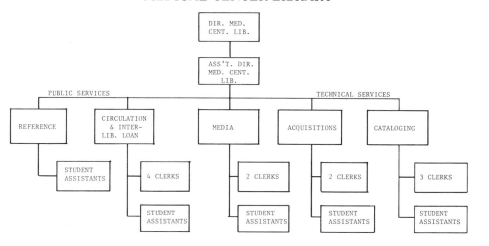

9

LECTURES ARE SO BROADENING

A glance at her watch told Layle Geddes, recently appointed Information Director of the Phyfe-Lilbourn Advertising Agency Library, that she had 10 minutes before her meeting with Una Feaver, the vice-president for Marketing Services to whom she reports. She picked up her list of activities for the previous day and gave them a quick scrutiny.

Time Log for Tuesday

8:30	Arrived at office
8:30-8:40	Spoke to copy editor about insurance campaign researched last week
8:40-8:50	Dictated replies to three letters
8:50-9:10	Discussed possible reallocation of work with assistants
9:10-9:30	Put finishing touches on report on optimal duration of cyclical "flights" of advertising
9:30-10:00	Attended meeting of product group to discuss copy for three low-calorie foods
10:00-10:20	Coffee in office—prepared daily clipsheet featuring important news items
10:20-10:30	Discussed outcome of product group meeting held earlier
10:30-10:45	Perused day's mail; signed letters dictated earlier
10:45-11:00	Discussed up-coming Special Library Association meeting with co-sponsor from hospital library
11:00-11:30	Studied market statistics
11:30-12:30	Clipped articles and competitive ads from periodicals and pamphlets
12:30-1:30	Lunch
1:30-1:40	Made travel arrangements for up-coming SLA meeting
1:40-2:50	Prepared visual examples of competitive low-calorie food advertisements
2:50-3:00	Monitored television commercial
3:00-3:05	Took telephone reference question from copy editor on best size for newspaper advertisement
3:05-3:30	Searched through material for material on the question
3:30-4:00	Consulted with staff on re-organization of picture and artist files
4:10-4:30	Reviewed suggested acquisitions by agency staff; read reviews
4:30-5:30	Examined new book acquisitions and identified sections of interest to various agency personnel
5:50-	Left for home
8:45-9:30	At home read current *Special Libraries*

As she finished her inspection, the information director of two months reflected that Feaver had asked her to keep this log as a prelude to a time management study she was to be involved in. This initial request was clear to her and Feaver had said she would explain more fully the nature of the assignment when they got together.

When she arrived at her boss's office at the appointed time, she learned why she had been asked for the breakdown of her day's activities. The president of the agency, Philip M. Claverhouse, had attended a two-day advanced management course Thursday and Friday of last week, and was most anxious to implement some of the ideas he had been exposed to. The course had concentrated on executive decision making, with a side excursion into the study and findings of Henry Mintzberg as reported in his book, *The Nature of Managerial Work.* One of the speakers during a presentation had touched on the subject of time management, pointing out that William James many years ago in his essay "The Energies of Man" had observed that "as a rule men habitually use only a small part of the powers which they actually possess and which they might use under appropriate conditions," and that "the human individual ... lives usually far within his limits; he possesses powers of various sorts which he habitually fails to use. He energizes below his *maximum*, and he behaves below his *optimum.*"

"Compared with what we ought to be," the speaker went on, quoting James, "we are only half awake.... We are making use of only a small part of our possible mental and physical resources." The speaker said that James estimated people function at only 20% of their capacity, and concluded that they could raise this percentage considerably if they knew how to manage their time more effectively. He also quoted from Peter Drucker's *The Effective Executive,* where Drucker says that "effective executives know where their time goes," and that they "work systematically at managing the little of their time that can be brought under their control." Drucker further says, he continued, "that effective executives ... start by finding out where their time actually goes" and that they "attempt to manage their time and to cut back unproductive demands on their time."

Not content merely to attend a lecture, applaud it at the end, and promptly forget what was said, the president is a pragmatist who believes that ideas should find expression in action—how else, he asks, could the agency be the success it is today? Hence, with the bloom of his enthusiasm for what he had learned still clinging to him, the first thing he did when he returned to the office Monday morning was assemble his vice-presidents and announce that he wanted the librarian (in the absence of a personnel director or department) to prepare a "package" on effective time management. This "package" was to consist of a list of fundamental principles of time management in the form of a presentation or a"talk" to the entire agency staff, and the design of "diary" or "time-log" forms that everyone could use. He would leave it up to the librarian to decide how best to present the material and to train the staff in the use of the forms—to work out all the details, in other words, including a rationale for the presentation. He would like to see what she came up with in writing, however, before anything was started, and have her give him her talk first.

Since, as the organization chart (Appendix I) shows, the company library falls under the jurisdiction of the vice-president for Marketing Services, it devolved upon Una Feaver to tell Layle Geddes about the president's request. In doing so, Feaver mentioned that she and Claverhouse frequently engage in some real "donnybrooks," as she put it, which invariably include a lot of amicable bantering, whenever they discuss anything. In this instance, she said she told him (staying after the meeting) that effective time management techniques seemed to her designed to harness people to treadmills, to make them slaves to their schedules, and to convert them into Type A's — crippled by anxiety, stretching themselves incessantly against unrealistic goals. The president countered with the view that most people fall somewhere between Type A and Type B anyway, and that effective time management and Type B behavior are not mutually exclusive. He suggested she reread *Type A Behavior and Your Heart* by Meyer Friedman and Ray H. Rosenman. Indeed, he pursued, stress is an inescapable fact of life and the reason one of every four persons suffers from chronic stress response is because people waste time. This makes them anxious, and anxious people can't do their best work.

Feaver was not about to be outfaced. She retaliated with the view that time management techniques run counter to the ideal 9.9 balance of concern for production coupled with concern for people that Blake and Mouton speak of in their book, *The Managerial Grid.* Such techniques, she opined, emphasize production over people and consequently turn managers into 9.1 types. The president disagreed. He observed that the practical wisdom and techniques of time management consultants — setting work goals; working toward these goals by establishing priorities; observing and analyzing time use; planning, organizing, and delegating; avoiding interruptions; and so on — interface with the theory, principles, and practice of behavioral scientists. Time management, he said, means self-management. He went on to explain his meaning:

Time is a constant in the management equation, and what managers must learn is not how to access more of a fully available resource but how to manage themselves *in* time, how to behave in the most effective manner in the time available. He produced some notes he had copied down from the speaker quoting R. Alec Mackenzie in his book, *The Time Trap*, to explain what he meant. He observed that he was paraphrasing: We all have all the time there is. There's a paradox to time. People don't have enough, and yet that's all there is. The problem is not time *per se.* The problem is ourselves — whatever we are: managers, salesmen, housewives, professionals, etc. The question is not how much time we have, but what we do with it and how we utilize it.

He continued: We must establish personal habits and self-managing practices that will control our environments and our behavior in the environment. The technique involves paying attention to ourselves in a very organized and systematic fashion. Research indicates that by recording data about desirable behavior we can increase this behavior. For example, he said, one study showed that when public school students were asked to keep precise track of the time they spent on studying, their study time increased considerably. When the recording procedures were removed study time fell off immediately. What is needed, then, is a methodology for designing logs and using time log information to help determine and analyze in a comprehensive fashion the locations, personal contacts, activity type, and work subjects involved in a manager's minute-by-minute life. An analysis of this data allows managers to profile their time use in a multitude of ways and determine any need for change in time management.

Still not to be outdone, Feaver complained that all this talk about measuring work, time-and-motion analysis, carefully planned activities, and such sounded like the "scientific management" or "dehumanizing" methods espoused by Frederick Winslow Taylor and Henry Gantt. She said she thought we had advanced beyond Taylorism and asked what had happened to the humanist approach to working.

Claverhouse retorted that he thought she was getting carried away, and suggested she study Taylor and Gantt more carefully. She would find, for instance, that such a recent innovation as PERT has its antecedents in Taylor's and Gantt's work. As far as he was concerned Taylor's methods comported well with the principles of humanism. He said that the debate between the humanist and the behaviorist is on the wane, and that contemporary behaviorism offers principles and procedures to help individuals increase their humanistic actions. By way of attempting to prove his point, he informed her that B. F. Skinner had received the Humanist of the Year Award at a meeting of the American Psychological Association.

Feaver remarked with the easy manner of familiars who are accustomed to sparring good-naturedly with each other that he certainly seemed to have picked up a great deal of miscellaneous information from that particular talk. Claverhouse chuckled a little, as if to acknowledge a hit, but added, unshaken in his opinions, that he had been motivated to spend Saturday morning browsing at his local public library among writings on behavioral humanism — nothing in particular, just a variety of sources. Yes, the talk had indeed kindled in him an interest in the subject! But he did concede that Feaver's demurrers were worth considering, and said he hoped she would pass them on to Geddes, who would in turn investigate them as well. Then, consulting his notes again, he said that the only other thing he had copied down was the name of Rosemary Stewart, "who has done some of the best work on the use of time logs and time management."

The Phyfe-Lilbourn Advertising Agency, located in one of the largest cities in the southeast, was founded 60 years ago by Bertram Emil Phyfe and Morton Lilbourn on the premise that an advertising agency should be a creative service organization rather than merely a broker for newspaper space. This concept of service (broadened to include radio and television) is still emphasized in the organization manual used by the agency's 68 men and women:

Goal No. 1 — To be the agency with the best record of service to its clients.
Goal No. 2 — To be the most efficiently organized agency.

Philip Claverhouse says of these aims: "We don't claim to have achieved them at all times, but we are forever moving forward and we are always alert to any methods that will help us achieve them." Claverhouse became president 10 years ago when Lilbourn retired, having worked his way up from copy editor, a position he took upon graduating from college. Under his direction, the agency has maintained excellent growth and has produced substantial loyalty on the part of both clients and employees. One of the reasons for the agency's continuing success is said to be the community of effort that goes into ad campaigns. Important decisions are made on an agency-wide basis. Claverhouse's experience has convinced him that advertising promotion and merchandising programs are most successful when prepared by the entire agency staff. Before any new campaign is launched, or any important change made in existing creative effort, it must win the approval of the "product group," which is made up of representatives of every department (including the library). These "shirt-sleeve conferences," as Claverhouse calls them, multiply the probability of more creative and successful campaigns by increasing the number of minds at work on an advertiser's products. His logic is simple: People need the help of others to be truly creative — thought breeds thought and ideas "piggy-back" on other ideas.

Phyfe-Lilbourn is primarily a consumer goods agency; its client list includes accounts in canned and frozen foods, fertilizers and other agricultural chemicals, paper and its products, costume jewelry, apparel and accessory stores, insurance, and plastic materials. The directors are elected each year by the stockholders, 93% of whom are agency employees. Because it is so largely a team operation—in ideas, in execution, in ownership—employees share a high degree of loyalty to the agency and turnover is low. An outside observer in discussing this aspect of P-L said that the agency's spirit "seems to be neither stimulated nor juvenile. The morale is high, and the feeling of being part of a team is widespread."

Much importance is placed by the agency upon the desirability of its personnel getting out into the markets. It is not unusual for account executives to spend as many hours in the field as they do at their desks, and to spend days taking the same sales-training courses that clients give their selling organizations. In this way the agency fuses itself with the client's business. It is not unusual also for the staff to take courses (at company expense and often on company time) that will keep them alert and mentally alive. This is in fulfillment of the Claverhouse dictum that unless staff members have the opportunity to develop as people their inspirational springs will become mere trickles. To this end employees are encouraged to accept and to seek out challenges, to expose themselves to new learning experiences. Not infrequently, individual staff members will put together presentations in the form of mini-courses for agency personnel.

The Agency Library was established when it was realized that a repository was needed to assemble, organize, and take care of the books and reference materials that were scattered about the agency. Over the years, people had been making their own little collections of books, pamphlets, and clippings. One person had an almanac; another had a folder of competitive ads; someone else had a directory; someone else a set of pamphlets and a thesaurus; and so on. But no one knew who had what or where things were, so a small 8x8-foot area was set aside to house this assortment of material. Soon, however, the collection outgrew its meagre quarters and a full-fledged library occupying a 40x60-foot area came into being. A librarian was hired to give it order. This occurred 36 years ago.

Now the P-L library is an indispensable part of the agency's operations. Philip Claverhouse believes that creative people depend on *information* as much as *inspiration*, and that a good agency library is one of the most important tools an agency can give its creative people. Layle Geddes and her staff of two professional librarians and two secretaries (all of whom report to her) provide a variety of essential services and functions. Their primary one is to answer questions, to supply information. She and her assistants must know what is to be found in their books and files, must be able to evaluate it, must produce it quickly, and must present it in an acceptable form. They must also be thoroughly familiar with the best sources of information in a large number of areas, and must be acquainted with sources outside the agency which can be used to supplement those within their own walls—government departments, public and academic libraries, institutes and foundations, research organizations, and the like. A sound knowledge of research sources is one of the chief requisites of the staff. A question may be answered in half a minute, a collection of clippings or of "scrap" may be selected in an hour or so, or a written report based on a thorough piece of research (conducted inside or outside the agency library) may take several days, or even weeks. Whatever the question or request, the work done in answering it must be thorough and accurate, and, usually, as quickly as possible.

The librarian and her staff try to keep in mind the special interests of their users by following up requests for information with later material on the subject, by sending them clippings of important articles, and by letting them know about new books and services they might like to see.

In addition to a relatively small collection of books, mostly reference, the library has general information or data files, made up of magazine, trade paper and newspaper clippings, pamphlets, and booklets. Advertisements or "competitive ad" files, brand preference studies, census releases, picture or "scrap," geographical and biographical files, market analysis studies, store audits, house organs, annual reports, and market letters are maintained. The library has also been given the duty of copyrighting advertisements, editing the agency's news bulletin, revising the employee handbook, and operating a suggestion box. All this is done while performing other routine library functions: assigning subject headings to file material and making new ones when needed; checking in, routing, and filing magazines; charging and discharging material that is borrowed; cataloging material—the 101 day-to-day jobs that have to be done if a library is to operate smoothly.

Every department turns to the library for help with its projects. For instance, a copy writer on an account picks a subject for an ad. He describes it to the librarian, together with any special angles he may want to develop. Within a day or two, all the necessary books, articles, and data are on his desk. Or a person in the Radio-Television department is working on building a program. The library staff provides her with the economic, educational, age make-up of the audience, with information and ideas on program appeals, with background information that helps to set the tone of the commercial, with facts and foibles of celebrities, with case histories of successful campaigns, with analogies, quotations, and anecdotes, and so on. It is thus that the library makes itself almost impossible to get along without.

As the organization chart demonstrates, under the P-L plan of operation there are three vice-presidents to whom the staff reports, through department supervisors. Each department is described below, along with its number of employees.

CREATIVE SERVICES

The vice-president in charge of creative services is responsible for the overall effectiveness of the advertising produced by the agency. She sets the philosophy, establishes standards of craftsmanship, and creates the environment the writers and artists work in.

Copy. The copy department is headed by a copy editor who has a staff of copy chiefs and copy writers. They prepare copy for all publication and direct advertising, working closely with the art department. Number of employees in the department: 6

Art. The art department is headed by an art director who has a staff of art buyers, studio managers, visualizers, letterers, artists, and layout people. They are responsible for the physical appearance of advertisements, preparing layouts, ordering and creating illustrations, lettering, and specifying type. Number of employees in the department: 7

Radio and Television. The radio and television department is headed by a media specialist who has a staff of program directors and assistants, musical consultants, talent people, and script writers. They write scripts, select artists from outside talent, cast them in their parts, and direct, rehearse, and produce shows. Number of employees in the department: 7

Print. The print department is headed by a mechanical production supervisor who has a staff of buyers of typography, engravings, electrotypes, printing, and so on, and proofreaders, and shipping clerks. They maintain contact with printers, typographers, typesetters, photoengravers, and other suppliers, and are responsible for putting together advertisements, securing proofs, procuring the matrices, electrotypes, and other duplicate plates needed for insertion in publications. Number of employees in the department: 5

Traffic. The traffic department is headed by a traffic manager who has a staff of traffic people. They are responsible for the smooth flow of work through the agency from the inception of a job to its appearance in scheduled media. It is a function of both the print department and the radio and television department; it sets work schedules and sees that they are met, so that advertising appears on time. Number of employees in the department: 4

ACCOUNT SERVICES

The vice-president in charge of account services is responsible for translating the client's wishes and programs to the agency so that it can carry them out in the form of advertising and merchandising programs. The work involves getting particular advertising campaigns or advertisements approved by the client, as well as overseeing the management of the agency office and financial matters.

Account Supervision. The account supervision department is headed by a chief account executive who has a staff of account executives. They are the representatives in the agency of the accounts and the representatives of the agency to the accounts—liaison officers who service accounts. Their work involves getting particular campaigns or advertisements approved by clients. They must have extensive knowledge of the client's business, of agency operations, and of advertising principles. Number of employees in the department: 8

Finance, Acconting, and Office Management. This department is headed by a general office manager who has a staff of accountants, bookkeepers, checking and billing clerks, comptrollers, and secretaries. They are concerned with matters of the agency's own business rather than creating services for its clients; hence they look after hiring of employees, compensating them, and so on, as well as administering billing procedures. Number of employees in the department: 7

MARKETING SERVICES

The vice-president in charge of marketing services, Una Feaver, is responsible for media planning and buying, research, and sales promotion. The job entails a high degree of knowledge and skill in analysis, strategies, and tactics.

Media. The media department is headed by a media director who has a staff of space buyers, time buyers, media analysts, and estimators. They have considerable knowledge of individual media and the markets they represent, offering clients the selection of the media best calculated to carry their message. Number of employees in the department: 5

Library. The library, or information center, described above, is headed by an information director who has a staff of two professional librarians and two secretaries, for a total of five people.

Research. The research department is headed by a research director who has a staff of marketing assistants, analysts, field investigators, and statistical clerks. They work closely with the library staff and study markets, copy, media, products, industry, and other subjects of interest to the agency and client. They include as part of their facilities the study of a client's product in order to determine its strong or weak points and how it compares with competitive products. Number of employees in the department: 4

Sales Promotions. The sales promotion department is headed by a merchandising manager who has a staff of sales promotion people and specialists in display and exhibits. They help the sales departments of clients with various aids, such as booklets, presentations, and so on, and aid dealers and distributors in the use of the clients' advertising. They also study the clients' products and the way they are sold and make recommendations for improvement. Number of employees in the department: 6

In relating the substance of her conversation with the president to Geddes, Feaver said she hoped the details of what was wanted were not too sketchy. She reminded the information director that frequently in the past the library staff had had to proceed with far sketchier outlines and that they had always carried all before them. The librarian gave her assurances they would do likewise this time.

APPENDIX I

ORGANIZATION CHART FOR THE PHYFE-LILBOURN ADVERTISING AGENCY

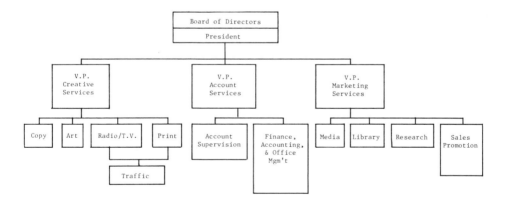

STAFFING

10

NOBODY EVER TELLS ME ANYTHING

Anthony Datto read the handwritten note he found in his mailbox from the principal of the high school at which he had been employed as head of the school media program for one month. He left the faculty mailboxes and walked down the hall to the office. His curiosity was piqued as he glanced at the words again—"Would you drop by my office at your earliest convenience? There is a matter I would like to discuss with you."

Since her secretary was not in the reception room, he marched directly to the doorway of the principal's office. Mathilda Panopoulos was wading through a batch of papers as he tapped gently on her half-opened door.

"You wanted to see me, Miss Panopoulos?" he said, his face cheerful.

She interrupted her scanning of the documents and waved him to take a chair.

"I understand that Dr. Dellaquila asked you to do some work for her," she began, right off, without a greeting.

Datto was startled to catch a note of annoyance in her voice. An inwardly feverish but outwardly calm desperation possessed him. He waited for her to speak again. "I wish she'd tell me when she asks one of my people to do something," she added in the same flinty tone. She put her pencil with a bang on the desk.

The young man raised his eyebrows with a gesture of deep concern. He could see that every muscle of her face was drawn tense. He offered no reply. "Didn't you learn anywhere along the line that a subordinate has an obligation to keep a supervisor informed about what's going on?" she flamed out indignantly. "You can imagine my consternation last night at the school committee meeting when the superintendent announced to everyone that you were looking into this question of merit increases, and I knew nothing about it. You were obligated to tell me."

There was a heavy and prolonged silence as Datto scrambled through his mind, trying to recollect the details of the event that had apparently triggered this violent reaction. Panopoulos put her arms on the desk, interlocked her fingers, and leaned forward, her eyes glinting with rage behind her thick spectacles. She was tapping with her foot on the carpet. He felt like a naughty school-boy. His first defensive impulse was boldly to deny any involvement. But instead he essayed to give an account of what had occurred, with an affectation of bewildered simplicity.

"The other day—Friday it was—when Dr. Dellaquila was in the building, she stopped by the media center. I hadn't seen her since you took me over to her office last spring, when you interviewed me for the position. She seemed interested to know how I was getting on. In the course of our discussion the topic

173

of merit increases and performance evaluation came up, and she told me about the teachers' reactions--"

"Can you speed this up?" Panopoulos cut his recital short. She had a habit of hurrying people when they were speaking.

Datto felt a wave of irritation engulf him, but he persevered, keeping his voice steady. "I offered to do some research on the topic for her." It was a lie; she had asked him to do it. And then he added, with a subdued laugh: "After all, we librarians are trained to do research for people!"

"Get on with this," the principal dictated, in a somewhat less severe tone. She sat back in her chair, crossed her legs, lighted a cigarette, and smoked herself into a cloud.

Hoping the gentler tone and the more relaxed manner meant that her anger was abating, the young man pressed on less apprehensively. "Well, it's just that," he said under a crawling canopy of smoke, trying to arrange himself easily on the hard chair. "I offered to give a report to Dr. Dellaquila on what I could find out about the pros and cons of merit rating plans and performance evaluations that could be used in a school setting—for teachers. I've heard about the controversy from some of the teachers. And Dr. Dellaquila confirmed it. She seemed most anxious for me to put something together for her. She said she thought a media specialist should undertake this sort of assignment. She really wants me to do this research for her." A special emphasis marked the last sentence: it was true; she had wanted him to do it, and *she* had initiated the request.

The principal sprang up from her chair and began to perambulate with swift, precise movements about her spacious office. But she did not speak. The walls of the room were hung with various pictures and sketches, chiefly unframed. She stopped and gazed absently as a Modigliani print. (Datto thought it odd that she would hang a Modigliani in her office—Modigliani with his struggle against bourgeois ideas. But he let that pass. He had not noticed the reproduction the two other times he had been in her office: once during his interview, and once two weeks ago when he had asked about the LMC budget. No problem those times, he recalled.) She let a long moment pass before speaking. "You had Friday afternoon and yesterday to tell me about this," she said to the painting.

The media specialist took thought. But before he could speak she turned toward him. "You are not to do it," she commanded, moving her head slowly from side to side in a firm negative. "You've got enough to do. You're new. You're feeling your way in your job."

This item of news penetrated his heart like a stab. "But I promised Dr. Dellaquila I'd do it." His eyes were full of appeal. "I told her I'd do it on my own time."

"What!" She fired the word at him like a bullet. "If you're going to spend your own time on school matters, you should spend it on matters pertaining to the library."

It was on the tip of his tongue to say: "Must you speak to me in this uncivilized fashion?" But he discreetly forbore. Consequences of challenging her at this time began to shape themselves vaguely in his mind. Clearly it was not the time. He could perceive that she was a person who was accustomed to having her own way.

A long silence followed. She was the first to break it.

"I tell you what, though," she announced, in a voice not quite so terrible. "I'd like you to come up with some way of evaluating *your* staff and assigning them merit increases. I think that would be a good thing for you to be doing. It'll keep you busy, and we need it. We don't have anything right now. Increases are automatic." She paused, and continued: "And I want to see forms and hear the advantages and disadvantages of different systems. I also want to know your thoughts on tying performance appraisals to merit increases. Somebody told me there was a problem there."

Datto felt the blood coloring his cheeks. He was extremely uncomfortable. He heard what she was saying, but his mind was occupied with thoughts of the superintendent. "What about Dr. Dellaquila?" he asked, dropping all his previous reserve like a garment. "Who will tell her?"

"I'll take care of that," responded the principal with acerbity, snubbing out her cigarette. She had moved back to her desk now, and was sitting on the corner, looking down upon him. "This isn't the first time she's pulled a stunt like this. I'll see her Thursday. I've been appointed to an ad hoc committee she's also on to look into the matter of merit increases and faculty evaluation."

She coughed discreetly. Then she said: "We also need a policy manual for the media center and job descriptions. I've been told that job descriptions start with job audits. I'd like you to find out about job audits and tell me what we'd have to do and what the final outcome would be. As far as a policy manual for the media center is concerned, I have no idea what they cover or consist of. Your job would be to tell me, and then to suggest how we might get one going. I have a feeling we'll be asked to do them." She laid a sneering emphasis on the last sentence.

The media specialist began to feel curiously self-possessed. He was determined that her arrogance was not going to paralyze his powers of speech or intimidate him any further. "I'd like to make sure I understand exactly what you'd like me to do," he began in a new brave tone. "You'd like me to—"

His sudden gust of audacity was quickly extinguished by her words and by her glance.

"Do I have to do it for you?" she snapped. "You had no trouble knowing what Dr. Dellaquila wanted." (Curious phrasing, he thought. Did she know that Dr. Dellaquila had requested him to do the work?) She returned to her chair and wheeled it close to her desk, twirling her wrist until she could see the face on her watch. "Look," she pronounced impatiently, "I have lots of work to do. Come up with the things I want and show them to me in a month." Then she bent her head down and confronted her papers.

Datto rose, bid her good-bye, and hurried away. Panopoulos grunted, without looking up.

As he traversed the length of the corridor to the media center, Anthony Datto reflected on the events that had brought him to this unhappy pass.

Pritchard, with a population of 50,000, is a community of strong social and economic contrasts. Until the mid-nineteen hundreds, it presented an almost feudal pattern of wealthy merchants and factory hands, with several gradations between these extremes. It occupies 15 square miles on the shore of Lake Tiemblo, and because of its location astride major rail and highway facilities is a center of industry and shopping. In "upper town" streets are broad, quiet, and tree-shaded; the homes are tall and heavy and look like battleships, each anchored in its private sea of grass. "Lower town," along the water's edge, is a district of crowded brick and frame structures of varied heights, an occasional old residence having had its ground floor pressed into commercial service. In the center of town are the usual cluster of banks, stores, and office buildings; shopping centers are sprinkled throughout the various neighborhoods. The city also boasts an excellent public library of 380,000 volumes, and a state-supported university with an enrollment of 14,000 students — which coincidentally is Anthony Datto's Alma Mater.

Mathilda Panopoulos, known as "Tilly" to her friends and colleagues but usually styled "Tilly the Hun" or just "the Hun" by her detractors, is a native of Pritchard. She was born in "lower town" 60 years ago of Greek immigrant parents, and holds a bachelor of arts degree in English, earned at night from a nearby state college. She has spent 35 years in public education in the town: 7 years as a junior high school English teacher; 4 years as an English teacher at the high school; 3 years as head of the high school English department; and 21 in her present position. She is a controversial figure, and has a reputation for being direct and gruff. Her knowledge of the technical aspects of her job is admitted by friend and foe alike; however, her strong-mindedness, dictatorial tactics, and attempts to dominate her teachers and staff have made her many enemies. She is a person of such strength of personality that few people have ever crossed her — including students, whom she controls with an iron hand. She is not a "progressive" educator in any sense of the word, and vehemently resists what she calls "undigested novelties" and "frills and fripperies" in teaching methodologies. Many parents appreciate her traditionalist approach, but others clamor for change. Two recently elected school board members have announced their intention of "ridding the high school of Tilly Panopoulos" — to which she replies, with a defiant shrug, "Let them try. They'll get the fight of their lives."

Few would deny that Amanda R. Dellaquila was the proper choice for the position of superintendent of schools when it opened a year ago. A woman of 38, who came to this part of the country from a school district 2,000 miles away, she possesses in addition to a doctorate in education two master's degrees: one in education and the other in English. Widely acknowledged to be an educator of the highest professional standing — as well as being in great demand as a speaker, she has published two books on education and numerous articles — she is a woman of unassailable integrity. Many times she has reminded her principals, department heads, and teachers to regard her as their "colleague with special responsibilities." Her office is always open to anyone who has a complaint, a suggestion, a grievance, or who "merely wants to chat." She enjoys talking informally with people — teachers, students, parents, and others — when she meets them in the hallways, or in the stores, or anywhere. She has made a habit of submitting proposed policies and rules to teacher organizations for study and suggestions before submitting them to the board for adoption. While teachers' recommendations are not always accepted, enough have been to assure them both individually and collectively that she is genuine when she says she wants a democratic school system. Rumor has it that she "tolerates" Mathilda Panopoulos, having tried many times to engage her in meaningful dialogue only to find her "hopelessly set in her opinions." As one wag quipped, "She came here saying, like Will Rogers, that she never met a person she didn't like — then she met Tilly the Hun!"

Anthony Datto was born 25 years ago in a village some 40 miles from Pritchard. He graduated from library school a year and a half ago, and served a one year stint as an assistant media specialist in a middle school media center prior to assuming the post at Pritchard High.

The Pritchard School District has under its jurisdiction approximately 4,000 young people from kindergarten through grade 12, and includes four elementary schools (K-6), two junior highs (7-9), and one high school (10-12). The board consists of seven members elected by popular ballot for three-year terms. Each school has a library or media center, which is headed by a professional librarian.

It was at the Monday night meeting a week ago – board meetings are held every Monday night and attendance by principals is mandatory – that the topic of merit increases and performance appraisal was introduced by one of the two new members who started their terms at the beginning of the school year. He inquired about the wage and salary policy, and how teachers are evaluated. The superintendent stated that this was an area she herself was anxious to investigate, because for all practical purposes salary increases were automatic and equal "across-the-board." The committeeman registered surprise. "You mean that good performance is not rewarded and poor performance not punished?" he said. "It is unthinkable to automatically give everyone the same percentage. Industry has developed ways of identifying good people. Surely some of these techniques will work for education."

In the ensuing discussion, the superintendent reminded the group that it is difficult to identify good and poor teachers, adding that she was always on the "lookout for effective ways."

"This seems hard to believe," was the committeeman's response. "Parents certainly know who the good teachers are, and so do the kids."

After an additional brief discussion, during which several questions and comments were aired, including a few by members of the professional association, who always attend the meetings, a motion was made that an ad hoc committee – to consist of one school committee member, one principal, one member of the professional association, and the superintendent – be appointed "to investigate the issue of merit rating plans and employee performance appraisal systems with a view to identifying and awarding larger increments to outstanding teachers." The motion passed unanimously among the voting members of the committee – the seven board members. Dellaquila's parting observation before they moved on to another item of business, which she announced with a faint air of mischievousness, was that Frederick Herzberg had found money not to be a motivator. Several people smiled – a few had no idea who or what she was talking about – but not one bothered to pursue the point.

At first blush, nothing seemed particularly ominous about the formation of the ad hoc committee. In its Wednesday edition, the Pritchard *Observer*, the bi-weekly newspaper which routinely covers board meetings, merely reported that the discussion had taken place. But later in the week, when teachers began to talk about the committee's purpose, apprehension began to mount among some of them. Battle lines were quickly drawn. There were those who favored the notion of rewarding the "best" teachers, but a larger number were opposed. The feelings of the opponents could be summarized by these typical statements: merit increases are unfair and destroy morale; there is no satisfactory way of measuring teacher effectiveness; and favoritism inevitably enters into evaluation. Before long the teachers were in a state of turmoil over the issue.

When he arrived back at the media center, Anthony Datto whisked straightway into his glass-enclosed office, to the right of the entrance. Instead of going to his desk, he proceeded to the window and lingered there idly watching the rain spatter on the pavement outside. The sky was completely overcast. He looked up and descried a gym glass, all wet and draggled, scurrying back across the sodden football field. But his mind, stimulated by the emotions of the encounter with the principal, ranged beyond his present world and sought satisfaction in the possibility of fleeing from her clutches. He perceived that his life threatened to be an interminable succession of these mortifying interviews unless he could discover a way or ways to deal with her surly and terrorizing ferocity. But how? He knew that he could not truckle to her forever. But what could he do? He did not want to leave. Quitting! The universal cure-all, employed by those who are not in the situation. He had signed a two-year lease on an apartment — unbreakable — and was making heavy monthly payments on a car. There were no jobs available at the public library or at the university. And anyway he wanted to be a media specialist in a high school. And he liked everything else about Pritchard High. It was out of the question. Think of what it would mean! No, he was not one to take off like a deer at the first warning of certain dangers. But why had he said he offered to do the work for the superintendent when in truth she had initiated the request? Why had he lied? The laconic question weighed upon him with a crushing weight. Why had he committed such an imprudence? Life is full of pitfalls, into which the innocent often tumble. Was it Mathilda Panopoulos' manner of making people feel like irrational children, guilty, apologetic, foolish, so that they bring disaster on themselves? Should he tell her the truth? But what difference did it make who the initiator was? Was the offense that monstrous? His thoughts covered again the round of questions, and again, and yet again.

A hesitant knock sounded at the door, bringing him with a shock to the level of earth. "Come in," he called out automatically, and looking around saw two of his three professional assistants, Madge Beck and Dorothy Lehmann, entering the office.

Madge Beck, a middle-aged woman with 18 years service, vaguely apprehending trouble, spoke first. "When you walked in here, Tony, you looked as if you had just seen a ghost. Anything wrong?"

"Oh, I'm okay, I guess," volunteered Datto cautiously. "I just had a royal dressing down by Tilly."

The assistants exchanged a quick glance.

"Need someone to talk to about it?" inquired Lehmann solicitously. She had been on the staff for a year, but had not applied for the head position because she felt unready for the challenge. The third assistant, Alfred MacIntosh, was recovering from a hernia operation and would not be back for two weeks; he has been on the staff for four years and, like Lehmann, did not aspire to the position. Lehmann and MacIntosh are in their late twenties.

"Yes ... thanks," replied Datto, as he removed an insecure pile of books from one of the two guest chairs. "Perhaps at the same time you could fill me in on some of our procedures."

The three sat down. Datto gave an account of both incidents — again omitting to mention that it was Dr. Dellaquila who had made the original suggestion. When she had finished Beck said reassuringly: "Don't let old Tilly bother you. She can be a rotter at times. She's a Jekyl and Hyde, if ever there was one. One minute she's fine; another, she's a monster. When you've been here a while, you'll see that it's hard to avoid run-ins with her."

Lehmann spoke up. "Alf is convinced that she chews broken bottles and wears barbed wire next to her skin." They chuckled. She continued: "You know, of course, that your predecessor left because she couldn't take her."

"No, I didn't know that," confessed Datto with surprise. "When Tilly interviewed me, she merely said that she had left to take a job in a college library."

"That's true," intervened Beck. "But the Hun drove her out of here. She stood it for two years. That was as long as she could take."

"And *you've* never wanted to be head," Lehmann reminded Beck, who nodded.

"I couldn't report directly to her," Beck grimaced. "I need a buffer between me and her."

"Funny," (he meant strange), "you didn't warn me about her when I spent some time with you during my interview. I've never encountered anyone like her in my life."

"We thought of it," the older assistant responded, "but we liked you and wanted you to take the job."

"Thanks a bunch!" he said, smiling self-consciously. "Actually, I'm flattered and pleased to hear that."

"And we certainly hope you won't consider leaving," interjected Lehmann, with an appealing, serious smile.

Beck concurred with an assenting nod. She continued: "We decided it wouldn't be professional to speak disparagingly to a stranger — which you were at the time — about a colleague, which after all she is." She smiled archly at her phrasing.

Lehmann's voice came in: "You remember we fudged when you asked about her. If I remember Alf did say something about her being a stern taskmaster, but that was all we indicated."

Anthony Datto signified that that was so.

"Alf thought we should have warned you, but telling you she was a taskmaster was as far as we agreed we should go," Lehmann explained.

"You know, Tilly wasn't bad during my interview with her," Datto said pensively. "A bit gruff, perhaps, but not bad. Inconsistent, I'd say. One moment she was fine, and the next ... well ... crotchety. And he added hurriedly: "I felt I could work with her though."

"If Alf had had his way," Beck supplied, "we would have given you the lowdown on Tilly the Hun."

"Well, you're certainly to be applauded for your loyalty," sighed Datto.

"I know that loyalty question is one that bothers Alf," Lehmann said. "We talked about it quite a bit."

Beck said, "I've always felt that professionals should stick together and not wash their dirty linen in front of others — particularly strangers."

"Even friends and relatives!" Lehmann chirped in.

Beck acknowledged the other's contribution, and went on: "I'd be disappointed to learn that my boss or subordinates — or peers for that matter — told tales out of school about me to others. I'd hate to have what they think are my faults broadcast around."

"I feel, too," Lehmann inserted, picking up on the sentiment, "that if we have a problem at work we should discuss it among ourselves and not go spreading it all over the neighborhood."

"Just one further point on this topic if I may," Madge Beck said, sensing that it was time to draw the discussion to a close. "I feel that librarians tend to be terribly critical and unsupportive of each other. Much as I hate to admit it," she added, her face creasing in a knowing smile, "some of my best friends are librarians, and I can't get over how they tear their colleagues to shreds when they're together. It makes one flinch sometimes."

"I know what you mean," Anthony Datto acknowledged. "It bothers me, too. I suppose it happens in every profession." Then, changing the subject, he wondered aloud whether he would be better off reporting to the assistant principal. Madge Beck said that the assistant had only as much authority as the principal gave him, and that was not much. "Besides," she appended, "his is a staff position, and he'd only have to clear everything with Tilly the Hun anyway." She added that she felt sorry for the assistant because he had so little power. Datto then said that if the system had a coordinator of media centers, he, too, would have a "buffer of sorts" between him and the principal. But this was just idle chatter he concluded; he would have to find a way to work with Mathilda Panopoulos. That said, he turned to a different topic.

"While I have you here," he said, "I wonder if you'd fill me in on how you've been evaluated and assigned increases in the past."　　　.

The assistant media specialists explained that no formalized appraisal procedures existed, and that previous LMC heads had merely engaged in informal (and infrequent) chats with them about their performance, individual strengths and weaknesses rarely being identified or discussed. They admitted that they did not evaluate their technicians and aides, and confirmed that increases were automatic and the same "across-the-board"; superior performance was not rewarded, nor inferior performance punished.

Anthony Datto thanked them for having permitted him to unburden himself; after a few desultory remarks about the nasty weather and nothing in particular, they parted. Thereupon, he reached for a pen and a foolscap pad and began to make some notes about the Pritchard High School Media Center and to draw a rough sketch of the organization chart (Appendix I).

When he had finished he looked down fixedly at his markings, but he did not see them. He fell again into a puzzled wonder as to how he should proceed with the principal's requests, and what he should do about the promise he made to Dr. Dellaquila. His mind flew back to the humiliating episode with Mathilda Panopoulos. It gave him to think most unpleasantly. How was he to explain her behavior? Would kinesics help? He had always viewed with suspicion the claims of nonlinguistic sign readers. As far as he was concerned the study of nonverbal communication, like the talk of "life positions" employed by the adherents of transactional analysis, was a pseudo-science, the work of dilettantes and other futile souls. And yet, had not the great Charles Darwin himself explored the meaning of facial expressions among humans and animals. And had not other serious investigators — eminent anthropologists, psychologists, sociologists, ethnologists — followed the Master's lead and delved into the syntactic language of gesture and movement. And are not the concepts of Eric Berne and Thomas Harris, the "I'm OK — You're OK" people, coming into their own as themes worthy of investigation? The thought of the "games people play" which Berne and Harris speak of brought a smile to his face. It occurred to him that both fields of endeavor might have something to teach him on how to understand and communicate with Mathilda Panopoulos, and he resolved to pursue them both thoughtfully posthaste. He would also complete the principal's desiderata. After all, it was his job to do so, regardless of his personal feelings toward her. There was also something not quite right about his discussion with his assistants. It seemed to him that they had violated some of their rules. But like Scarlett O'Hara, he would think of that tomorrow. He began to probe himself again for answers to the Amanda Dellaquila matter.

The bell rang. A new class would be arriving. He got to his feet and walked out into the media center, the Dellaquila matter unresolved.

APPENDIX I

PRITCHARD HIGH LMC

Students: 1,100

Professional staff: all library school graduates
all properly certified
tenured: Beck & MacIntosh

Head of the LMC: Datto (equivalent to department head)

Media Professionals: Beck, MacIntosh, Lehmann (equivalent to teachers)

Media Technicians: Gottstein; Nesbitt; Wright, J.; Sharp (equivalent to skilled maintenance personnel)

Media Aides: Wright, P.; Welch; Foley (equivalent to clerks, office staff)

Student Assistants: 4

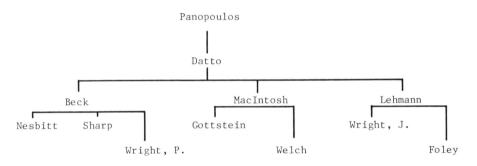

Responsibilities:

Datto: Overall administration

Beck: Technical services, circulation

MacIntosh: Planning and implementing curriculum, instruction (for students) and in-service (for teachers), reference and reading services

Lehmann: Production and design

11

HELP WANTED

"Just one letter today!" the mail clerk announced as she handed an envelope to Assistant Professor of Library Science Leslie Remington. The young professor said thanks with a smile and glanced at the name and address at the top left-hand corner: Sara H. Braver. In Hamilton's Harbor—all the way across the country! Wasn't she a former student and recent graduate? Yes, about a year ago. She must want a letter of reference! Extracting the contents, Leslie Remington began to read.

This is what Sara Braver wrote in her sprawling hand:

March 17

Dear Professor Remington:

I am writing to inform you about a couple of problems I think could be classified as sexual harassment and to seek your advice and counsel. A year ago, I was a student of yours, and as I recollect we discussed the subject briefly in class. The discussion didn't make that great an impression on me at the time, because I had never to my knowledge experienced any form of sexual harassment. But now that I have, I wish I could be there to share my experience with you and a class of students. I would love to know what you and they would advise me to do. Since I can't do that perhaps the next best thing would be if you could share my letter with them and get their suggestions. I'd really appreciate it!

After working at Royalty College for six months as a reference librarian, I have reason to believe that my boss, the head of reference, has been sexually harassing me. He repeatedly comments on my appearance, makes sexual innuendoes, and touches me. His actions have bothered me to the extent that I have difficulty working with him without always being apprehensive. I'm afraid my work will suffer if something isn't done. (By the way, in case you haven't heard of it, Royalty is a small coeducational private college with a student enrollment of 2,400!)

First, I should make it clear that I have not provoked him in any way. My skirts are always far below my knees and I usually wear a jacket. But when he speaks to me he always scans my body and stares at my breasts. I avoid being alone with him, because another reference librarian told me he recently tried to kiss her. Apparently they were alone in his office and he had told her he had "needs," and that her performance evaluation would be affected if she didn't comply with them. From what I can gather—she's *very* reluctant to talk about it—she was able to wriggle away, but now she won't go into his office unless someone else is there with them. She admitted he's asked her outright to have sex with him. But she's a shy person and she really won't discuss the episodes. At any rate, she's *definitely* not prepared to do anything—whatever that anything might be. She says she needs the job and she couldn't stand up to a public confrontation. I even think she regrets having told *me*, because now she won't even discuss the matter with me. She's sure she's going to suffer though when appraisal time rolls around.

Now he hasn't tried to kiss me, but he's always putting his hand on my shoulder or my arm or my back. I did tell him once that I didn't appreciate being touched in this way, but he merely smirked and said that was my problem. He still does it. (While I think of it, he also has one of those posters of a semi-nude Bo Derek up on his closet door.)

The problem is compounded by the fact that his boss, my second-removed boss, the director of the library, has asked me out! He gives me that old line about his wife not understanding him! He says he needs someone to talk to, and since his wife won't listen and he likes me as a person so much would I go out with him after work? How does one handle situations like these? I get the feeling from both of them that my job may be in jeopardy if I'm not a better sport.

I don't know where to turn. I suppose I could go to the president of the college—also a man—who is the director's boss. But is that advisable? Don't I need some sort of proof? Should I threaten them with going to the president? How does one get started? How does one bring a harassment suit against one's employer? Are there laws protecting women in these circumstances? I wish I had paid more attention in class that day!

I have discussed this situation with five confidants, both male and female, on the staff. Most of them—there are 24 people on the library staff; 6 in reference (3 males and 3 females)—have not personally experienced sexual harassment and haven't been aware that it exists. A couple of them have reacted as if it was my fault, as if I bring it on. I don't consider myself sexy. I have always maintained a business-like approach and attitude, so it can't be my actions or my physical appearance. From what I can gather that other librarian and I are the only two people the head of reference has bothered.

I should mention too that he seems to treat the women work-study students unfairly. (By the way, he always refers to women as "girls," and he won't stop. He's amused that it bothers us.) He frequently asks them to shelve books upstairs on the balcony and then stands there looking up their dresses. They complained to me, so I told them to wear slacks or jeans. Isn't it ridiculous that they have to think about what they wear? The head of reference told me that he's going to see about a dress code for the staff, prohibiting slacks for women. Can you believe it? Are dress codes legal?

To return to my own experiences with him. As I indicated he makes lewd comments in front of me. One time he showed me a photograph in an art book of a woman's bare breasts and said "Nice tits, uh?" I gave him a look of scorn and disgust, but he merely laughed at me. I've tolerated his remarks and his wandering hands because, frankly, I need the job. I'm in a bind financially. I'm also trying to establish myself in the profession. For instance, I'm running for president of our regional library association. I can't quit and I don't want to quit; my future is important to me. I like the job. It took me almost a year to get it. I couldn't tell you how much it cost me in postage, resumes, airfare for interviews, etc. But it was a bundle. I'm worried about the publicity I'd get if I brought some sort of suit against both of them. What makes the situation particularly sensitive is that the head of reference is established in the field. (He's a bachelor, by the way!) He has been at Royalty for five years and is well-known and respected. Everyone thinks he's great! Also, there are no unions at all at Royalty, nor do librarians have faculty rank and status; there are also no grievance committees, women's groups, or a Civil Rights Office. I did visit the woman who heads up the Personnel Office, she told me I'd have to inform the head of reference that I'd like to bring it up at a Trustees' meeting. What kind of suggestion is that?

This letter is getting very long, and I apologize for it. But I must ask you about one other thing, and what I might do about it. There is a male reference librarian who started the same day I did in exactly the same position. He graduated from another library school about the same time I did. He, too, has no previous experience. But in talking one day over coffee, I learned to my horror that he is being paid $1,000 more a year than me. Is there anything you or your students would advise me to do about that? What makes this one difficult is that when I registered my horror, the fellow told me he didn't want me to tell anybody that he had told me his salary. Being a private institution, salaries are treated as confidential. He told me that if I mentioned this to anyone, he'd deny he ever told me and that I was making it up. He gets along famously with the head of reference, by the way.

Professor Remington, I'm sure you can see I'm desperate. I haven't made any friends yet; most of the people I socialize with are co-workers, and I've told you their reactions. My family is 1,500 miles away, and I'm not sure they'd know what to do anyway. That's why I'm turning to you. If you want to read this letter to one of your classes please do so. I very much look forward to hearing from you.

Yours most sincerely,

SARA BRAVER

12

CONVERSATION AT LUNCH

Vere County, in the heart of the hard wheat country, is a fairly large county in both area and population, with the focal point being a major city—Constantia—which has a population of 75,000. The population of the county approaches a quarter of a million. The Vere County Department of Public Libraries is a joint city-county system which serves both Constantia and Vere County under the county government—specifically a five-member board of commissioners. There are no library trustees. Financed with taxes voted by the county and with state and federal aid, the library department maintains a central collection in Constantia and extends services through 8 branch collections, 4 deposit stations, and 3 bookmobiles. Service is further supplemented by materials provided by the state library extension agency.

The system is headed by a director, 42-year-old Beatrice R. Coy, who has been in the position 12 years. Responsible to her are three divisions—public services, technical services, and extension services—each headed by a chief. The normal chain of command has department heads reporting to division chiefs, Librarians II to department heads, Librarians I to Librarians II, and Library Technicians and Clerks to Librarians I. All positions from Librarian I above are classified as professional, and all professional librarians hold master's degrees in library science. The total staff numbers 201, of which 78 are professional.

Civil service was instituted in the county 45 years ago. At its inception it was applied only to clerical and mechanical jobs; but as time passed it was extended to include positions at all levels, except directors of departments. (In the library department, only Coy is not a civil servant.) Promotions are arrived at by seniority, written examinations, and oral interviews before the County Civil Service Commission, which is composed of five members.

Florence Meek joined the staff of the Vere County Library Department a week ago as a reference librarian (Librarian I), working under the supervision of senior reference librarian (Librarian II), Simone Jergens, who has been there a year and a half.

The two women were having lunch together when a turn in the conversation made Meek's statement "Tell me about Vijay Sethi and Rowena Kobitsky" seem entirely appropriate. Jergens waited until a piece of apple pie was chewed down. After the wait, her first words emerged with an amused laugh. "You've noticed something is amiss!" she grinned, tapping her forehead. "Very shrewd!" Then, consulting her watch, "We have time. Let's get another cup of coffee."

Their cups refilled, Simone Jergens said she would tell her assistant all she knew.

Vijay Sethi, head of the public services division, is 34 years of age and has six years of service with the library department. He had left the system five years ago when he was a reference librarian to work in a nearby academic library, but after two years he returned. He rose quickly to the position of chief of the public services division, which he has held for two months. During his ascendancy he was accused of sycophancy by other staff members, partly because of the many hours he spends with the director in her office and partly because they and their families socialize outside work.

Rowena Kobitsky, chief of the technical services division, has been in the system for 20 years, is 43 years of age, and has served in the department under two previous directors. She is married and has a family, but does not spend much time in the director's office or socialize with her. Prior to her present assignment, she was the chief in charge of public services. Sethi and Kobitsky have the same date of rank, although Kobitsky scored the highest on the oral and written civil service examination of all persons competing, while Sethi scored next to lowest.

Florence Meek looked puzzled and asked how that could be. Her companion responded that she was only reporting what she herself had been told. Meek made a mute signal of assent and the other went on.

The director has recently instituted the practice of transferring division and department heads periodically so that, as she puts it, "each person will know the functions of several or all divisions or departments." She feels that this will help to alleviate misunderstandings and tensions between division and department heads as well as provide a better balanced staff. However, when Sethi was moved two months ago from chief of technical services (a position he held for one year) to public services, the grapevine carried the story that "Sethi got his way again." The chief of public services is the unofficial "prestige" position among the three divisions.

Here Meek interrupted to ask whether Jergens thought job rotation of this sort was desirable. Jergens made a delicate shrugging gesture for answer. She resumed.

When Kobitsky was in charge of public services, morale was high and the division operated smoothly. She was always available to her subordinates and tended to back them in the majority of situations. Discipline was good, and she was well liked and respected by the staff. The remark was frequently made that "If Rowena leaves public services, she will be a hard person to replace."

"How does Ms. Coy treat her?" Meek asked suddenly with real curiosity.

Jergens considered for a while. "It's interesting you should ask. Let me tell you something our department head told me about."

Meek took her glasses off and twiddled them as her supervisor related the following incident. As head of public services, Kobitsky had six months ago prepared a detailed report showing that the department was short of staff; the most pressing needs were for two additional reference librarians. When the request was submitted to the director at a regular staff meeting of all division and department heads, Coy rejected it saying, "When are you going to learn to administer your department properly?" Kobitsky was disappointed by not getting the additional staff, but was even more hurt by the director's attitude. The director had on several occasions praised the public services department for its outstanding performance in her talks to various groups around the county; however, Kobitsky had only learned of this from other people. Coy has never praised her directly or at staff meetings.

The new reference librarians' eyes widened. "Why would she behave like that?" she asked, assuming her glasses.

"Beats me!" responded her listener with a shrug. "There's more!" She went on.

When Rowena Kobitsky and Vijay Sethi changed jobs, morale in public services fell immediately. There was open criticism of the move by the staff, but Coy either did not hear it or chose not to hear it. Sethi is never available for consultation. He spends more of his time with the director than in managing the division. Efficiency has deteriorated. "We're all very unhappy," Jergens frowned perplexedly. "And we don't know what to do about it."

"I find this all baffling," Meek commented, arching her eyebrows.

"There's more still," continued her companion. She picked up her story.

When Sethi requested more staff, including two reference librarians, the request was granted and he was praised for his progressiveness in reorganizing the division. "You're one of the two reference librarians to be hired because Vijay got his way!" Jergens told Meek, letting a significant smile wander over her lips.

The new reference librarian swallowed hard. "I can't believe all this," said she, scarcely knowing what else to say.

Simone Jergens took a sip of coffee and began afresh. When Rowena Kobitsky took over as chief of technical services, the division was in a state of extremely low morale. She met with the members of the entire division and explained several changes she was about to implement to increase effectiveness. She encouraged suggestions from the staff; those she felt were worthwhile were implemented. At the end of her first month, the division was operating at a much higher level than before and morale had become considerably higher. Since the division was short of staff, Kobitsky spent many extra hours doing some of the jobs that needed doing. Soon others began working overtime without compensation, due to the example of their chief. Each time Kobitsky put in requests for additional people, however, she was turned down.

Marilyn Tribble, head of the cataloging department, in discussing the rejected requests for more staff with Kobitsky, asked that she be allowed to represent the requests to the director. Her thought was that perhaps another person might find the director responsive to the requests, and she had always gotten along satisfactorily with her. Kobitsky reluctantly agreed because of her sincere feeling that more staff was an absolute necessity.

When Tribble met with Coy, she presented data supporting the requests and, at the same time, asked the director for a transfer because of the immense work load she was carrying. The department head had hoped the latter request would lend credence to the seriousness of the situation.

Both requests were turned down, and the director was most angry about the incident. At the next division and department head meeting, Kobitsky was reprimanded and told that she should learn to be an administrator and conduct herself accordingly. She was further instructed to correct the "morale" problem in the division — the director's interpretation of the department head's request for a transfer. "That's all I know," Jergens finished.

A bewildered look crept into Meek's face. "I — I can't — " she faltered, "I can't understand why Ms. Coy would treat Rowena like this."

Jergens said: "There are many things I don't understand, either. For instance, I always thought the civil service system was created to eliminate any possibility of favoritism."

"Me, too."

"As I see it — and remember I'm only reporting to you what I've heard second-hand — Coy has made a lot of mistakes. I'm not sure, for example, that it's a good idea to rehire a former employee."

"I suppose it depends on who it is. If it were you or me — fine! But Vijay!"

Jergens smiled. "And how about the way Coy handled Rowena in front of the department heads?"

"Unforgivable. But what can anybody do about it?"

"Our department head asked me the other day if I had any thoughts on what we could do. She and Rowena are friends, and Rowena asked her. It's common knowledge there's a problem. But what to do?"

"Is Rowena doing anything?"

"Apparently not. As I understand it, she doesn't know what to do. She's been beaten down so many times, she doesn't know how to approach Coy. Anyway, she's not a 'street fighter.' She seems to believe that if you treat people decently, they'll treat you decently. Her approach seems to work with her subordinates, but not with Coy. Do you have any thoughts about what she — or we — could do? I'll pass them on."

Florence Meek fell silent. "I suppose we could go to the board of county commissions," she hazarded, after a longish pause.

"Who's 'we'?" asked Jergens in the tone of one seeking an answer of utmost importance.

Meek looked at her dumbly. "Good point. I don't know." Then, changing abruptly, "What about the chief of extension services? What's his relationship with Ms. Coy like?"

"I don't know him too well, but I'm told he gets along all right with her. He seems to be staying out of it, from what I can gather."

Again there was silence. Simone Jergens was the first to speak:

"Something has to be done, because this is affecting us all. I suppose if we had a union we could do something, but we don't."

"Well, what if we start by finding out whether there's any sort of grievance procedure under civil service. I'd be glad to investigate this."

"I think it wouldn't do any harm. I don't think it's important to see *our* specific civil service agreement. You could find out about civil service generally."

"That's what I was thinking. I don't know, for instance, whether civil service regulations differ from place to place."

"Now, there's another consideration here. Supposing Rowena won't pursue any suggestions we come up with because she won't fight. It's likely, you know. Can we — should we — do anything on our own? And what? We can't live under Vijay. We've got to do something. But he's Coy's pet. What *do* you do when you can't even discuss the 'pet' with a boss. The sun seems to rise and set on Vijay as far as Coy is concerned. People who have been around for a while say that morale in our department has never been lower. No one really wants to leave — including apparently Rowena. Anyway, quitting is the very last resort. It does get *you* out of the situation, but it doesn't solve the problem."

"And I don't like the option of just 'knuckling under,' and walking around smiling as if everything was just hunky-dory," Meek put in. "That's the solution most people take most of the time."

Simone Jergens dropped back in her chair and covered her assistant with a sombre stare. "No question," she said meditatively, "we have to do something."

"Like more coffee?" proffered the waitress, the coffee pot hovered above Jergens' cup.

"Good grief! What time is it?" Jergens brisked up.

"Ten to two," said Meek.

"No, thanks," Jergens said to the waitress. "We have to go." And picking up the check, "Lunch is on me today, Florence—no arguments!"

"Thanks," smiled Meek.

As they debouched into the street and hurried back to the library, Jergens thanked Meek for being someone she could share her concerns with. "Let's see if we can find an acceptable way to resolve this dilemma," she added as they tripped up the stairs to the entrance.

13

HOW AN EMPLOYEE GOT SELECTED

When she became head of reference and adult services at the Dorado Public Library five months ago, Melanie B. Stanton thought her dream of a more peaceful life filled with absorbing work had been realized. Compared to the turbulent and impatient manner of Willington (pop. 300,000), the state capital where she worked as a reference librarian in the State House Library, Dorado, itself a busy city of 25,000 some 80 miles to the south, has an almost rural serenity about it. Indeed, she was delighted to forsake the urban reality of steel and glass, traffic and crime, aspirin and litter, for the sort of over-the-fence friendliness of the smaller city. It was a just reward, she felt, for the two hectic years she had spent since graduation from library school under the capital dome, answering telephones that never stopped ringing and bustling from one reference source to another.

Standing in the early morning on the balcony of her apartment, she was smote as she always was by the grandeur of the sky turning to scarlet as the rim of darkness in the east released the sun for its sluggish trek through the heavens. How she ached to be a poet and by some wizardry of pen capture the mysteries going on out there. But lines were not hers; she was inarticulate in the face of overwhelming beauty.

No, she must think of other things, of the day ahead. Reluctantly she gave herself over to the more mundane concerns of the moment. Today, for the first time in her career, she would be the interviewer rather than the one being interviewed. She returned to the breakfast table, filled her coffee cup again, and abandoned herself to her thoughts. She reflected on many things. On her new assignment at the library. On her departing assistant, Samuel Warren. On the professional staff association and its procedures.

It had all started when the Dorado Public Library was selected to become a new regional center for interlibrary cooperation, and when Warren announced he was leaving to take a job as a special librarian in a distant city.

Spurred by the need many years ago for the public libraries in the state to provide a wider range of services and materials to their communities, and with a mix of federal and state funds available for its use, the State Library Commission divided the state into three regions for purposes of developing a cooperative library system. At the hub of each region is a single public library charged with the responsibility of satisfying requests from its member public libraries for materials and reference information. The member libraries have complete autonomy and their boards function as usual.

Under the plan, Dorado was one of 28 libraries assigned to the Aukurville public library as the regional center for that part of the state. Then—as now—regional centers were asked to provide only the following services: interlibrary loan of books, films, recordings, and tapes; photocopying of periodical articles; and assistance with reference questions. Aukurville is equipped with a teletype, which connects with the two other regional centers (one of which is the Willington public library) and the State Library, which serves as the central reference resource—the library of "last resort"—for the state. Materials are forwarded through the mail.

Due to the number of libraries assigned to it, and the consequent demands made on its staff and resources, Aukurville officials asked the commissioners if its area might not be better served by creating another regional center. The commissioners agreed, and saw this as an opportunity to establish a model for the ideal regional center.

By virtue of standing an easy first among the libraries of the region—first in size of collection, first in financial support, and first in that mysterious quality known as "excellence"—Dorado was asked to assume the role. The city's governing authorities, honored by the request, had complied readily.

When the announcement was made two weeks ago, Marsha K. James, Dorado's library director, asked Stanton if she would take charge of developing the center, retaining her position as head of reference and adult services. Having performed ILL activities at the State House Library, she welcomed the added responsibility, especially since it involved a pay increase.

"Now what you'll have to do, Mel," James had explained when she outlined the details of the assignment, "is come up with a preliminary plan of how the department should be configured and administered. The commissioners would like us to think in terms of developing a multitype network. They would like something more than we have in the regional centers now. They view this as an opportunity to provide for the coordination of the resources of not only the public libraries in the area, but of the academic, school, and special libraries as well. In other words, they want us to start from scratch and come up with a plan for a full-service center, which might then be used as a model for the other regional centers. Think in terms of the ideal. Staff. Equipment. The kinds of services we should provide. Union lists of serials, union catalogs, technical processing, truck delivery, institutes, workshops—what have you?"

"Stanton had smiled, but she also cast a rather desperate look at James, who had ignored it.

The director went on: "What we need you to do is sit down and prepare an outline, which I can then submit to the commissioners. Base your thinking on what you can find in the literature, selecting from it the kinds of services we could provide our member libraries. Maybe you could interview some people as well. The commissioners have said not to worry about financing at this point; they're merely interested in seeing how we think a regional center should operate—along with a timetable for the implementation of what we propose. See if there's any funding available, too, okay?"

Stanton felt a bit like someone who, after boasting that she could dive into water from a great height has climbed to the height and dares not jump, but knows that she must jump. "I think I can manage it," she smiled. But it was a reserved smile, which said: "I *hope* I can manage it!"

James gave her what amounted to a grin. "Look at it this way," she said, "you won't be starting off with any preconceived notions, and there are advantages to that. The sky's the limit!"

The young librarian merely nodded a friendly affirmative to the director's concluding observation. She kept saying to herself, "Where do I start?" "Where do I start?" A peep into her mind would have revealed that she was quite apprehensive about the immensity of the assignment.

Melanie Stanton sat alone at the table, remembering.

She also remembered that there were to be 13 public libraries in the Dorado region, with the largest having a population of 28,000 people and the smallest 1,200; and that in the service area were 48 school library/media centers, 6 special libraries, and 1 four-year accredited private academic institution, none of which belonged to a resource-sharing network. The Dorado public library was to remain in the Aukurville region until it started functioning in its new capacity. And she had two months to develop her plan!

The kitchen was full of glancing sunlight and clean color; and as she sat there her mind recurred to her attempts to get her assistant to stay. She was seeing him standing in front of her at the reference desk. He had been her assistant since she arrived, and she was going to miss him.

"You know," she had said amiably, "there might be a better job for you here once things get rolling with this new regional setup."

To this Warren had laughed politely and said, "No thanks!"

"But didn't you say that one of the reasons you wanted to leave was because you were tired of macrame and wanted to get into computers? In our capacity as centerpoints for local activities, we may be equipped with card production equipment for producing catalog cards through the state division of OCLC. Here's your chance!"

"Look, Mel," he had smiled with entire good nature; "thanks for the offer, but I've signed a contract and made a deposit on an apartment."

Melanie Stanton broke into a gentle laugh as she recalled him executing a shuffling fandango and announcing mischievously, "Women in the SLA, get ready, here I come!"

As her mind swept back to her discussion with Marsha James concerning a replacement, she grew more sombre. Together they had decided that Warren's Librarian II (L2) position would retain programming and desk reference work, and probably—it was a little early to tell—have some ILL duties added, including possibly the supervision of clerical staff (Appendix I). The Librarian I (L1) position of the third member of the reference and adult services department, occupied by Albert K. Y. Lo, would remain unchanged. With the thought of Albert Lo, her mind turned abruptly to the union.

The Westbourne Valley Professional Association (WVPA) is the union which represents 52 professional librarians in 17 libraries in Almus County, of which Dorado is part. Founded 10 years ago, its members work under separate contracts in each town or city. One of the WVPA's most important acts, other than sending its officers to help in bargaining sessions, collecting dues, and retaining a law firm to help in personnel matters and negotiations, has been to mandate the posting of all vacant or new positions for application by members of the WVPA before a town or city may seek candidates outside the bargaining unit.

Melanie Stanton's position had been posted in accordance with the clause of the contract, that states: "Vacancy is defined as any opening in a position within the bargaining unit and shall include any position to which new duties have been added." Although there had been several applicants for her "vacant" position, no one had the qualifications and experience for the job. She had been a trifle nervous until it was formally announced that the position was hers, even though the director had assured her that she had been her choice from the start.

"After all," James had explained, "the contract protects my selection of an applicant to a great degree (Appendix II). It says that we, the management, shall be the sole judge of the qualifications and ability of candidates as they relate to the vacancy, provided we don't exercise this judgment in an 'arbitrary and capricious manner.' And Bob Jackson says—"

"I'm not sure what 'arbitrary and capricious' means," Stanton had cut in reasonably. "I wish contracts would define their terms! Ours doesn't."

James had stared at her rather blankly. "I agree with you. But let me go on. We can look into that some other time."

Stanton had turned on her an eye that appealed for justice. There were times when she disliked James, and this was one of them. The director had a habit of postponing certain questions and never returning to them. "As you wish," she had temporized, in a resigned tone.

James gave her a curious glance, and resumed:

"Bob Jackson says we should be really careful about how we interpret 'arbitrary and capricious.'"

Robert Owen Jackson is the attorney who represents Dorado in contractual disputes that are unresolved through the lower levels of the grievance procedure; disputes, in other words, which are brought before the impartial judgment of an arbitrator from the American Arbitration Association. The WVPA is represented by Pearlstein, Chrarin, and Cline. This legal firm, one of the largest in Willington, specializes in labor law and represents most of the major unions in that part of the state. Customarily legal questions concerning contracts are channeled to the firm from members of the WVPA through the union's president.

"Time to get going," said Stanton, reorienting her thoughts to the present. She put the dishes in the sink, locked the balcony door, found her purse, and sallied forth. When she arrived at the library, she went immediately to Marsha James's office. The director was not there, but she went in and sat down.

In a minute, James burst into the room in her usual emphatic way, threw her briefcase on the desk, and said: "Hi! Ready to select your L2?"

After chatting idly for a few moments about the weather, the two women looked over once again the applicant information forms (Appendix III) they had prepared on the WVPA members who had responded to the ad.

"Everything seems ready," said James presently. "Let's get on with the trench work!" Then, noticing that Stanton looked uneasy, she added: "Don't worry, Mel, there's nothing to this. Just ask them what they've done and what they plan to do—it's that simple."

"Isn't there more to interviewing than that, Marsha?" inquired Stanton gravely, and yet good-naturedly.

Came then the familiar retort, "We'll go into that some other time."

"Okay," said Stanton feebly, making a mental note to investigate how to conduct a job interview, now that she would certainly be doing more of it.

James gave her a faint smile and reached for the phone and asked the front desk to send in the first scheduled interview—Albert Lo, the L1 in Stanton's own department, who had been in his job 14 months.

During the next two hours they saw, in addition to Lo, three other people: a reference librarian who had received his degree a year ago and had been working for three months in a public library 12 miles from Dorado; a children's librarian from a small library nine miles away, who before becoming a librarian four months ago had taught elementary school for eight years; and a young adult librarian, Cindi Kass, from the nearby Dumais public library, who had begun employment there eight months ago.

After Kass left, James turned to Stanton and said: "Well, that wasn't so bad was it?"

"No," was the other's reply. "But I sure wish I had a better handle on this contract language. The part about candidate selection is trickier than it looks at first."

"Well," said James, sidestepping the issue, "I think Kass was quite impressive, and Albert handled himself very well, too. But we can eliminate three people immediately, because they don't meet the minimum service requirement of two years professional work and they don't have the requisite ILL experience. Therefore, I think we should offer the job to Albert right away."

Melanie Stanton looked both shocked and alarmed.

Marsha James comprehended the expression. "I gather you don't agree," she observed wryly.

Stanton nodded. "There's no question at all about the reference librarian and the children's librarian," she said. "They don't qualify. And there's no question that both Lo and Kass did well during their interviews. But there of elements of Kass's experience that can't be passed by easily."

The director sat up straight, as if preparing to debate. "Bob Jackson says that when applicants are looking for promotions rather than lateral transfers the main thing is first to determine who the senior candidate is. Then he wants us to take a hard look at the quality of the experience of the top candidates. If we feel the senior candidate's experience is relatively equal to that of the less senior candidates, then the contract language says we have to take the senior candidate."

Of a sudden, Stanton felt she knew which candidate had the superior experience, even if she could not at the moment understand what was meant by "relatively equal." There was another knot in the contract language which needed untying. No point in asking James what it meant. All she would get would be the conundrum of her vague smile and the familiar retort: "We'll look into that some other time."

"Well," Stanton tendered, "one candidate clearly has the superior experience—Kass."

The director frowned. "Mel," she said wearily, "Kass doesn't satisfy the minimum service requirement. I know she worked for over two years in the ILL department of a library even larger than the Willington Public. But we can't consider most of her experience as professional. She worked in an internship position while she was attending library school. When you consider her strictly professional experience, you come up with under two years of service."

Stanton listened respectfully, then said: "But the library she worked at is the center of a regional library system. Don't forget, even if her first job there wasn't professional it certainly was a full-time job. She worked full-time and attended library school part-time. She had a lot of time to learn the library business from the professionals in her department. We can't deny that she knows something."

James sat silent and peered out the window, as though at some object of great interet to be seen thence. "Anything else you want to say on behalf of Kass?" she bade, turning to face Stanton.

Stanton drew a breath and went on. "Well, the job description language we've written for the L2 position does say that we'll accept equivalent experience in lieu of professional experience. Let me get the exact wording"—she fumbled through some papers in a folder—"so long as it, ah! here it is, quote, is sufficient to indicate ability to do the job, unquote. I'm convinced Kass is the person for the job. Her references are superb. I would like *her*."

The other seemed not to hear. After a little, she proclaimed with significant emphasis: "I want Albert." She settled back in her chair and folded her arms.

It did not behoove the young reference department head to relinquish her position too quickly. Having failed apparently with her trump card, she fell back on a finesse. She smiled broadly, an engaging, open, friendly smile. "Can we debate this further?" she pressed, hoping her smile was disarming.

"All right," responded her listener, with neutral calm. "But let me give more of my reasons first."

Stanton fell in with the suggestion readily. "Okay," she laughed, "but I get a rebuttal!" She felt a small thrill of triumph.

Unexpectedly the director's face softened. "Now look,' she commenced, "if we accept Kass's pre-professional experience as a relevant consideration, then we have to be fair and look at Lo's work experience in library school. You can see from his sheet that he did ILL work, too, at his library school. Maybe we even have to go back to his work as a library assistant when he was in college — if we want a liberal interpretation of what our 'equivalent experience' language means. I say professional work can never really have any sort of equivalent in pre-professional or non-professional work. As a matter of fact, I think we should excise this bit of the job description next time we advertise an L2 or higher position. It leads to a lot of hand-wringing. I think we should simply ignore the non-professional work experiences of both candidates, and do what the contract says — simply take the senior person, Albert, who is the only qualified candidate. Albert will be fine in the position. He's been enthusiastic about the regional experiment. He's expressed his interest to me on several occasions. I think he's a fine young man."

"My turn?" asked Stanton, feeling adventurous.

The other woman nodded, smiling slightly, and began to make concentric circles on a pad of paper.

Stanton went on at once. "Common sense compels me to say this, Marsha." The director looked up; Stanton continued. "I'm going to be the one who will have to live on a day-to-day basis with whomever we select. I think it's more important that I be able to get along with the person...."

But here she stopped. The import of what she was about to say was clear. "Than me?" finished James, with a gleam of amusement in her eyes.

"Well, yes," acquiesced the other, relieved. The spark of warmth had emboldened her. The words wanted to tumble out now. "Marsha," she rolled on quickly, "I can't deny what Kass has in her head. Her knowledge of ILL is simply more comprehensive and relevant than Albert's, and that's what this whole selection process is about, isn't it?" She leafed through her copy of the WVPA contract as she spoke, stopping at the section on grievances (Appendix IV). "And what if we take Albert for the position, and Cindi decides to file a grievance? Can't she claim we've broken the agreement through our 'arbitrary, capricious, and unreasonable' consideration of her qualifications when we deny that her experience as a pre-professional isn't equivalent to professional experience? Don't you think that if the WVPA took this question in front of an arbitrator, somebody who is detached from the idea of the MLS mystique and who would look at what she did and what we would ask her to do in this new job, that such a person might agree with the grievance?"

There was a pause. The director was obviously thinking. "All this is not very likely," she observed at last, "not only because of the strength of the selection process language—its imperviousness to proof before an arbitrator. The union would have to make me out to be nearly a criminal in order to make that sort of proof. But also, there's one sticky detail: Albert is the vice-president of the WVPA—or did you forget that? I think that if we pick Kass, then Albert might not only attempt to make his case for our 'arbitrary and capricious' treatment of his qualifications, but he might make another cause of action out of the anti-discrimination clause of the contract" (Appendix V).

Having said that, she picked up her pen and fiddled with it. She looked at her employee in a weary, wordless way, so that it was hard for Stanton to tell whether she was angry.

She was not long in doubt. "Look, Mel," said James after the hiatus, "I'm irritated at the convoluted mess this simple case of filling a vacancy has become. I feel my control over the situation is slipping away. I've always felt I could resolve nearly any problem in my professional life within half an hour, and then move on to something else. Most of my life I've done this. You know, I had half a hundred other things to do today. I'd decided within the first few minutes of our receipt of applications for the position that the job would go to Albert. We don't have references on him because he's here, but I rate him very highly."

Melanie Stanton had always paid her supervisors without question the deference their positions demanded. But there was a principle at stake here, and she too felt obligated to express her honest thoughts.

"I don't want Albert," she negatived, swallowing hard.

The two regarded each other. James sighed and glanced out of the window. Stanton changed her position, and leaned her chin upon her hand. Thus they remained for what seemed like an eternity. Finally, Marsha James broke the hush. "Look," she began, rousing herself from her secret contemplation, "Cindi Kass doesn't strike me as the type to grieve. She doesn't seem the union type. She may not even know what the contract means. And besides," she added, her voice taking on a curious quality of childlike appeal, "I'll give you that new typewriter if you agree to Albert."

This slightly off-balance, whimsical remark was a Marsha James trademark. They both exploded into laughter, thereby releasing the pent-up tension. But Stanton knew that the remark belied James' impatience with the situation.

"Seriously," the director continued amid the embers of their mirth, there are practical considerations that reach months beyond right now. If we take Cindi, Albert will almost surely grieve. And how in heaven's name will we get any work done around here if we have to worry about grievance hearings, to say nothing of the grievant being in the same building. He'll be sitting in the corner and brooding. And we'd have to give him all sorts of time off to investigate and process the grievance (Appendix VI). As if we need that. I want to get this ILL thing on the road, in the smoothest possible fashion. There will be other opportunities for Kass."

Stanton, however, was unmoved by the argument; she detected inconsistencies in the other's reasoning. "How can I broach them?" she wondered to herself. "You commented earlier," she said ingenuously, aloud, "that Kass didn't strike you as the union type." Then, without waiting for an acknowledgement, "Well, I think Albert is *too much* the union type."

James expressed surprise. "What do you mean by that?"

"He spends too much time doing union work."

"The contract gives him that."

"And he knows it. I can't speak to him about anything he does in the union. Everything is simply very important — has to be done right away. I'm really afraid he won't do the work in the new position. It's going to require someone who can devote his or her full attention to the work. And he's such a job-hopper. He's had three professional jobs in his three years since getting his degree in three different libraries. That must be some sort of record. I can't plan the center and do his work too, while he trots off somewhere on union business."

"I'm surprised to hear you talking like this," said the director, not quite understanding. "After all, you're a member of the union. Only people above your L4 level aren't in the WVPA. I thought you people stuck together."

James waited for a response.

Thus brought to bay, Stanton hesitated. "I don't know what to say," she owned, and lapsed into silence. She sat back in her chair and considered her supervisor's gentle prods. Her ambivalent feelings toward Albert and his union activities flooded her brain. What *were* her thoughts? she wondered. First, it was the time he had spent running for office. It wasn't quite campaigning, but what else could it be called when he arranged parties twice a week, called people all day — on the pay phone, of course, which was proper — which meant he wasn't always on hand to take care of reference questions. Then there was his endless processing of grievances, photocopying time sheets for heat relief disputes, more talking on the phone to stewards, to the union president. How was she going to appraise him? For one fleeting second, she wished she had taken the job she was offered at the last ALA conference.

Her abstraction finally provoked James to speech. "You were far away, weren't you?" spoke the director across the desk fetchingly.

Stanton eyed her. "Yes," she replied. "Sorry. I was just thinking of what I will say about him on his appraisal. I haven't been here long enough to complete one on him. And since my predecessor had left when Albert reached the 12 month point, he hasn't had a formal evaluation. I'm thinking I won't be able to give him a good appraisal. I don't think he's that good a worker. And of course his problem is compounded by the amount of time he spends on union activities. Do I mention that in the appraisal?" She lifted her shoulders; the lifting was eloquent of her confusion.

The director chuckled an evasive chuckle before she made answer. It was her familiar retort. "We'll go into that some other time." And then, "Right now I want you to consider this. If we turn Albert down, the union could make the roof fall in on us. And you, as a member of the union, may become something of a pariah. Albert's popular, you know."

"I know," conceded Stanton, smiling with recovered assurance. "Maybe the answer is to reject everybody in the WVPA who applied and advertise for outside applicants."

"I think Albert would definitely grieve then. And if we took an outside candidate, then Kass wouldn't be able to grieve at all. The union's contract stipulates that only the 'seniormost' unselected candidate has the right to grieve. But that wouldn't be my problem."

Stanton darted a sardonic glance at her antagonist. "But that isn't fair."

"Look, Mel, these are your people, not mine," said the director with an assumption of nonchalance. "I really believe in the idea of giving the people in this union as many chances for advancement as possible. After all, to fairly allocate limited job opportunities was one of the main reasons librarians formed unions. It's an idea I agree with completely." She adjusted the gooseneck lamp on her desk. "Look, we don't have to decide today. Let's sleep on it. We'll get together tomorrow and go at it again. I'm still for Albert."

Melanie Stanton smiled. "And I'm for Cindi Kass."

APPENDIX I

Announcement #32

To the Members of the WVPA:

The Dorado Public Library intends to fill the following vacancy. The appointment shall be made by the Department Head with the approval of the administrators of the Library. Employees who believe they are qualified may apply for the position by sending a resume to the Dorado Public Library, c/o Director Marsha James, not later than Monday, September 23rd.

> Marsha James,
> Director,
> Dorado Public Library

September 16

Professional Service:
Senior Adult Services/Interlibrary Loan Librarian (L2) (temp.)
(Note: This position will be reviewed within a one year period from the date it is filled.)

Position Description:
Essential Functions: Under supervision, to implement and direct interlibrary loan services relating to the Dorado Public Library's function as a regional center within the state system of library cooperation; to plan and implement adult services, including reference work and programming; to supervise professional and non-professional staff, as assigned. Substantial evidence of the ability to apply professional knowledge and experience is required.

Reports to: Administratively to the Director; functionally to the Coordinator of Adult Services/ILL services.

Typical Duties:
ILL:
1. As assigned, answers reference inquiries from member libraries with appropriate media: photocopies, written replies, etc.
2. Keeps records of photocopying, in compliance with Copyright Laws.
3. Processes requests for book titles, as well as for monographic material about stated subject areas.
4. Assists in coordinating acquisition of resources purchased with state funds, in accordance with the

APPENDIX I (cont'd)

overall goals of the Dorado Public Library's acquisition program.
5. Assists in the development of bibliographic resources aiding access to materials within the libraries of the state.
6. Related and comparable duties, as assigned.

ADULT SERVICES:
1. Assists in the development of the collections of the Dorado Public Library.
2. Provides reference services to adult patrons. Includes instruction of patrons in the use and interpretation of catalogs, reference sources, as well as public service files and directories.
3. Participates in planning programs and exhibits.
4. Related and comparable duties, as assigned.

Minimum Qualifications:

Bachelor's degree from an accredited college or university, and a master's degree in library science from an accredited library school. In extraordinary circumstances, other education, training and experience may be substituted for part or all of the educational requirement.

Two years of professional library experience, or any equivalent combination of education, experience and training sufficient to indicate ability to do the job.

Demonstrated knowledge of bibliographical tools and reference sources; knowledge of interlibrary loan techniques.

Broad knowledge of library methods, procedures and issues; maturity, tact, ability to work well with public and staff.

Equal Opportunity Employer M/F/H

APPENDIX II

SELECTED CONTRACT CLAUSES. BASIS AGREEMENT BETWEEN THE WVPA AND WESTBOURNE VALLEY MUNICIPALITIES.

ARTICLE VII   VACANCIES/SELECTION PROCEDURE

Section 1. Notice of all vacancies within the bargaining unit will be given to staff. Sufficient time will be allowed for the purpose of candidates' application for said vacancies. Notice will be given by posting vacancies for seven working days on bulletin boards throughout all libraries that employ bargaining unit staff. This notice will describe duties, location of position, together with pay grade and minimum qualifications. Interviews of personnel who have applied for posted vacancies will begin within a reasonable time after the final date of the posting period has elapsed.

APPENDIX II (cont'd)

Section 2. METHOD OF SELECTION. Definitions. Seniority, for purposes of promotion shall be measured by the length of continuous service commencing with the date of employment in a position covered by this Agreement. Vacancy is defined as any opening in a position within the bargaining unit and shall include any position to which new duties have been added. In order for a position to be considered as a vacancy in the latter case, the new duties cannot be reasonably considered to be part of any existing job description for positions covered by this Agreement.

Section 3. METHOD OF SELECTION. Procedure. The selection of an employee for promotion or lateral transfer shall be made on the basis of qualifications and ability. Where qualifications and ability are relatively equal, seniority, as defined in the above Section 2, shall be the deciding factor. In the event that the senior applicant for the position is not selected, the appointing authority, or his delegate shall upon request of the Association submit reasons in writing why said senior employee was not selected to fill the vacancy. The appointing authority or his delegate shall be the sole judge of qualifications and ability, provided that such judgment shall not be exercised arbitrarily, capriciously or unreasonably. Any dispute hereunder shall be subject to the grievance and arbitration procedure.

Section 4. Selection from among the eligible candidates shall be made within a reasonable time, in any case not to exceed one month after the close of the posting period. Notice of selection shall be sent by the appointing authority to each applicant and the Association. If no selection has been made among candidates, the Association President shall be notified in writing seven working days after the close of the selection period.

APPENDIX III

APPLICANT INFORMATION FORM FOR ALBERT K. Y. LO

Education: M.L.S. (36 months ago), M.A. (English), B.A. (English)
Library Experience (from most recent to earliest):
  Dorado Public Library (pop. 25,000)
    Title: Adult Services/Reference Assistant (L1)
    Duties: Reference and reader's advisory services; adult programming
    Duration: 14 months
  Hailfield Public Library (pop. 40,000)
    Title: Adult Services Assistant Librarian (professional)
    Duties: Reference and reader's advisory services
    Duration: 13 months
  Bruton Public Library (pop. 17,000)
    Title: Reference Assistant (professional)
    Duties: Reference services
    Duration: 9 months
  School of Library Science Library
    Title: Library Intern (10 hours per week)
    Duties: Assisted in processing ILL requests; reference work; circulation duties

APPENDIX III (cont'd)

Duration: 12 months
Tainter Memorial Library, State College
Title: Library Assistant (20 hours per week)
Duties: Circulation duties; shelf search for reserve requests; responsible for re-shelving of reserve readings
Duration: 16 months

APPLICANT INFORMATION FORM FOR CINDI KASS

Education: M.L.S. (21 months ago), B.A. (Sociology)
Library Experience (from most recent to earliest):
Dumais Public Library (pop. 18,000)
Title: Young Adult Assistant Librarian (L1)
Duties: Plans young adult programs; selects materials; answers reference questions
Duration: 8 months
Stanbury Public Library (pop. 400,000; library of "last resort" in state)
Title: Assistant ILL Librarian (professional)
Duties: Fulfillment of ILL requests; supervised delivery system; selection of materials
Duration: 13 months
Stanbury Public Library
Title: Pre-professional Library Assistant, Interlibrary Loan Department (full-time)
Duties: Clerical tasks; opening mail; securing materials; preparing for delivery
Duration: 18 months

APPENDIX IV

ARTICLE X   GRIEVANCE PROCEDURE

In the case of a dispute over the Municipal Employer's selection of a candidate for a vacancy, the following procedure shall be used to determine who among the unselected candidates shall have the right to file a grievance.

The grievant will be considered to be the seniormost unselected candidate for the position in question. If the seniormost candidate declines to file a grievance, then the option of filing a grievance shall be offered to the unselected candidate who has the next greatest level of seniority. This procedure shall be followed until one candidate has accepted the option to grieve, or until all unselected candidates have declined to do so.

APPENDIX V

ARTICLE XXV   NON-DISCRIMINATION (excerpt)

Section 4. The Municipal Employers and the Association agree to the general principle of good employer-employee relations. Both parties agree that there should be no discrimination practiced against employees covered by this Agreement, on account of membership or non-membership in the Association's aims and goals, or participation in their attainment. No discrimination will be permitted on account of race, religion, creed, color, national origin, sex, age, or physical handicap.

APPENDIX VI

Section 8. Time off with pay shall be allowed for the investigation and processing of grievances. Up to six representatives of the Association may engage in the investigating and processing of grievances.

14

A WORD TO THE WISE

Drew Pope put down his pencil, pushed back in his chair, stretched his arms overhead, and swung in a half-circle so he could look out the window. It was a warm Indian-summer day. The maple trees that lined the Allenby Public Library parking lot reached toward the sun like a hedge of orange fire. The smell of their dry, aromatic leaves spiced the gentle breeze. "What a day to be inside!," he said, meditatively addressing the emptiness of the room. With considerable reluctance, he spun his chair around and was about to return to his papers when Preston Huish put his head into the room.

"Have a minute, Drew?" the selectman asked, perkily.

"Sure," smiled the library director, "Glad to see you. Won't you sit down, Preston?" He didn't know the selectman well, but they were on a first-name basis.

Pope studied him with questioning eyes, his hand reaching for the coolish remainder of his coffee.

Huish spoke: "My daughter, Lisa, applied for a page's job at the beginning of September, and yesterday she stopped by to see the circulation head to find out when she would be starting. Ms. Wren told her that she was number 18 on the waiting list and that it would be quite some time before she would be called."

The dim thought at the back of the director's mind was: "You're about to ask a favor of me. I can tell." But he kept his own counsel.

The selectman continued: "Would you personally look into this and see if she can't be moved up on the list? She's in her final year of high school, and she's saving to go away to college next year. She's bright and a really reliable kid. I'd appreciate it if you'd move her to the top of the list." He fully expected the director to acquiese, for his eyebrows mounted ever so slightly.

A choking emotion, partly made up of incredulity and in part a burning resentment filled Drew Pope. This—this isn't right, it isn't fair. You can't ask me to do this. Something within him brought him to his feet. He was shocked, hurt, but his calm tone disclosed nothing of that. He explained to the selectman that pages were hired on a "first come, first-take" basis, and that while there was considerable turnover he doubted 18 would be needed in the year, perhaps three or four at best. He added that hiring pages was the delegated responsibility of the head of circulation, and that he left it entirely up to her, seldom becoming involved, except when there was a problem, which there rarely was.

The selectman received this explanation in silence, but he fastened on the librarian a glance full of sinister meaning. It said: "Look, pal, I can do things for you. Don't forget I'm chairman of the budget committee. Your budget will probably be one of the first to be cut in these budget-slashing times. If you want to fare reasonably well, you better play ball with me."

The logic of the thing was spread out plainly and irrefutably before Pope. And yet the thought of what he was being asked to do to salvage the jeopardized budget outraged his every fiber. How he had always anathematized those who took unscrupulous advantage of their positions, and those who succumbed to their insolent methods.

All this filled his brain and throat, and clamored for expression; but not a protesting word escaped his lips. He merely said, striving to conceal his anger: "I'll see what I can do."

Preston Huish smiled approvingly, expressed his thanks, and walked away with suave confidence.

The director returned to his paperwork, nothing in his heart but hot shame at having permitted himself to be bullied into submission by this disagreeable public official.

After a time, he went to the circulation area.

"Hilda," he said, approaching the department head, who was computing next week's schedule at her desk behind the charge-out counter, "Mr. Huish, one of the selectman, dropped by earlier today and asked me if his daughter, Lisa, who has applied for a page's job, could start immediately. I told him I'd look into it. He says she's eighteenth on the list."

Hilda Wren looked up, acknowledged that was so, and added, "We won't get to her by the time she graduates. She came by to see me yesterday and I told her not to hold out any hope."

The director reached up and scratched the side of his head. "Are we hiring anyone soon?" he inquired.

"Yes, we need someone to start next Monday," was Wren's answer, curiosity and challenge in her voice.

"Well," he responded quietly, turning his face away, "I think it would be advisable to offer the job to Lisa."

"What!" she exclaimed, on a hard and inimical note. It was as if she had been given a dizzying blow.

The director saw at once that he must tread warily.

"I needn't tell you," he suggested tentatively, with brow creased, "that Preston Huish is a very influential person in town. We need all the help we can get to save our budget. We can't risk alienating him. He's chairman of the budget committee and he wields a lot of power. I've been working very hard to establish good relations with the powers-that-be, and I don't want to see my labors wiped out by denying one of them a request. If I expect them to grant me requests, then I must be prepared to grant theirs. With these assorted tax-cutting propositions being voted in right and left, we'll be the first to have our budget cut for sure. Common sense dictates that we play ball with him. Don't make this more difficult than it is. A word to the wise should be sufficient."

"I've already contacted the first person on the list," she said, with a low but intensely clear and precise articulation. "He's coming in Monday." Her lips closed resolutely into a firm line.

Pope wasted not a second in responding. "You'll have to call him and tell him there's been a mix-up and that he'll be called as soon as there's another opening."

Her eyes swept the room and then enveloped him in an icy glare. "I don't think it's right," she said with that maddening clearness of articulation. "The kid I've called has been waiting patiently for a year and a half for the job. He was thrilled to be called. He's a neighbor of mine. I know him and I like him. He's a good kid. He's conscientious and takes his work seriously. He's been our paperboy for years, and he's never been late one morning. I never moved him up on the list, although I could have many times and no one would have known. I've never done this for anybody."

The director ran his hand along his cheek. He often did this, almost unconsciously, to avert an immediate sign of reaction to an irksome confrontation. "Let's go to my office," he enjoined, noticing that the circulation clerks were beginning to take an interest in the dialogue.

Therein, Pope closed the door. "Look, Hilda," he began in a rather pleasant style, as he sat down and as she sat down. "Let's be reasonable about this. I think we have to make an exception here."

The woman seemed to be trying to hide a growing personal anger toward him, and it kept her cool and reserved. He waited for a comment, an acknowledgement — something. None came. He continued: "There are two ways you can react to this: you can accept it gracefully or you can accept it unpleasantly. Whichever, we're going to hire Lisa Huish, and that's all there is to it."

Wren found speech. "This is an order then," she said defiantly, "even though I'm supposedly in charge of pages."

"Yes, if that's the way you want to take it." Neither of them relaxed the grip on each other's eyes.

"Very well, then, I'll do it," she responded sternly. "but I think it's wrong. It isn't fair to those who don't have 'pull' that those who do get preferential treatment. I don't care who's involved. I think they should wait their turn like everyone else. I'll call the young fellow and tell him there's been a mix-up, as you suggest — I hope *his* parents don't raise a stink — then, I'll call Lisa Huish." And then, after what had almost become an unbearable pause, "Yes, I'll do it, but I want you to know that it really sticks in my craw. It violates all my principles."

A feeling of unshielded relief filled Pope's whole being. "Don't think I like it any better than you do," he said, as it were appealing for approval. "But you can see, can't you, that we have to do it?"

That was not the thing to say. Wren threw him another malevolent look. "No, I don't see. I'm doing it because you're the boss and I'm following orders. I want you to know that. I think you're usurping my authority."

The library director decided to let well enough alone; after all, she had agreed. They parted with Pope saying, by way of offering some consolatory remark, "Her father says she's reliable."

Lisa Huish was hired and started at the appointed time. She was to work every weekday afternoon from 3:00 p.m. to 6:00 p.m.; no Saturdays, at her request. (Wren felt she had compromised enough that she didn't even blink when Lisa announced that she would like to have her Saturdays free. Pages usually work every other Saturday. The library is closed Sundays.)

Four weeks later, on a Friday, Hilda Wren came by the director's office to say that she didn't think Lisa — her tone was distinctly facetious — was as reliable as her father thought. She was frequently late for work, and she spent so much time talking with other pages and other people in the library that she was not getting her work done. And she'd been absent five days in the month. When she called in sick the third time, a week ago, the circulation head decided to have a talk with her. "As I approached her in the stacks the following day," Wren related, "I heard her saying 'We spent yesterday afternoon at the movies; we went from one theater right into the other, and got home at 6:30.' I didn't confront her with that, because we can't afford to alienate Mr. Huish, can we?" Pope observed that her manner was mocking and not the slightest bit sympathetic; a conspicuous coolness had existed between them since they had exchanged views on the hiring of Lisa Huish. Wren went on: "I spoke to her about missing work and being tardy, and she promised me she'd watch it. She's been absent twice this week and late twice, so obviously my words haven't had much effect."

Pope flushed hotly at this disclosure. Wren translated the look on his face. It was a look of horror. He looked up the selectman's telephone number at his dairy and dialed him.

"Hello, Preston," he began brusquely, "Drew Pope at the library. Look.... Fine, thanks.... Look Lisa isn't working out as a page. She's been consistently late, she's usually behind in her work, and she's been absent 5 days out of 20. One of those days she was at the movies when she was supposed to be home sick."

Hilda Wren ahemmed when she heard that, as if to indicate what a silly thing to say. "Rhinoceros!" she said under her breath, shaking her head.

Pope continued speaking to Huish: "Last week sometime.... Ms. Wren overheard her say it in the stacks.... Well, that's what she heard...." He cupped his hand over the receiver and asked Wren what day it was. "Thursday" was her reticent response. "Thursday," he said, speaking into the mouthpiece. "Uh, huh...." He began to tap his fingers nervously on the desk. "Well, anyway, she's been absent 5 days out of 20, she's frequently late, and she talks so much with her co-workers and the patrons that she doesn't get the work done.... I suppose it is Ms. Wren's word against Lisa's.... Ms. Wren has spoken to her and she's been absent twice since, and late, too.... All right.... Yes, I understand.... Perhaps that will do some good.... Okay.... Goodbye."

"Preston's going to speak to her about it," Pope said as he clicked back the receiver. He proceeded to relate the other side of the conversation: Huish was upset, not so much that Lisa wasn't working out but that they, Pope and Wren, were bothered by it. He accused them of lying when they said she was at the movies when she had called in sick. The reason Huish asked about the specific day was that Lisa had to stay home with her mother on that day. Her mother hasn't been well lately.

"Lisa didn't say she was staying home to take care of her mother when she called in sick that time, did she?" Pope asked Wren.

"No," replied the other, "she said *she* was sick."

"Well, I don't know what's going on," Pope continued disgustedly. "Anyway, to make a long story short, Huish said he knows Lisa has been a little flighty at times. But he said she's a good girl and a good worker. She just needs a good talking to. He said he'd be very disappointed to learn we were thinking of letting her go. He said he'd speak to her himself. Let's see if *he* can whip her into shape."

Consistent with her conduct in this affair, Wren agreed to go along. "There's one thing I should add," she threw in. "Several other pages have been complaining to me about Lisa. I thought you should know this, too."

The library director strove to master his frustration. "Keep me posted on how she makes out," he said resignedly.

Two weeks later, Wren popped her head in at his door. "I thought you should know that Lisa has been out two days in the past two weeks," she announced, "one time not even calling in, and late three days."

DIRECTING

15

TO WHOM IT MAY CONCERN

Cecilia (Cissy) Bogardus poured a cup of coffee, plugged the pot back in so that refills would be ready, and joined the other staff members around the table. It was a sweet, sharp, sunshiny morning in early October, and Bogardus felt good: she had just put the finishing touches on a draft of a study of the possibilities of automating personnel records which she had inherited from her predecessor and which she had been working on intermittently during her three weeks on the job.

"You look cheerful!" someone said as Bogardus added two lumps of sugar to her cup.

The personnel officer smiled. Just as she was about to explain the reason for her high spirits, the library director's secretary approached her and asked if she could come at once to the director's office. "Bring your coffee with you," she advised good-naturedly.

"Duty calls," announced Bogardus as she got up and made her way cautiously toward the door, taking care not to spill any of the steaming liquid. Harboring the employee's instinctive fear of abrupt summonses like this, she asked if the secretary knew why Rachel Bough wanted to see her. As they insinuated their way through the stack area that would take them to the elevator to the administrative offices, the secretary responded that all she knew was that the director had just returned from a meeting of all department heads with the president, and that she looked glum. She said that Bough had been sitting in her office for the last half hour, alternately gazing at the ceiling and making notes on a pad. "Something's up," she frowned. "I can see it in her face."

A vague sensation of apprehension seized the newly appointed personnel officer as she knocked on the director's door.

"Oh, come in, Cissy," the director said, glancing up; her forehead revealed disquieting lines of concern. She inclined her head toward a chair by her desk. Bogardus moved into it quietly.

"Well, it's happened," Bough began. "The word's out: all departments have to cut their staffs by 10%." Her voice was weak and laden with woe.

The young librarian's face crimsoned, and a physical wave of emotion seemed to sweep downwards through her whole body. "Oh, no!" she exclaimed.

Old Orchard University was organized under the auspices of the Methodist Church, but like many early colleges which were intended to qualify a ministry for their respective sects it has long since divested itself of sectarian supervision. Housed in an abandoned warehouse, instruction was begun on November 1, 1860, with a faculty of 3 and 30 students. Today OOU consists of 36 buildings on 54 acres, and has a faculty of 816 (58% of whom hold doctorates) and a student enrollment of 8,119, approximately half men and half women. The university buildings are grouped about stretches of greensward crisscrossed by paths and canopied by impressive trees, making the campus a sylvan retreat in the midst of a small commercial center (population: 19,000) for a mineral and agricultural hinterland in the northern plains area. A privately supported and largely residential institution, it offers a full roster of degrees in its three main academic divisions: the College of Liberal Arts, the School of Business, and the School of Law.

Not unlike several other institutions of higher education today, OOU finds itself beset with an array of problems, most of which turn on two closely linked axes: student enrollment is declining and costs are rising. The euphoric years of affluence and expansion in the decades immediately following the midpoint of the century have given way to traumatic years of austerity and contraction. The consequences are not unexpected. Some private colleges and universities have responded by eliminating academic programs, reducing faculty and staff, and shifting priorities, while others, acting out their total desperation, have been forced to close altogether.

When OOU's president and governing board recognized earlier this year that some form of retrenchment was inevitable, they set up a Task Force (composed of five department heads, one trustee, one graduate and one undergraduate student, and the academic vice-president) to analyze the situation and make recommendations for keeping the school viable. Below are excerpts from its final report:

"Old Orchard University is a private residential university, and as such its problems are almost exactly the same as those confronting most similar institutions of higher education. We articulate them as follows:

• **The halt in the boom in enrollment.** Owing to the end of the post-World War II 'baby boom' and the subsequent decline in the absolute number of births, there is no question that the traditional college-age cohort of the population will be smaller in the years ahead. It is clear now that OOU's enrollment projections, made during the 'good old days of growth,' far exceeded reasonable expectations. Emptying elementary and secondary classrooms portend an analogue for higher education. Unless the current trend is reversed, we conclude that things are likely to get worse before they get better. While it is more difficult than usual to forecast the behavior of the American economy, our best projection, offered with the hope that it might be wrong, is that enrollment by the end of the next decade can be expected to be no more than 75% as great as the present enrollment of two years ago.

• **The rapidly rising cost of higher education.** Unrelenting tuition increases are pricing private institutions out of the reach of many middle-class parents. The gap between what private and public institutions charge means that private schools are at a big disadvantage in recruiting students. Faced with paying five times more a year to attend a school like OOU, many parents are having to send their sons and daughters to lower cost state supported schools. OOU is thus in danger of losing touch with its traditional constituency — upward-mobile students whose academic and socioeconomic backgrounds would have previously indicated nearly automatic attendance.

• **The changing social and economic aspirations of high school students.** The base of higher education is shrinking not only because of the drop in the birthrate and rising costs, but because of an evident disinclination on the part of growing numbers of eligible students to extend their education. Suddenly 18- and 19-year-olds are not going to liberal arts colleges — unless they really want a liberal education or unless they see it as a first step toward a professional career. Simply put, the drive to keep everyone in school is losing much of its force. Since two-thirds of all college graduates earn no more in their lifetime than their counterparts with high school diplomas, and since employers are increasingly disposed to drop the college degree as a criterion of employment, many students are bypassing traditional institutions. OOU is tied to professional rather than technical training, whereas large numbers of the "new student population" are choosing short vocational courses in community colleges or trade schools. The unavoidable conclusion of all this is that more than ever before young people are seeking to escape from the academic environment and move out into the world as soon as possible."

Having set forth in broad outline the key issues and problems as it saw them, the Task Force proceeded to make the following comments and recommendations:

"Old Orchard University stands today at the hinge of its history. The new realities identified above are fraught with momentous implications. Unless the academic community demonstrates a willingness to address them openly and realistically and an ability to change, our viability may be jeopardized. Hard times lie ahead. The halcyon days are gone—perhaps forever. Survival is our main imperative. While we lament the changed environment in which we live, we must not permit inertia and rigidity to prohibit us from meeting head on the demands it makes on us. We are all too familiar with rhetorical substitutes for substantive innovation.

Listed below are a number of alternatives which could be implemented to maintain our vitality under the conditions of declining enrollment, spiraling costs, and different outlooks. They call for flexibility in our thinking.

• Liberalization of rules to permit deferred admissions and 'stopping out' of students in the midst of their college careers.

• Tapping of new pools of potential students: high school graduates who are nonattenders; college dropouts; transfer students from two-year colleges; adults.

• Intercampus registration that would permit a sharing of faculty and students.

• Giving credit for work done in surroundings other than the college classroom.

• Reexamination of the time when courses are offered, fee structures, ancillary institutional services, child care, off-campus locations, and the like.

• Expanding the market by offering continuing education courses for nontraditional students.

• Relaxing admission standards.

• Increased student-to-faculty ratio (by reducing faculty and/or proclaiming a moratorium on future hiring).

• Considering changing our status to that of a public institution.

• Reducing support services: holding the library collection to standing orders and "essential only" purchases and/or reducing staff; curtailing athletic programs; holding back on the purchase of new equipment; reducing student services; cutting back on supplies for the physical plant.

Very hard decisions will have to be made. Though these suggestions, taken separately or together, cannot guarantee that we will successfully ford the current crisis, they may help us avoid some of the rocks and shoals on which other private institutions have foundered."

While conceding that some changes were unavoidable, the governing authorities reacted negatively to what one called "this unholy set of options." They acknowledged the accumulating evidence that higher education appears not to be a growth segment of society at the present, but they were reluctant to pursue some of the "more drastic" measures suggested by the Task Force. They rejected totally the notion of deferred admissions, intercampus registration, giving credit for work done off-campus, relaxing admission standards — indeed, everything but reducing faculty, staff, and support services. They argued that any projection of enrollment must recognize that there are extraordinary uncertainties in the murky future of higher education, and that to change the character of the institution at this stage would be too extreme a measure.

Thus, they would "wait out" the present crisis. However, they announced that all departments were to reduce staff and faculty by 10% by the beginning of the academic year — July 1. There were to be *no* exceptions. In addition, they decided to act on the other part of this suggestion. The library budget, for instance, was to be reduced next year by 10% as well.

"I've been sitting here wondering how best to select the people to be laid off," Rachel Bough said blankly, after she had informed Cissy Bogardus of the administration's decision. "They've delegated the matter to us. There are many ways we could do it, and I want to tell you what I've come up with and get your reactions. If you have other ways, I'd be delighted to hear them. I need and want your help. We'll have to let both professionals and non-professionals go."

Bogardus maintained a fatalistic silence while the director consulted her jottings. Bough continued:

"First, we could call the department heads togther and say 'Well, this is the way it is; there's going to be a 10% reduction of staff, effective July 1 of next year. This is what the president and trustees call coping with declining enrollments and increasing costs. In plain English, it means we don't have enough students and expenses must be cut. Therefore, we must let 10% of you go. I don't like to do it, you don't like to hear it, but that's the way it is. The decision as to who goes will be based partly on seniority and partly on ability.' "

The personnel officer experienced an involuntary shiver as the lancinating reality of the board's decision sank in. The director noticed the shiver. "It's not easy is it?" she said ruefully. Then: "The second thing we could do is call them all together and say that word has come down from on high that 10% of the staff is to be let go, and that we'll have to decide which are the most important jobs and let the people who aren't doing them go, regardless of seniority."

Bogardus interrupted, looking puzzled. "What *are* the most important jobs? How would we go about identifying them? They're all important to me."

"Well, to me, too. I don't have the foggiest idea how one would go about it. Think about it, though, and give me your thoughts."

Bogardus nodded.

The other went on with gloomy hesitation. "On option two again. I could say that I'm doing what I've been told to do, and that I've got to do it. I could tell them that I hope they understand how it is with me — that my hands are completely tied. I could say that the people who are lowest on the seniority list—regardless of ability—would have to go, and that I'm sorry the authorities think this is necessary, but that I have to go along with them."

The personnel officer could see that the director was passing through adversity. A feeling of sadness overwhelmed her. The director resumed:

"Thirdly, we could post a notice on the bulletin board, explaining the situation and telling them that 10% of the staff will be laid off. The notice could contain the list of the poorest performers, based on the most recent set of appraisals. We'd know they're the poorest performers; others wouldn't necessarily."

Bogardus privately resolved that nothing would induce her to assent to this monstrous possibility. She thought the director had got to the point of catching at straws. The director amplified: "The personal touch would probably take some sting out of the layoff, but if I did it this way I could avoid involved discussions."

"I don't know about that one," Bogardus said, politely argumentative.

"Well, as I said, I'm just trying to think of as many ways of doing this as I can." Bough consulted her notes. "The fourth approach I have here is the opposite of the last one, almost. I could make my decision on the basis of the importance I assign to the various jobs, and *privately* inform each person affected." She looked up and turned her face toward the window; her voice was uncertain. "The problem with that is that I'm not sure how to determine the importance of the various jobs. That's where you could help me."

Bogardus drew a deep breath in an effort to feel less uncomfortable. "Boy, that's a toughie," said she to herself. Then, aloud, languidly: "I'll see what I can come up with."

"Good," was Bough's only comment to that. She went on:

"The fifth option I have here is to let some of the older people go, not necessarily the most senior, but the oldest. People who are approaching retirement."

"We don't have anyone who's closer than 10 or 15 years from retirement, do we?" Bogardus asked.

"That's right. Jeannie's the oldest among the professional librarians. She's in her mid-fifties. And Leslie's the oldest among the non-professionals. She's in her early fifties."

"If you did that, how would you let them know?"

"That's the problem. We could send them letters, or distribute notices with their paychecks, or call them in—something like that."

"There's no easy way, is there?" Bogardus sighed, dejectedly. "But we certainly have to establish some fair criteria to determine who gets the tap on the shoulder."

"Now, you know, I could merely turn this over to the two division or all the department heads and let them decide," reflected Bough. "They could do the dirty work."

The personnel librarian nodded solemnly. "True."

"What would you advise them to do, if they asked you?" Bough inquired, gazing reflectively at her.

The junior librarian leaned forward, and resting her elbows on her knees, put her chin in her hands. For a moment she sat bewildered, in a dream, staring at the floor and other unresponsive objects. Finally, she said:

"I honestly don't know. I have to think about it." Suddenly she piped triumphantly, almost getting to her feet: "We could let the student assistants go!" She said it with sparkling eyes, as though the problem was now solved.

Bough negatived the suggestion instantly. "I thought of that, but we just have 80 hours of student help a week. That translates into a ratio of 1 : 0.98, with our full-time staff of 84. That doesn't take care of 10% and I'm not sure it's the answer anyway."

Bogardus felt crestfallen. "I'll give it more thought," she said with a sharp frown, resuming her former posture.

"Please do," the director urged. "Now, in general terms, how would you go about reducing the budget by 10%? What sorts of thing would you look at first? How would you establish priorities? I know you're not familiar with the budget. I'm merely interested in how you'd start the process of determining where the cuts should be made. Perhaps there's some literature on it. After all, we can't be the first in the country to face a problem like this."

Bogardus felt a sudden chill as if someone had opened a door. "I wish I could be of more immediate help," she felt impelled to say. "I have to think that one over, too."

"Administrators have some hard decisions to make, don't they?," summed up Bough.

Bogardus agreed with a weary nod. "I'd like to return to the possibility of letting the oldest members of the staff go, if I could, Rachel," she said. "If the library staff had faculty rank, then they'd be protected, wouldn't they?"

"I suppose so, if you mean they'd have tenure," replied the director, curious. "They do have tenure-in-fact, which means that appointments tend to be renewed annually automatically, but that's not quite the same as being on the tenure track. I know what you mean. We do have academic status and the privileges that go with it—TIAA, faculty club membership, and so forth—but not full faculty rank, that is, professional titles, Sabbaticals, nine-month appointments, and such."

"Well, in case this ever happens again—or even if it doesn't—wouldn't it be desirable for the staff to have faculty rank?"

"I've always thought so. I have a problem with it, though. Faculty competence is frequently judged by peers within or beyond a college or university, by professional activities, by students. How do you reconcile faculty activities and library work? What I mean by that is we simply don't do the same things. Faculty are in the classroom, oh, let's say, 7 or 8 to 10 or 12 hours a week. We work a 40 hour week. They're expected to engage in professional and scholarly activities—consult, write, conduct research, speak, review books—things like that. Some librarians do these things, but not all by any means. How would you establish criteria for promotion and tenure?"

The personnel officer nodded. "Even so, some library staffs do enjoy faculty rank."

"Well, I certainly wouldn't be opposed to it," returned the other. "It's certainly worth looking into."

Bogardus caught the oblique directness of the statement. "You'd like me to do it—right!"

"Yes," Bough said with a smile. She had a pleasing smile. "There's no real hurry, though. But see if you can build a case." And then she added, "Perhaps when you start investigating the pros and cons, you'll change your mind about its desirability. What would it mean? How would we judge competence? Anyway, let me know what you come up with. Put it in the form of a proposal to the president."

"That's if I agree we should go for it!"

"Either way, I'd like to know your reasons and what you find out. I guess you better make the presentation to me, outlining pros and cons, and then justifying what you recommend."

"All right," Bogardus said.

They were both silent for an instant. Then, with a kind of energetic abruptness, Bough said, "You know, even though the president and trustees have said there are to be no exceptions to the 10% reduction of staff, perhaps we could try to build a case for keeping the budget intact. I'd like you to give some thought to that, too. How have other librarians coped with budget cuts? See if you can find out something that would be of use to us. What have they had to do by way of adjusting?"

Bogardus jumped to her feet and smiled drolly. "I better get out of here before I wind up with more jobs!"

Rachel Bough gave a short laugh. Then she grew serious again. "Let me know how you think we should break the news, uh?"

Cissy Bogardus replied that she would, and took her leave.

Old Orchard University Library has a staff of 84 — 28 professional librarians, 54 nonprofessional personnel, and the equivalent of 2 full-time student assistants. The expenditures for library operations during the present academic year total $1,806,534 or 4.62% of the University's $39,102,467 support expenditures. A detailed breakdown of expenditures follows:

Salaries and Wages:

Professional Librarians	$ 448,690
Clerical and Sub-Professional Ass'ts	584,400
Student Assistants	18,720
Staff Benefits	122,437
	$1,174,247

Operating Expenses:

Books	$ 322,551
Textbooks	1,374
Periodicals	139,975
Binding and Book Repair	36,076
L.C. Cards	4,557
AV Materials	5,626
Documents	2,228
Microforms	48,636
Maps and Pamphlets	1,132
Supplies	36,243
Interlibrary Loans	683
Equipment Service	765
Equipment Rental	7,071
Travel	1,670
	$ 608,587

Equipment:	23,700
TOTALS	$1,806,534

APPENDIX I

OLD ORCHARD UNIVERSITY LIBRARY—
ORGANIZATION CHART

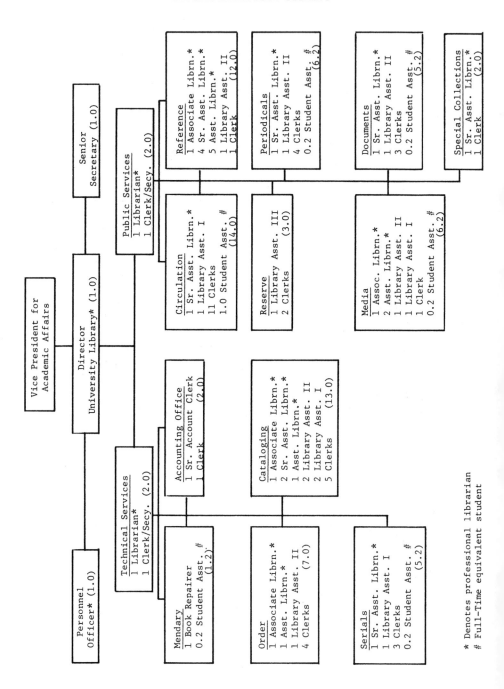

* Denotes professional librarian
# Full-Time equivalent student

16

INCIDENT AT SQUIER MEMORIAL

Wanda Bragge was rather pleased with herself — not terribly pleased, because she was very conscious that as president of a real estate firm she had to keep a close rein on all evidences of pleasure when she herself made a big sale. She restored the Williams folder to its place in her file cabinet, and as she turned around she saw the slender figure of Arnold Carmichael standing on the threshold of her office. His usual open countenance was marred by a frown, and there was a quiet desperation in his tone as he said: "Wanda, may I have a few minutes of your time, if you're not too busy?"

"Arnold!" she exlaimed. He had never visited her office before. "What a pleasant surprise! Certainly. Come right in. Take a seat. What brings you over?"

"I hate to bother you like this," said Carmichael, easing himself into a chair, "but I have to talk to someone." Bragge took her place behind the desk.

Thirty-eight-year-old Arnold Carmichael has been director of the Squier Memorial Public Library for seven years. He is a gentle, sensitive person, intelligent, scholarly, and conscientious. Yet he is not a dynamic leader and he tends to shrink from controversy. However, the trustees are not dissatisfied with him in any way because he is competent in a quiet, effective way, and the library seems to be well, if unimaginatively, run. No, there is nothing about him or his performance which can be seriously faulted. And now, sitting in the office of the chairwoman of the board of trustees, he appeared distraught.

The room was a bit cold, and Bragge pulled her sweater closer about herself. She offered Carmichael a cup of coffee, which he declined. He sat rubbing his forehead along the creases, and his voice was unsteady as he started to tell his story.

"It's finally come to a showdown with Stuart Wronski. I guess you know he's been a thorn in my side for a long time. But he's finally gone too far, and I've got to do something about it." He bit his lip, and looked at the floor.

Wanda Bragge, who is the same age as Carmichael, was well acquainted with the library and its problems, having served as a member of the board for four years and chairwoman for two. She also knew something about Stuart Wronski. She knew, for instance, that he was considered to be the unofficial leader of the library and that his hold on the staff was a factor to be reckoned with. She also knew that he was an excellent worker. There was no aspect of library work he couldn't do — and well. She had been told from time to time that he seemed to derive satisfaction from needling the staff, but this always reached her second- and third-hand, and she had never been able to pin down specifically what he does that irks them. To her and other board members he was unfailingly courteous, helpful, even charming. Still, the reports had come frequently enough and from enough different sources for her to be sure they had some validity. However, as far as she and the other trustees were concerned, he was such an asset to the library that they were willing to overlook whatever it was about him that bothered the staff. Moreover, no one had ever registered a formal complaint. She was surprised then that things had come to a "showdown," for it appeared that over the years Arnold Carmichael not only had managed to live with him but had even learned to handle him successfully. Hence it was with considerable interest that she settled back to hear the director's story.

"Let me give you some background information first," Carmichael began, his perplexed forehead beginning to smooth out. "Of course, from periodic reports I've given you and other trustees you already know something of Stu's history, but unless you've been associated with him on a daily basis over a period of years as I have, you couldn't possibly know the whole story. That man is a menace to the Squier library."

"What do you mean by that?" asked Bragge, almost with an air of alarm.

The library director continued, appearing to ignore her question. "You know Stu doesn't have a degree in library science. He came into the library when he was 22 and no one on the staff had a library degree, including the former director. She, however, got her degree by going to library school part-time and working full-time. He's never seen fit to get the degree—he does have a B.A. in English—although others who joined the staff after him did get their master's in Library Science. In fact, he boasts that he knows more about library work than all of us who have our master's degrees put together. And, of course, he never passes up an opportunity to disparage us. He says the library science degree is a racket; that there's nothing taught in library school that can't be better learned on the job. And his definition of professionalism is interesting. He feels you should never question a professional—or at least him."

The chairwoman stopped him with a half lifted hand. "I don't for a moment doubt what you are saying, Arnold," she sympathized, "but I must ask you this. It's been bothering me for some time, and since we're speaking frankly I might as well bring it up." She learned forward and focused her eyes full upon his. "What mystifies me—" she paused, searching for the proper words—"what mystifies me is the hold he seems to have over you and the staff."

"It's not mystifying if you know him well," Carmichael reflected, shuffling uneasily under her steady gaze. "There was a time—under my predecessor—when he was the undisputed unofficial leader. He fully expected to get my job when she retired after 40 years, and was most disgruntled when he didn't. There was no question in the minds of the then trustees that he could have done the job—and some definitely favored him—but in order to qualify for state aid, as you know, the library must have in charge a graduate from an accredited library school. He doesn't even have the professional standing awarded by the state; he refused to apply when all that was needed was a degree and experience, and he wouldn't hear of it when the examination was introduced. The trustees and the former director never pushed him—or anyone else, for that matter. He still has 10 years or so to work—he's 55—and he'll never do anything about it. When I was appointed, he was made Associate Librarian as a gesture of some sort. No one on the staff reports to him. He does everything—reference, cataloging, selection, collection development—as a sort of 'floater.' There isn't even a job description for his position—and ours are in a state of disarray anyway. He has a lot of latitude to do what he wants. In complete fairness to him, he always keeps busy on things that have to be done, and he takes his turn at the reference desk like everyone else. He's never absent or late. He cooperates in every way—works two evenings a week, every other Saturday, and one Sunday afternoon in four. He even takes work home with him. He can't be criticized for his devotion to the place and the work he does – until yesterday."

A gust of wind flung a powder of snow from the window-sill into the room. Bragge got up and closed the window. She lingered there a moment and watched the cars move on the highway with a hushing swiftness against the cold gray sky. "Continue," she prompted, returning to her chair. "What happened yesterday?"

"Well, as you know, we usually close in bad snow storms. Stu looked out the window about eleven and saw that it was snowing. Fearing that he might have trouble driving home at five, the time he was scheduled to go off duty, he asked me for permission to leave immediately – he lives 12 miles away in a rather isolated area. I said the storm didn't look that bad to me, but that I would keep watching the situation and would give everyone notice if the snow got really bad. I also said that I would check with the weather bureau every half hour and with the schools. If the schools close early, we usually do, too. This didn't satisfy Stu. Shortly after lunch, he went home without permission. As it happened, the snowfall was moderate and all the rest of us worked all day and got home without difficulty. None of the schools closed early, either. He wasn't scheduled on the reference desk yesterday afternoon, so no one had to cover for him."

"Well, what did you do?"

"I spoke to him first thing this morning when I met him at nine in the foyer, and told him I didn't approve of what he did and that I didn't want such a thing to happen again."

"And ... and what did he say?"

"He listened to me and then said 'Are you finished?' and just walked away."

The woman sat up, as if stabbed. "What did you do?"

"I went to my office and had my secretary call him and tell him I wanted to see him in my office at once."

"And?"

"She came back and said he said he wasn't coming, that there was nothing more to say."

Bragge looked at him curiously, as if she meant to say something, then changed her mind.

He continued, "I waited half an hour, and then called your secretary to see if you were in. I asked him to notify me when you arrived."

"What did you do in the meantime – until I arrived, that is?"

"I worked in my office."

"Has anything like this ever occurred before?"

"Well, more or less. Whenever I've had to discuss anything with him about his work, he creeps into a shell and refuses to answer me. He's not amenable to correction – from me anyway. He takes a 'we've-been-through-this-so-often-before' attitude."

"You mean he doesn't pay any attention to you at all?" She was interested.

"That's his tactic – the silent treatment. Occasionally he argues." And then after an interval: "You see, that's why some people consider him the unofficial leader of the library. Nobody wants to cross him. If they do he becomes remote and unfriendly. He makes his feelings abundantly clear by sullen silences and glances that indicate complete disgust." Again, he stopped, this time shaking his head. "No," he resumed. "There's more to it than that – he becomes vicious, cutting people up behind their backs if they cross him in any way. I guess you'd have to say he has the staff cowed."

"I know his family is a power in town," the chairwoman commented. "I've had business dealings with them. When they speak, people sit up and take notice."

"That's part of the problem, but—"

The chairwoman clipped him off. "Don't staff members ignore him when he speaks against others—or challenge him?"

"No," responded Carmichael. "You see, they're glad it's not them he's complaining about. Some even go so far as to curry favor with him, to keep him off their backs. I find it disgusting. But I guess that's human nature."

The trustee said, "I've heard of things like this, but I never suspected they were going on at the library. Don't you cover this sort of thing with him in his annual appraisal?" Her tone expressed incredulity. Trouble slithering underfoot in the Garden of Eden?

The librarian shook his head sheepishly. "I don't give him appraisals," he answered truthfully. "I've found him always on the defensive; instead of taking my comments as well meant, he argues. He doesn't seem to want to hear praise either. Since appraisal forms don't have to be signed by the appraisee, I don't even bother filling one out on him. What good would it do? He's one of those people who can't realize that a problem exists."

"We're getting away somewhat from yesterday's incident," Bragge remarked suddenly. "You came over here as soon as my secretary told you I was in?" She glanced at the clock; it was 10:10.

"Yes. But there's one other thing I should mention. Just before I came over, one of the reference librarians came to my office and said he was going around calling me an incompetent. She said that morale would plummet among the rest of the staff if I permitted him to get away with taking off the way he did yesterday. She said they've tolerated his moods, his viciousness—everything else—but that this was the last straw. The staff frequently complains to me about him. She said they would lose respect for me if I didn't take some action. I have to do something, but frankly I'm not sure what." He was silent for a moment, his eyes on the floor; then timidly he advanced the thought that had come to him. "Would—would you speak to him?"

Bragge did not answer right away. She leaned back and stared straight into the core of the light above, her eyes squinting. "Arnold," she pronounced, bringing her eyes down to him and speaking very slowly. "Are you sure that's what you want?"

"I'm at my wit's end." He spread out his hands in a gesture of hopelessness. "You know I'm an easygoing person, but this has made me furious! I don't know what else to do." Silence again enveloped him.

Compassion shadowed the trustee's face—she could see he was desperate—and compassion was in her voice as she made answer: "All right, I'll go over this afternoon. I must warn you though that this might not solve anything. I'm not even sure I should be doing this—after all I'm only one trustee—not your only boss." And then, with hesitation: "I hope you won't take what I'm about to say to mean I doubt you, but there are usually two sides to a story. I'll regard this as an opportunity to hear his side—that's all."

On Carmichael's face came the look of one who sees the immediate fulfillment of a wish. "That'll be fine," he replied. "There is probably something to be said on both sides. There usually is."

After a few tangential remarks apropos of nothing, Carmichael left, a considerably less anxious person.

Seated later on opposite sides of the table in the trustees' room of the library, Wanda Bragge, in a friendly, impartial voice, expressing neither disapproval nor approval nor anything, asked Stuart Wronski about yesterday. He had greeted her courteously, as was his wont, and had inquired if she minded his smoking. She told him to go ahead and slid over an ashtray.

"I'm rather surprised that Arnold would have bothered you with such a trivial matter, Ms. Bragge," Wronski said with a reassuring smile which had an almost fatherly quality. "I don't think I did anything wrong." He adjusted himself comfortably in the chair, overlapped his legs, and blew a smoke ring that dissolved two feet above her head.

The chairwoman invited him to go on. This was what he said:

"Well, since I do professional work—and do it very well; no one can say I don't—I consider myself a professional librarian. Is it only the possession of a degree that makes a person a professional?" Then, without waiting for her answer, "Professional people don't live by the clock. They don't punch in and out. You wouldn't tell a doctor or a lawyer that he couldn't make a decision to call it quits on a particular day. As a mature, responsible professional I was acting quite within the bounds of proper professional behavior. I'm not a child, you know. Professionals are expected to be highly skilled and motivated, which I certainly am, so that little external surveillance over us should be required. When I asked to leave—and I really shouldn't have had to ask—I knew I was not scheduled on the reference desk. No one had to fill in for me. I do lots of library related work at home—particularly the selection of material—on my own time. I don't expect to be patted on the back for this—it's my job."

He smiled politely, but Bragge could not help but feel that his expression was one of low cunning. She sensed that something was wrong with his logic, but she was at a loss to explain it. She strained to think of something she had read about the difficulty of equating professionals who have considerable autonomy and professionals who are clearly subordinated to an administrative framework and have relatively little autonomy, but her memory stubbornly refused to perform the simple, necessary act of producing it for her. So she said nothing and moved on to another of Carmichael's concerns.

"Since I've been on the board," said she, "I've heard comments to the effect that you belittle other members of the staff. Specifically, I'm told you delight in putting down the professionals." And she added, quickly: "Those with degrees."

Wronski stared at her blankly.

"Do you have anything to say about that?" she questioned. The battle was joined.

"Arnold and the others are too sensitive!" he sneered, spreading his hands in a fantastic gesture of disdain. "Can't they see I'm just having sport with them?" Then he smiled, just a quirk of the corners of his mouth.

Bragge regarded him coldly. "But it bothers them," she asserted, hoping to draw him out further. But she waited in vain for any comment.

What a strange colloquy! It seemed unreal to her. Strange that so helpful and charming a person in his capacity as a librarian could behave so monstrously; but behave thus he did. His manner positively carried with it a chill as palpable as that now in the streets. Perhaps he had the protective coloring of the chameleon and the adaptability of the amphibian that can breathe both air and water. She began to suspect that his instinct of self-preservation was so strongly developed that he could without difficulty select the tone, the gesture, and the look that he felt would best serve his purpose.

It dawned on her that what she was doing might be a mistake, and she began to think of how best to extricate herself. She asked whether there was anything he would like to say.

"About what, specifically, Ms. Bragge?" he asked superiorly.

"About anything," was her exasperated answer.

Wronski remained silent for a moment, looking at the thin gray threads of smoke that were rising from his cigarette. "No-o," he answered, drawing out the word. "I can't think of anything."

An angry flush burned in her. She was overpowered by a feeling of impotence. How disagreeable this was. No wonder Arnold hates any contact with him. "Well, I guess that's about it," she heard herself saying. "Thank you for coming in."

"Thank *you*, Ms. Bragge," Wronski replied, squashing out his cigarette.

As they made their way to the door, she tried to give no indication of the emotions she felt. He let her pass first. They said good-bye.

She returned directly to her office. By the time she got there she had resumed her self-possession. She suddenly remembered the monthly trustees' meeting that night. She called the four other members and asked if they could meet with her a half hour early to discuss "an important matter which I would prefer not to mention over the phone."

In the half hour before Carmichael would join them, the chairwoman transmitted what had occurred. "What do you think about it?" she inquired. "And what should we do?"

The Squier Memorial Public Library has a staff of 24 people, which translates into 16 full-time-equivalents. No one on the staff belongs to a union. At the end of a six-month probationary period, letters are issued making employment permanent. There are seven librarians (including the director) with degrees in library science—three in reference, one in the children's room, one in technical services, and one in young adult service. Carmichael does not have an assistant; all professionals and other department heads report to him. Wanda Bragge has served longest on the board.

17

IN-SERVICE WITH A SMILE

The Mt. Rova Community College District is a 52-year-old system, consisting of five community colleges. The campuses are situated to provide maximum access to the million and a half residents of greater Mt. Rova. Four colleges have permanent campuses: Hayes Valley Community College, located near the center of town; Gould Park Community College, located 15 miles from the center of town on the southern fringe; Fieldview Community College, 10 miles to the west; and Pewabic Community College, some 20 miles to the north. The fifth, Trail Blazer Community College, utilizes classroom locations throughout the five-county, 500-square-mile area and has no permanent campus. These five colleges, each with its own president, staff, facilities, and distinctive characteristics, together enroll more than 20,000 full-time-equivalent students. They form a consortium that offers programs in the broad areas of general education, vocational technology, and personal and social enrichment. Their purpose is to provide the kinds of learning opportunities that will enable the area's citizens to correct educational deficiencies, to develop marketable skills, and to enhance their lives.

A five-member board of trustees governs the district, each trustee a resident of the district. The officers of the district are the five college presidents and three members of the central chancellor's office: chancellor, vice-chancellor of Planning and Educational Services, and district treasurer. Since the academic structure of the district involves five somewhat autonomous colleges and a central chancellor's office, the responsibilities and authority for academic programs are shared between the colleges and the chancellor's office, with recognition of different decision-making functions. It is the district's responsibility to provide an overall, comprehensive program of education and services suitable for all segments of the district population, and to assure that these offerings meet individual and community needs. The colleges, on the other hand, have responsibility for developing and operating all educational programs and services in their service area.

Each college (with the exception of Trail Blazer) has its own library/media center, with its own director, staff, and collection (Appendix I). The four directors report in a direct line relationship to the coordinator of library services, Edward L. Wood, who in turn reports to the chancellor. The chancellor and his staff, including the coordinator of library services, his administrative assistant, and his secretary, are located on the top floor of the main building at the Hayes Valley campus.

The administrative assistant position is a new one, and its first occupant, Booth Slye, has been on the job one week. Slye was recently graduated from a nearby library school, and this is his first professional position. He was pleased to accept the "staff" assignment, because it afforded him the opportunity to serve as apprentice to a man who has the reputation for practicing a democratic pattern of administration. The directors of the college libraries had verified this when Slye was interviewed, and attested to the fact that they felt free to make suggestions and to criticize policies and programs with impunity. Their recommendations, they had stated with pride, were discussed openly and acted upon whenever possible. On those few occasions when Wood had not been able to accept them or carry them out, he made thorough explanations. No evidence of resentment could be found toward the coordinator, who himself has only been in his position a year. The general opinion of Edward Wood seemed to be summed up in the words of one staff member, who said, "Ed Wood's a prince of a guy. You couldn't ask for a better boss or mentor."

By the exercise of all his persuasive skill, Wood had been able to convince the chancellor and trustees that the interests of the district would be better served if he had an administrative assistant to perform specified routine and detail activities and to carry out special assignments and projects. When the position was advertised, previous experience was not identified as crucial; hence Slye applied and was ultimately selected.

The new administrative assistant spent the bulk of his first week in consultation with Wood and visiting the four library/media centers. During one of their talks, Wood mentioned that he had been wanting for some time to discuss with the directors the possibility of implementing an in-service training program for their staffs. He went on to say that this was a topic for the next bimonthly meeting of the directors and the coordinator, which Slye would be regularly attending. If the idea of launching a program was accepted, it would be the administrative assistant's job to plan, organize, and implement it.

In his journeys around, Slye spent a few hours with each director, meeting staffs and touring premises. Each director possessed a library degree from an accredited library school. At Hayes Valley, he met Alma Pottie, a woman of 45, who had worked her way up to director in a period of 8 years from an entry position as cataloger; at Gould Park, he met Hugh Cermac, a man of 32, who had been a high school librarian until he took this position two years ago; at Fieldview, he met Kevin Bain, a man of 34, who had joined the staff of the Fieldview library/media center four years ago as reference librarian; and at Pewabic, he met Cara Argyle-Bates, a woman of 39, who had been director of a community college library in another state for six years before assuming the position at Pewabic seven years ago.

As soon as the minutes of the previous regular meeting had been read and approved, Wood proceeded to the first topic of new business — "In-service Training."

EDWARD WOOD: As you know from talks I've had with you individually, and from some of the books and articles I've been routing around to you, I've been thinking it might be a good idea to embark on some sort of continuing education training and development for our staff. We haven't done anything in this regard, and now that we have Booth with us, if we think it's worth exploring, we can get him working on it.

KEVIN BAIN, Fieldview: I guess one of the first things we have to do is determine why we would want to do anything — establish a purpose.

CARA ARGYLE-BATES, Pewabic: I think we have to decide – if we agree to do something – whether we want to include everybody on the staff or just the professionals.

HUGH CERMAC, Gould Park: We're jumping ahead of ourselves here. I'd like Ed to tell us what he has in mind before we start getting into the kinds of questions Cara and Kevin are asking. What *are* you thinking of specifically, Ed?

WOOD: I'm sure we're all in agreement that one of our functions as managers is to develop our people, to help them become what they're capable of becoming, and to help them better achieve their personal goals and at the same time the goals of the organization. I see training programs as attempting to do three things: impart knowledge, develop skills, and change attitudes.

ARGYLE-BATES: You know, I read in one of the books you routed around – and, by the way, I very much appreciate how you always do that before we take up a topic at our meetings – that training is often treated as a luxury and is undertaken when things are quiet. According to the author – I wish I could remember his name – it's usually given up, if it's ever started, when the demands of work make it inconvenient. Too many people subscribe to the idea in principle only. Who can be against training one's staff to make them more effective? It's like being against motherhood and apple pie. But still, as whoever it was points out, it's often considered a nuisance. If training is to be accepted, it has to be accepted by everyone on the staff.

BAIN: I don't think it will be – by everyone. I have some older staff members who would resist any form of formal education – if that's what we're talking about.

ALMA POTTIE, Hayes Valley: Could I suggest, Kevin, that that might be because they're afraid of failure and of not looking good. Older people have suffered some losses in sensory and physical capacity, and newer teaching techniques might intimidate them. There's a legitimate danger there, Ed, as I see it. I'd like to see somebody – Booth maybe – put something together on the characteristics of adult learners. After all, our people are adults and most of them have been out of school for a long time. Our training activities have to take that into consideration. Malcolm Knowles and J. R. Kidd have done quite a bit of work in this area. A summary of their findings would be helpful.

WOOD: Well, it would seem to me that one of the challenges of implementing a program of this sort would be to allay the fears of people who are anxious about learning. And I think everyone should be included in the planning stages. If they aren't, they won't have the same commitment to it. And not only that, they'll have some good ideas on how we should proceed and what we should do.

BAIN: I have to express my doubts about the effectiveness of training and development programs. The only way to learn a job better is to spend time doing it. Experience is the best teacher.

WOOD: In one sense you're right, but you must admit that when you live with one way of doing something you develop a rigidity toward it. This results in a lack of perspective. Which of the authors said that it's not sufficient to teach the "how" of a job without giving the "why"?

BAIN: I think practical experience is everything. All the theory in the world is meaningless if you can't *do* anything.

WOOD: No one'll argue that experience is not important, but it's not enough.

CERMAC: I'm still confused about what we're talking about here. Are you suggesting, Ed, that we should be identifying the skills and responsibilities that go with each job and evaluating peoples' abilities in terms of them?

WOOD: That's part of it, yes. One of the first things to be done is to identify individual training needs.

BAIN: If we're talking about programs that would take people away from their jobs for periods of time, then I see a problem. It's difficult to spare people for any stretch of time.

WOOD: True, but there must be ways. Before we go any further, let me attempt to sum up and try to state more clearly what I have in mind in laying this proposal before you. The purpose of training and development — and this is not original; I think I copied it down from somewhere, but I didn't write down the source — is for employees to acquire and maintain the necessary skills, capabilities, and personal capacities to more adequately contribute their services toward the fulfillment of their objectives and the objectives of the library. Newly hired employees need training to begin their work; and older ones need training to keep them aware of the changing requirements of their jobs.

BAIN: Can I interrupt for a moment? A couple of times, Ed, you've mentioned this business of employees serving the goals of the library and at the same time satisfying their own needs and aspirations.

WOOD: Yes.

BAIN: Well, there's a basic conflict between the objectives and needs of an organization and those of its employees.

WOOD: That's why I think training and development programs are important. They can help resolve this.

BAIN: It seems to me they're irreconcilable. The organization wants employees to be dependent and the employee wants to be independent.

CERMAC: I think Kevin's on to something there. Some training programs are designed to convert employees to the organization's point of view. To hell with their personal goals.

POTTIE: This discussion is getting off the track. Let's get back.

BAIN: I don't agree. I think it's highly relevant. And another thing, I'd like to hear of some successful training ventures. Perhaps, Booth, you could track some down and tell us how they've worked—what they've done, how they've proceeded, and so on.

SLYE: I'm sure I could.

ARGYLE-BATES: There's another thing to consider here, and that's whether training programs seek to prepare people for wider responsibilities or make them more effective in their present jobs. I'm a little afraid that if you prepare people to take on greater responsibilities you create false hopes that they're going to be rewarded by promotion or more money.

WOOD: I think the questions you all have raised are important and must be investigated. I have to admit that you've given me much to think about. I do think, though, that most people at all levels appreciate the opportunity to broaden their perspectives and improve their skills.

POTTIE: I'm concerned about something Kevin brought up earlier—the point about taking people away from their jobs for periods of time. I'm wondering who would coordinate the training and what methods would be used. We have to consider whether the programs—or at least some of them—would be "in house," or whether we'd send people to conferences or seminars and such. I also wonder what teaching techniques would be used.

ARGYLE-BATES: There's a lot of controversy over the best way to develop people—whether to lecture to them or have them participate in some way. I keep hearing about "business games" being used.

SLYE: The best method, it seems to me, depends on what's being taught, and the aim of a particular course. When Ed mentioned earlier about training programs attempting to do three things—impart knowledge, develop skills, and change attitudes—I think each would require a different methodology.

WOOD: True, and as a British writer has suggested, training and development programs include three types of training—induction training, job training, and development training.

POTTIE: He also says feedback and evaluation are important.

ARGYLE-BATES: You know, this discussion points up the need for us to have something to react to.

WOOD: I agree, and that's where Booth comes in. You can see from the discussion, Booth, that several things have to be considered. I've jotted down a few that came up and added a few that occurred to me while we were talking. This is not a complete list by any means. We have to determine whether the training and development will be for all members of the staff—professional librarians and clerical. Who will undertake it—outside experts, or us, or both? Will it be carried out on one of our campuses or off-campus? The library school that three of us went to is only 50 miles away; they might be doing something we could take advantage of. Library schools are doing quite a bit of continuing education.

POTTIE: And state library agencies, too.

BAIN: Could you find out about these, Booth?

SLYE: Be glad to.

WOOD: A couple of other considerations are: What would the objectives be? How can we create an atmosphere in which the idea of training would be accepted? How are training needs identified? What are the steps in developing a program? What learning methodologies should be used? What are the characteristics of adult learners? Who will coordinate all this? I suspect you, Booth! It's quite a list!

CERMAC: Good luck, Booth! I'd like to add something to your list if I could, Ed. It ties in with something Kevin suggested earlier about successful ventures. Could you, Booth, work up a few hypothetical outlines and give us illustrations of how a few programs might work? What I mean is, could you map out a few programs for us, showing us what they would consist of, who would participate, what they'd be exposed to, what methodology would be used—for instance, would we have people read articles or books before they get together? I agree we need a proposal to react to.

POTTIE: Good idea! Maybe, Booth, you could work up examples of the three types of training you and Ed mentioned. I think the more detailed you could be the better.

WOOD: That's a great idea! It would be of enormous help to us if you could put a few things together for us to look over.

BAIN: And if you could find some answers to some of the issues we raised!

POTTIE: I hate to burden you with more work, Booth, but if you have time and can fit it in I'd like to know not only what the characteristics of adult learners are, as I suggested before, but something about learning theories as well. It seems to me that this would tie in with the different types of methodologies you mentioned earlier.

SLYE: I don't promise anything, but I'll see what I can do.

ARGYLE-BATES: I'm quite excited about this.

WOOD: Excellent. Thank you all for your comments, and suggestions. Don't worry about money at this stage, Booth. That's not a consideration now. The agenda for our next meeting is quite full, but perhaps you could have something ready for us for the meeting a month from now.

SLYE: I'll certainly try.

WOOD: Good. Well, shall we move on to our next item of new business?

APPENDIX I

STAFFS OF THE MT. ROVA COMMUNITY COLLEGE LIBRARIES/MEDIA CENTERS

	Hayes Valley	Gould Park	Fieldview	Pewabic
Director	Alma Pottie*	Hugh Cermak*	Kevin Bain*	Cara Argyle-Bates*
Assistant Director	Kerr Watman*	Hazel Atcheson*		
Acquisitions	David Rush*			
Clerical Assistants	Ina Almeida, Louise Volkov, Wilma Sankey			
Media	Helga Stoklasa*	Dudley Cuxham*		
Clerical Assistant	Iona Freneau			
Reference	Lenore Willis*	Lois Buck*	Lillian Massey*	Manuela Lopez*
Reference Assistant	Maxine Supka*			
Technical Services	Eugene Saito*	Charlotte Dehaan*	Rodney Klein*	Effie Nhan*
Clerical Assistants	Mildred Bound, Wendy Ulrey, Iris Van, Daisy Hazzard, Lucille Mure, Kay Cheyne	Leah Traquair, Esu Hu, Lavinia Vogel, Lorna Hunter, Celia Baumann, Grace Legrand	Mabel Modeora, Isabel Nunn, Giselle Aimard, Rhea Beeching, Rose Ekwall	Xenia Payne, Mona Crowder, Sybil Hood, Mary Lilbourn
Student Assistants (FTE's)	4	3	2	1
Total Professionals	7	4	3	3
Total clerical	10	7	5	4
Student enrollment	7,440	5,870	4,020	2,670
Faculty	248	147	124	96

*Designates professional librarian.

N.B. No name beside a position means the library/media center does not have such a position.

18

O'BRIEN'S LUCK

"Ms. Modjeski's telephone, Ms. Giddings speaking."

"Hi, Joyce, this is Muriel. Would Polly have a few minutes for me right now?"

"She's in her office, Muriel. I'll check and see. Hang on a sec, okay?"

Muriel O'Brien, senior assistant librarian in charge of the Serials Department at Heaton University, tapped her pencil gently on the desk while she waited. Polly Modjeski is chief of Technical Services, her supervisor.

"Come right over," she heard the secretary say. "She can see you now."

"Be right there," said O'Brien, hanging up the phone.

The Serials Department consists of five people in addition to O'Brien: a Library Assistant I, Wade Erskine, and four Clerk-Typist II's, Inez Benefield, Merle Delaney, Sarah Vanzandt, and Zoe Tabary. There is also a student assistant who works the equivalent of one day a week, his hours spread over the entire week and his tasks are highly routine—unwrapping current issues, stamping with ownership marks, alphabetizing in bins, placing on book trucks, sending to check-in records, etc.

When she arrived at Polly Modjeski's office, Muriel O'Brien came promptly to the point. "You won't believe this," she announced, slumping into a chair. "Sarah was rushed to the hospital early this morning with a ruptured appendix and peritonitis. She'll be out for at least a month. What luck!"

The division chief's face expressed disbelief and honest concern. "Oh, no!" she gasped. "I hope everything's going to be all right for her. Give me a report as soon as you know."

O'Brien smiled a positive, and went on: "With Wade in traction and Merle having just had her baby three days ago, we're really in a bind."

Smothering an excusable curse, Modjeski asked: "How much longer is Wade likely to be out?"

"He thinks six more weeks."

The two women breathed a simultaneous sigh.

"Well, let's see now," said the division chief, her lips moving in silent calculation. "That leaves you, Inez, and Zoe. And you have some student help."

"Right," agreed O'Brien, "but there's not much the student can do." Then: "As you know, Sarah, Inez, Zoe, and I have been working two extra hours a day for several weeks, to try to keep up. And even with that we're way behind. Now with Sarah out, I don't know what we're going to do. I can't ask Inez and Zoe to work even more hours. They've been very good sports. I've been working every Saturday as well as two extra hours a day."

"I'm sorry about that," Modjeski said with a note of apology in her voice, "and I greatly appreciate what you're doing. Since we can't pay you overtime the way we do the clerks, I'll try to arrange some compensatory time when things get back to normal." And then, emitting a short laugh, "if they ever do!"

The two women reviewed the work the department had to do. Because serials contain the results of new research and scholarship, their prompt appearance on the shelves is essential. Their handling, from the time of arrival until they are made available, must be fast, efficient, and careful. In addition to their regular tasks, which keep them working at full tilt at all times, the major bill containing 89% of the 15,000 periodical titles received had arrived and had to be processed; also, each department head and division librarian had to be notified that it was time for renewals, cancellations, and new titles. They concluded that it would be impossible to do all this work without extra help.

Since a freeze on all hiring was in effect, taking on new people was out of the question; student assistants would not solve the problem because they cannot handle the complex problems involved in the work; but borrowing someone from another department loomed up a possibility—if anyone could be spared. Familiarizing the person with the procedures would consume precious time, but it was better than nothing.

"Let me call around and see if someone can be transferred in for several days, or possibly weeks," Modjeski suggested, her face lighting up.

Her expression turned progressively more solemn as one after another department head told her that it would be a virtual impossibility to part with anyone without leaving their own departments understaffed. "I hate to order anyone to give up an employee," Modjeski felt impelled to say as she returned the receiver to its cradle after speaking to the last person.

The two sat gravely in silence, Modjeski fingering the stars on her necklace while she thought. Suddenly a thought arose in her brain. "Didn't Justine Asadorian in the order department used to work in serials?" she almost shouted, with a sudden access of excitement.

"Yes!" returned O'Brien with eagerness.

"Well, I'll see if I can prevail upon Jack McSpadden to dispense with her services for a while."

The senior assistant librarian in charge of the order department, McSpadden, was sympathetic to O'Brien's plight, but he reminded Modjeski that releasing Asadorian would create problems in his own department. Once Modjeski heard him express sympathy, she knew she could wheedle him into acceding.

"Justine will be over tomorrow morning," she said, rubbing her hands with a complacent smile. "You're lucky because she's Jack's best person."

"That's wonderful!" said O'Brien, relieved. "She worked in serials before I started working here, but I know her."

"Good! Let me know how things are going," Modjeski requested as the other departed.

Justine Asadorian accepted the temporary transfer willingly; she remembered the work and performed it well. But at the end of the day—5:00 p.m.—as she got ready to leave, a problem arose. Inez Benefield and Zoe Tabary told her that they were working two extra hours a day, and that they were sure she would be required to do the same. Asadorian drew back and stiffened. She approached O'Brien and asked if she was expected to work overtime. O'Brien replied that she hoped she would.

"I'm not working overtime," said the employee firmly. "Nobody told me about this yesterday."

O'Brien glanced swiftly at the woman standing next to her. She knew from the peculiar expression on her features that she was extremely annoyed. She gave a little nervous laugh. "But we have a new deadline to work to," she said, as if to encourage her. "We've already had an extension. We've all been working a couple of extra hours a day. You'll get time-and-a-half." And then she added in a casual tone: "Is there any reason why you can't work overtime?"

The employee's answer came at once, perfectly certain, perfectly controlled. "I don't have to give a reason. Jack never told me about this." And she seized her sweater and purse and vanished.

Benefield and Tabary had been watching the encounter. They whispered to each other across Benefield's desk, and forthwith approached O'Brien. "We couldn't help but hear and see what happened, Muriel," spoke up Tabary. "We don't think it's fair that we put in all those extra hours and she doesn't have to."

"We've decided that if she doesn't work overtime, we won't either," warned Benefield. "It isn't fair."

"We don't have to remind you how we're inconvenienced by all this overtime, Muriel, but fair is fair," Tabary added.

"Having her for her eight hour day is better than nothing," O'Brien hastened to explain. But her words fell on deaf ears: The two employees remained adamant — either Asadorian worked overtime too, or they would not.

O'Brien prevailed upon them to stay that night with the promise that she would take the matter up with Modjeski first thing in the morning. They returned to their desks, unhappy.

Muriel O'Brien was in early the next day. Eight o'clock arrived and Asadorian was nowhere to be seen. Inez Benefield and Zoe Tabary had arrived on time and were working. O'Brien went to Modjeski's office, detouring by way of the order department. She spied Asadorian in earnest converse with McSpadden. She continued on, hoping they had not spotted her.

"We've got a problem, Polly," she proclaimed, entering the latter's office. "Justine refuses to work overtime. And Inez and Zoe say they won't anymore unless *she* does. And Justine didn't come to our department this morning. I saw her sitting with Jack as I came over here."

Modjeski made a gesture of annoyance and waited a little before speaking. "I'll get in touch with Jack and find out what's happening. Why don't you go back, and I'll call you later."

When she returned to her desk, O'Brien was acutely aware that her two staff members were wondering what had happened. Asadorian was not there. "Polly's looking into it," was all she said as she picked up a pencil and bent over her papers.

About an hour later she was summoned to Modjeski's office. When she arrived, Jack McSpadden was also there. They greeted each other courteously. O'Brien took a chair. They were all three seated around the division head's desk. No one spoke. Then after a minute that seemed like 10, Modjeski cracked the silence.

"Justine refuses to work in your department, Muriel, if it involves overtime," she said crossly. "She argues that it's not fair to her to be expected to work overtime, since she's on loan and not a member of your department. And Jack supports her in this decision. He doubts that you could borrow anyone who would agree to work overtime. I've called around, and he's right. Now what are we going to do?"

Heaton University is a large private university in the Southwest, with an enrollment of 15,000 students. All serials work is done by Muriel O'Brien and her staff. As head of Technical Services, Polly Modjeski supervises the following departments (in addition to serials): Cataloging, Order, Searching, and Mendery. The library staff is not unionized; contracts, which take the form of salary agreements, are issued annually. No mention is made of overtime being required in either the contract or the staff manual. Modjeski has 12 years service; O'Brien 1 year; and Asadorian 5 years. This is O'Brien's first professional library job.

CONTROLLING

19

THE TRYING-OUT OF LAURA CARPOZZI

On a Tuesday in September Dexter B. Rundle was walking up Church Street at about a quarter to ten. It was an incredible day, a warm and benign day of earliest autumn. The street was thronged by people who had not a moment to spare. Dexter Rundle had plenty of moments to spare, however, for his next appointment was not until half past eleven. He had transacted his first item of business much earlier than expected, and had decided to walk back to his office.

Dexter Basil Rundle is a vice-president of the Garrett National Bank in Garrett, a practical, progressive, hard-driving city of 122,680 in the Midwest. He is a small, slender man, with a pencil-thin moustache and whitening, scanty hair. His bespectacled face bears the marks of decades of administrative decisions and manipulating markets. His age is apparently about 65.

He had walked two miles, but he felt no fatigue. As he stood waiting for the lights to turn from red to green at the corner of Hawley Street, he glanced casually at the ill-balanced frontages of the buildings ahead that stretched on and on until they melded in an indistinguishable mass of gray at Lawrence Street. This section of Church Street between Hawley and Lawrence had always fascinated him. Hidden away in lairs behind the chaotic jumble of facades of all styles from stately Greek classical to the severe straight-line school of modern architecture, a thousand businesses plied their mysteries. The lights changed. He was swept across the intersection by a miscellaneous crowd of anxious, energetic persons in search of business or raiment or nourishment or whatever. When he reached the curb, he fell behind and began to stroll at a leisurely pace. He and a police officer who was controlling the traffic light switch agreed upon the fact that it was a glorious morning. He was happy, absurdly and splendidly happy. He regretted that he did not walk more.

Before the Garrett Public Library at No. 786 Church Street he stopped suddenly. He hadn't intended to stop, but he did stop. He had never before taken the time to examine the immense two-story granite structure of modified Romanesque design, with its massive arched and deeply recessed entrance generously treated with carved ornament. Astounding that he had never really noticed how beautiful the building was! He observed that despite its noble proportions it was somewhat drawfed by several colossal neighbors. Neither had he entered the building before—even though he had worked only a few doors away for 32 years. He and his family lived in an exclusive suburb of Garrett, and while he frequented its public library he never had occasion or reason to visit the larger one on Church Street. Some hypnotism beckoned him in, and since he was in no hurry he submitted to it.

He mounted the six broad steps to the entrance, passed through an "In" door into a vestibule, and then through a second "In" door into the vast interior. The cathedral-like hush contrasted strangely with the clamor and movement outside.

He noticed the circulation desk on his left, and on the wall to his right a display board on which were posted the multifarious events the library was sponsoring during the month. He stood for a moment and watched the calm, efficient activities of the circulation desk. At the end of the passageway he hesitated whether to turn to the left or to the right. He chose the right, and wandered down the corridor. Soon he found himself fronting a door, on which were elaborately patterned the words "Newspaper Room." It occurred to him that the library might subscribe to his boyhood hometown newspaper. He pushed open the door and stepped inside. The room was large, and contained tables, newspaper shelves, and leather-covered chairs. He saw that the papers were arranged alphabetically by city. Finding the one he was looking for, he gathered up several issues and found a place to sit.

So ensconced was he in his reading, as he told his lawyer later, that he forgot his 11:30 appointment. He saw a clock. It was 11:35. He picked up his briefcase, returned the papers, and hurried off.

As he strode assertively toward the exit, he noticed several people queued up to charge out materials. Since he had not borrowed anything, he made his way past them — to find himself accosted by a young man in casual clothes entrenched behind a desk. He had not observed the desk or the young man on the way in.

The young man pointed to him and said in a sharp, curt tone: "Let me see your briefcase." And simultaneously he curled his index finger up and down that in the vocabulary of his gesture was meant to signify "Come over here."

"I beg your pardon?" Rundle said, genuinely surprised.

"Open your briefcase!" ordered the young man impatiently. Whereupon he cocked his head in the direction of a sign above the exit, which read: "All bags, packages, and briefcases must be opened for inspection. Gladys R. Lachaise. Director."

"But I haven't taken anything out," the banker explained calmly. "I was just reading some newspapers."

"I have to see for myself," the checker maintained coldly. "Open your briefcase."

"But I'm telling you I'm not taking anything out," returned the banker in a low, controlled voice.

The young man looked at him, and he looked at the young man, and not a word was said.

Dexter Rundle thought:

"The day was progressing serenely. I was feeling not at all belligerent. Then I came within this disagreeable person's atmosphere, and lo! before I know what's happened I'm involved in an unpleasant altercation. Talk about charm! This fellow has about as much as a pailful of hissing snakes. (It was in such terms that his thoughts ran.) Why don't they give these people some lessons in common courtesy? Pointing at me! Tilting his head! No please! No smile! Commands! And he's dressed as if he just made a killing at a rummage sale! At 11:30 I was feeling that all was well with the world, and then at 11:35 I'm all tightened to a smarting tension by having been treated like scum. Such is my introduction to the great Garrett Public Library. I must remember this next time they canvass the bank for funds."

Finally, the checker spoke. "You can't leave until you show me inside your briefcase." This in a voice charged with bitter callousness.

While they were thus argufying, a few people had started to line up behind Rundle waiting to get out. Some of them were conversing together in soundless whispers. Rundle remained stationary, too confused to move.

"Let these people by!" shouted the young man with angry, exasperated brusqueness. Startled by the tone, Rundle obliged.

Laura Carpozzi, head of the circulation department, who was on the far side of the desk, heard the checker's outburst and espied the bottleneck in the stream of traffic. She moved over and asked if anything was wrong.

"This man won't open his briefcase for me," the checked answered resentfully, jerking his head in the direction of Dexter Rundle, who was standing off to the side as immobile as a statue.

Laura Carpozzi approached the banker with an equable, friendly smile. "The checker's just following instructions, sir," she said in her best diplomatic manner. "It's the library's policy that all parcels and briefcases be opened for inspection."

"I gather that," replied Rundle, with an air of tired resignation. He handed her his card. "But shouldn't you have a notice over the entrance informing people that they will have their parcels checked when they leave?" (This was accurate, Carpozzi reflected. The regulation is not posted by the entrance.) "And I must say I was appalled by the rudeness of your young man—his tone, his manner." The crowd has frittered itself away.

After a pause Carpozzi resumed. "I'm very sorry this has happened, sir," said she, with such an air of eager sincerity that Rundle glanced at her suspiciously. And then in a tone good-naturedly informing, "You wouldn't believe the number of people who try to make off with things without charging them out. That's why we have the rule."

"I understand that," Rundle said, relaxing his features, "but shouldn't my word be good enough?"

Her calm confident eyes silently invited him to relieve his mind, and he could not resist the temptation.

"You know," he said, hurrying the words out, "I wonder if what you're doing is legal. I wonder if this is not a clear case of unreasonable search."

Then he paused and adjusted his eyeglasses. "Your sign says that all bags and briefcases must be opened for inspection, and this is apparently authorized by the director of the library. But I question whether the library has the legal right to do it. I'd like you to tell the director—Ms. Lachaise, is it?—that I'll be back in a day or so to see her to challenge this policy. I'd do it now, but I'm late for an appointment. I'd also like to discuss with her this young man's atrocious behavior."

She could see that his improved humor was still precarious, still insecurely re-established. A clumsy remark on her part might bring down a storm of anger which should ruin all. Tact is essential at this juncture, she reminded herself.

"I can certainly understand your concern," she ventured, speaking with a certain amiable casualness which she hoped would keep the edge off his annoyance, "but we're really trying to protect the taxpayer's investment and the library's materials. Some items are irreplacable."

"Oh!" said Rundle, allowing a vague smile to flit across his face. "But, you know, this may be an invasion of people's right to privacy. And also I'm opposed to the idea of the innocent suffering for the guilty. It's my understanding of the Fourth Amendment that people and their possessions can't be searched unless law-enforcement officials have information that they've committed a crime. I'm going to check this with my attorney when I get back to my office. I'm not sure you're on secure ground when you frisk people's briefcases this way. But"—and here an acerbity entered his tone—"if you do have the right, then you should at least train your people to do it pleasantly. Really, that young man was terribly rude." He made this last comment in a lower tone, and emphasized it by an ominous frown.

Laura Carpozzi hesitated whether to comment further on the checker's behavior, or whether to let his comment stand. She was in a dilemma. She decided to say nothing, feeling that was the best thing to do under the circumstances.

Dexter Rundle went on:

"As I said I'm late for an appointment and have to go, but tell Ms. Lachaise that I'll be in touch with her." Then he added, yet again frowning, "You should do something about this young man's attitude. You should be concerned with the image he projects of the library. I'd never for an instant tolerate this kind of behavior in one of my employees."

He bade her good day and issued out into the street.

"Do you ever let anyone leave without inspecting their bags?" Carpozzi asked as she sidled up to the checker.

"Never," he answered quickly. "Mind you, quite a few people complain—like that old geezer—but they do it anyway. I've been called a few names. That's about it." He shrugged his shoulders indifferently, as if to say "So what!"

"Old geezer!" exclaimed Carpozzi, staggered, dumbfounded. She was on the point of saying "How dare you call him that?" but she checked herself and substituted, "That's no way to speak about a patron, Mike." He turned on her a look of sublime unconcern. Perhaps it was a ludicrously inadequate expression of her profound surprise; perhaps it was best for now to have said no more. But whence had that attitude toward patrons sprung? The young man's casual nonchalance utterly confounded her. Her face, which had been calm, changed and then composed itself again. She gave him one long piercing glance and started up the stairs toward the deputy director's office.

As she wended her way through the corridors, she pursued an inquiry with herself as to what she ought to have done with Mike. She ought to have—ought to have done what? Fired him on the spot? Blasted him for his incivility?.... She could not decide what she ought to have done. Anyhow, there was a problem with the checkers. She must pay them more attention and observe them more closely. Perhaps it wasn't Mike's fault. He and the others are put there without training.... But still what possible justification is there for unprovoked rudeness?

She reached the deputy's office. Yes, he could see her now. Yes, we've had a few complaints about checkers before. Yes, we must do something. Yes, perhaps Mr. Rundle has a point. Yes, let's check the rules and regulations which were established by the trustees when the library opened in 1902.

He produced the *Rules and Regulations for the Garrett Public Library*. The first part contained a short historical sketch of the library—how it was founded, who the first contributors were, etc., etc. The second part contained sections on the selection of trustees, the operation of the library, and the duties of the librarian. Under "Operation of the Library" they located the following statement:

"The Library shall be free to all residents of Garrett, who shall agree
to observe the rules and regulations adopted from time to time by the
Trustees and who shall comply with said rules and regulations at all
times."

After detailing the length of the borrowing period, the way people should "demean" themselves in the library, the hours of operation, the number of books that could be borrowed at any one time, and such, they came to Article 17, which read:

"Persons entitled to the privileges of the Library shall, upon request, open their parcels for inspection upon leaving the Library. Anyone who willfully or wantonly and without cause writes upon, injures, defaces, tears or destroys any book, plate, picture, engraving, or statue belonging to the Library shall be punished to the full extent of the law of the State."

Carpozzi, grinning from ear to ear, asked when a person would have cause to write upon, injure, deface, tear, or destroy a book, plate, picture, engraving, or statue. The deputy detected her satire, and wondered aloud why the authors would have appropriated that particular language. They laughed.

He then turned to the end of the pamphlet and read a short statement referring to amendments:

"These regulations may be amended at any meeting of the Trustees. The changes shall be entered in the minutes of the Trustees' meetings."

Pushing himself back in his chair, he concluded that the library had the right to inspect bags and briefcases, and as far as he knew (and he had been with the library 37 years) subsequent boards had not changed the rule. (He would check it however.) Carpozzi reminded him that Dexter Rundle was questioning the library's "legal" right to search personal belongings. The deputy said he would take the matter up with the director and get back to her.

In addition to the downtown library on Church Street, the city of Garrett is served by 7 branches and a bookmobile. The main library, which has the one public entrance and exit, is open from 9:00 a.m. to 9:00 p.m. Monday through Friday, 9:00 a.m. to 6:00 p.m. on Saturday, and 1:00 p.m. to 5:00 p.m. on Sundays; it closes 10 days a year for legal holidays. During the last reporting year, it circulated 947,578 items. The budget was $1,279,853, with $321,779 being spent on books, $29,554 on periodicals, newspapers, and microforms, $5,860 on binding, and $15,911 on AV materials; $717,699 was earmarked for salaries. The collection consists of 378,332 volumes, 1023 microforms, 6961 micro-fiche, 7934 reels, 978 AV-Recordings, 630 films, 1237 slides, 313 art reproductions, and 89 VF items. Books (save reference books), films, and recordings are the only items that circulate; stacks are open. Overdue materials are fined at the rate of $0.10 a day.

The "Checker's Desk" is staffed at all times by college students and other part-time help; they receive no training, are paid the minimum wage, and are permitted to read or study during slack periods. Mike, for instance, is a college student.

Laura Carpozzi became head of circulation three weeks ago to gain administrative experience in a large public library system. She had been a reference librarian in a small neighboring town since graduation from library school three years ago. She is 27. Her staff consists of 15 circulation clerks: 9 full-time (working a 37½ hour week) and 6 part-time (working anywhere from 15 to

25 hours a week, for a full-time equivalent figure of 2.3), as well as 22 checkers. She devotes half an hour a week to the checker staff, mainly scheduling; if checkers wish to change their schedules, they work them out among themselves. Her annual salary is $24,500, and she gets four weeks vacation. The circulation staff also looks after overdues — sending out reminder notices, making follow-up telephone calls, etc. — but does not read the shelves.

About four o'clock that afternoon, Carpozzi received a call inviting her to the deputy director's office. When she arrived, the director was there too.

"Come in and sit down, Laura," the deputy said, motioning for her to take a chair.

"You had quite an experience this morning, didn't you?" observed the director sympathetically.

Carpozzi straightened her shoulders and smiled. "I think Mr. Rundle would have come right up to see you if he hadn't had an appointment," she informed her. "He seemed quite annoyed."

Gladys Lachaise smiled, but said nothing.

"Laura," the deputy started, "Mrs. Lachaise had her secretary go through the minutes of the Trustees' meetings to see if the rule on inspecting belongings had ever been changed. It hasn't."

"It took her three solid hours," murmured the director, with a manufactured sweetness of tone.

"The question remains whether that rules and regulations document is legally binding," stated the deputy.

"It should be," observed the director. "The trustees are a legally constituted body with authority to make rules. And anyway I'm sure there must be state laws permitting libraries to detain people if they're suspected of leaving with hidden material. I know there are laws making it illegal to mutilate material."

The deputy director spoke:

"You might check a few states for us, Laura, to see how the laws are worded and to get chapter and verse. We have to be ready for Mr. Rundle!" Then, after a pause, "But we also have another assignment for you."

The young head of circulation waited in keen anticipation.

He went on: "We've been questioning our use of checkers lately. The incident with Mr. Rundle has brought the issue to a head. We know the checkers aren't catching everything. The last time we did a sample inventory, five or six years ago, the loss rate was 0.9%. What we did was determine the number of volumes lost from a sample number during a one-year period. We sampled every thousandth book. Now we'd like you to investigate theft detection devices for the main library — we'll worry about the branches later — and give us a report and a recommendation. Our thinking at this stage is that we'd like to eliminate checkers — unless of course as a result of your investigations you feel they're more effective than electronic checkers."

The director said:

"There are quite a few aspects to this assignment, and we feel it would be good training for you to get in and do the kind of digging necessary to come to an intelligent decision."

The deputy went on:

"What you come up with will be a preliminary plan, but we'd like you to try to anticipate everything that must be planned for — costs, training, implementation schedule, renovations in the charge-out area, and so forth. Use for now the 0.9% loss rate for any calculations you might have to make."

"Concerning that," the director counselled, "we should plan to measure the loss rate again. So we'd also like you to identify various reliable methods of inventory control, and suggest how we should do it this time."

"Also," the deputy put in, "feel free to redesign the circulation area. Leave the walls and doors as they are, however. If additional electrical outlets are needed, no problem. We'll be staying with our photocopying charging system." ("Our photocopying charging system" meant the Eastman Kodak Recordak Starfile Microfilmer and disposable transaction cards.)

Said the director in turn:

"You may find yourself needing some additional information in order to proceed, but maybe not. If you do, make a list and present it to us after you've done what you can. You should be able to do a cost-benefit analysis without any additional information, though. I've been working on next year's budget, and it would be fair to add eight percent to materials and salaries."

The deputy smiled. "We've been loading quite a few things on you, Laura! Do you have any questions?"

The young woman cogitated. "No, not right now," she said, and left a pause. "Well, maybe," upon more sober reflection. "Do you want me to consider costs and therefore recommend only the least expensive system?"

"I'm glad you brought that up," answered the director. "No! Go ahead and base your recommendation on what you think is best."

Carpozzi nodded.

The deputy director pushed back his chair and stood up. He seemed extremely well satisfied with the course of the discussion. "It will be interesting to learn if we could cut down appreciably on our losses with an electronic device. It will also be interesting to know not only what the initial outlay is likely to be, but the continuing costs compared to the checkers."

"And of course," said the director, brightening as his idea gave birth to another one in her mind, "it will be interesting to know how efficient electronic systems are at catching people." Then, taking breath for a new start, "I wonder if they've found ways to beat them!"

"Good point!" exclaimed the deputy. "And there's the legal question, too. We'd still be checking people. But I wonder if people object to them."

"Answers to all these questions should be in your report, Laura," commented Lachaise. "And while you're at it," she appended, as a sort of afterthought, "what about exposure to radiation? Frank Munch over in Parkwood was telling me that he has a patron who refuses to pass through his Tattle-Tape gate because this worries her."

"I've heard that people with cardiac pacemakers are concerned," said the deputy. "I've stopped having dental X-rays because small doses of radiation are supposed to be cumulative. There's much to consider."

"Well, Laura, it looks as if you have your work cut out for you!" remarked Lachaise, a knowing smile spreading over her face. She rose and started toward the door. "If there aren't any more questions, I'll be on my way."

"I have a pretty good idea how to proceed, Mrs. Lachaise," said Carpozzi, with an admirable assumption of light and easy casualness.

"Good!" said the director. And off she went.

As Carpozzi turned back to the deputy, she said: "I'll get right to this." And she got up and moved to leave.

"Feel free to consult me if you have any questions," he assured her, soothingly. "Make a list of them."

"Fine," she said, standing at the door. She signaled good-bye.

"Don't forget some sort of training program for the checkers!" he called out as she started down the hall. She smiled to herself.

When she arrived back at the circulation area, she noticed that Mike had been replaced by someone else. She proceeded to her office along the corridor and took a tape measure from her desk. She returned and walked up a few stairs in front of the desk. From an elevation of four steps she could survey all the details of the immediate area (Appendix I). There was a steady flow of people charging out materials, and the checker was inspecting their bags as usual.

The ceiling must be easily 15 feet high (she thought), and the recessed fluorescent lights provide excellent illumination. People can't get out the "In" door because there's no inside handle. Of course, if they waited until someone came in and then slipped through the open door they could. But the checker would catch them. I better count the number of electrical outlets and make some measurements.

Armed with the tape measure, she wrote down the following measurements:

Loan side of desk: 72"	Checker's desk width: 24"
Registration side: 72"	Left and right walls: 120"
Return side: 104"	Width from walls to desk: 54"
Loan side to exit: 48"	"In" and "Out" doors: 36"

She then looked for electrical outlets and found one on each wall, exactly halfway along; there were also three at the circulation desk: one at the floor level on the inside of all three sides.

Well, she mused, I guess I can get started now!

APPENDIX I

CIRCULATION FLOOR AREA

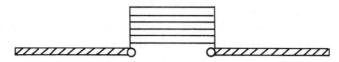

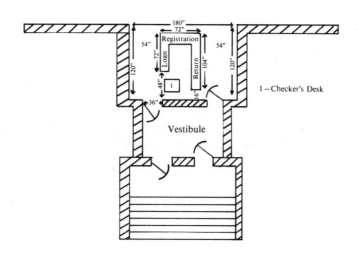

1 — Checker's Desk

20

TO PUFF OR NOT TO PUFF—THAT IS THE QUESTION

Gerould College, an independent and mostly residential co-educational undergraduate institution, is located on the outskirts of a peaceful, hideaway village in the Northeast, far from the rumbling tempo of industrialism. It was founded in 1891, and has a current student enrollment of 1,900. The 11 college buildings form a harmonious group in the Georgian style about an oval-shaped campus. The library, a detached two-story structure, is fast approaching the time when its useful life will expire. Massive architectural stairways and thick walls have given it a rigidity which has virtually precluded any rearrangements in the internal design. A new building program is in the "talking" stages, and in the meantime all the changes that could be made have been made.

The library office is in the basement, "downstairs" as it is euphemistically referred to, along with a staff lounge, the washrooms, heating equipment, and electrical and janitor's closets. The lounge, where employees take their breaks and lunch, is across the corridor from the office in a space 20x18 feet. Along one wall are a sink, an oven, a small refrigerator, a counter, and cupboards. The remaining walls are occupied by an assortment of comfortable chairs and sofas; a table which seats four is in the center of the room. There are two windows, accessible only by standing on an object, such as a chair, along the one outside wall. The college cafeteria is 10 minutes away by foot; members of the library staff seldom, if ever, eat there.

The library has a staff of 23 people—5 professionals, 11 clerks, and 8 student workers. The professional staff consists of a director, a cataloger, a technical services librarian, a media specialist, and a reference librarian. The circulation department is headed by a senior circulation clerk; he is assisted by two clerks and three students, who share two desks in the loan area by the entrance. The media specialist is assisted by two students; her department is behind the reference desk on the first floor. The remainder of the staff—13 people—is located "downstairs"; the director has a private office (14x14 feet) at one end of a large (80x42 feet) open rectangular room. The rest of the building is occupied by bookstacks, interspersed with tables and chairs. All employees make use of the staff lounge.

Juan Flores, the cataloger, and Blanche Demongeot, the technical services librarian, were waiting in the office of the director, Emma Ruttenberg. As Ruttenberg hurried in she said "Hi, sorry to keep you waiting. I was tied up in the library committee meeting longer than I expected."

"That's all right," Demongeot said, cheerfully. "Your delay gave me time to muster more ammunition!" Flores merely smiled.

"Well, what are we going to do about the smoking problem?" asked Ruttenberg, as she sat down. "I gather you're representing the smokers, Blanche, and you the non-smokers, Juan."

The two nodded assents.

"Well, let's hear your arguments," the director invited.

FLORES: I think smoking should be forbidden in the office and the lounge.

DEMONGEOT: Why the lounge, too?

FLORES: Because the air in there is always poisoned by smoke. The place stinks of cigarette smoke all the time. Even the furniture has taken on the smell of smoke.

RUTTENBERG: Now, you two! Let's try to talk this over calmly and coolly.

FLORES: I don't know if it's possible to be reasonable about this topic.

RUTTENBERG: Well, let's try to be, at least. Now how many smokers do we have, including me?

FLORES: Twelve.

RUTTENBERG: Of twenty-three. And how many work down here again?

FLORES: Seven. Two of my four people, three in Blanche's department, you, and your secretary.

RUTTENBERG: That leaves six who don't.

FLORES: Right. But all twelve smoke in the lounge.

DEMONGEOT: I'm very much resenting the suggestion that we stop smoking altogether during our working day. I don't think the college has the right to set standards on our personal habits—particularly in the lounge.

FLORES: I don't see why that bothers you so much. We don't allow smoking anywhere else in the library, and the students who study here seem to be able to survive.

DEMONGEOT: What you don't understand, Juan, is that smoking is a tension reliever. If we can't smoke....

FLORES: For us, it's a tension creator. Actually, it's more than that. For one thing, it gives Lily chest congestion. She probably hasn't told you, Blanche, because after all you're her boss, and she can't afford to fall from grace.

DEMONGEOT: Well, speaking of things like that, your Fred has often said that your exaggerated coughs and annoyed looks and the oh so dramatic flailing about of your hands and arms when he lights up drive him up a wall. Talk about tension creators. If that doesn't do it, I don't know what does.

RUTTENBERG: I don't like this at all. Let's be careful now and not go overboard. Let's discuss the issue without bringing in the names of other staff members.

FLORES: Okay, but I think that smoking should have a subordinate priority where the health and comfort of non-smokers is involved.

RUTTENBERG: No matter what we do, we're going to displease some people.

FLORES: I don't see why the smokers can't leave the building briefly when they want to smoke.

DEMONGEOT: Oh, great! I can just see us all standing outside when the temperature's ten below.

RUTTENBERG: What if we have carrels constructed for everybody?

FLORES: They'd have to be enclosed. The walls would have to go from ceiling to floor and have doors. Smoke has a habit of not staying put. It wafts into other areas. And how would the people in those cubicles breathe, anyway? There wouldn't be enough air.

DEMONGEOT: Even if we did that, we'd still have the problem of the lounge. But going back to the carrel idea. So much of our work involves talking to each other and passing things back and forth. You weren't serious about that idea, were you, Emma?

RUTTENBERG: Not really! I'm just thinking aloud, I guess. I forgot to ask how many of the non-smokers are bothered by smoking. How many complain?

FLORES: I'd say three in the office down here, not counting me. Two don't. I think there are also four among the other staff. Even the ones who don't complain say they have coughing fits at times, and itchy eyes, and headaches. Did you know that a non-smoker in an enclosed space can inhale the equivalent of one cigarette an hour?

DEMONGEOT: But there's no evidence to prove that non-smokers can get diseases from "second-hand" smoke.

FLORES: Boy, have you been brainwashed! You've been taken in by the tobacco industry. They'll say anything to keep sales up.

DEMONGEOT: Why don't you produce some proof that smoking is harmful to non-smokers?

FLORES: What good would it do? You'd merely neutralize my proof by producing studies to show it doesn't.

RUTTENBERG: Whether it does or doesn't is not the point here, right now. The point is we have a problem. And we have to do something about it.

DEMONGEOT: I think the question of harmfulness *is* important, Emma. If smoking causes heart disease, lung cancer, and emphysema, why do non-smokers develop them?

RUTTENBERG: I suppose the evidence is inconclusive. But in the meantime, I'd like to get back to our immediate problem. Don't you think, Juan, that when the reference librarian or somebody from the circulation desk comes down to the staff room after a tough morning, they should be able to put their feet up and enjoy a smoke?

FLORES: Well, we non-smokers also like to put our feet up and relax, too. But we have to breathe in their foul fumes.

RUTTENBERG: Separate facilities would be the answer, I suppose. But we have to live with the space we have. There simply isn't any other area in the building where we could segregate smokers from non-smokers.

DEMONGEOT: Maybe Juan and his merry companions would be happy to relegate us to the boiler room, or a janitor's closet!

FLORES: Sounds fine to me! That's the first time you've made sense today!

RUTTENBERG: Well, at least you're smiling now. But this is serious business. How about staggering lunch hours and break times? We could send smokers at one time and non-smokers at another.

FLORES: I don't know if that would work. As it is now, we don't have set times for breaks and lunch. That might be fine as far as the lounge is concerned, but what about smoking in the office?

RUTTENBERG: There's no official college policy on smoking. They're having the same problem in some of the other offices around the campus. They're all trying to negotiate some sort of compromise—like us.

DEMONGEOT: I've been making a list of possibilities while we've been talking. Here are the options as I see them. There are obviously pros and cons to each. First, we could possibly relocate the smoker and the non-smoker. Have the smokers at one end of the room and the non-smokers at the other.

FLORES: It wouldn't work. You have both smokers and non-smokers in your department, and so do I.

RUTTENBERG: Let Blanche finish her list, Juan.

DEMONGEOT: Take no action at all. Leave things as they are.

FLORES: Oh, that's a great one!

RUTTENBERG: Juan! She's just listing the possibilities.

DEMONGEOT: Set up "smoking/no-smoking" areas.

FLORES: How would that work in the lounge? The space is too small.

DEMONGEOT: Let me finish my list. Install smoke collection devices.

RUTTENBERG: What on earth are they? Are you being serious? Would people blow their smoke into a tube?

DEMONGEOT: I don't know, but there must be some sort of mechanical air flow system that could be installed. The next is to declare "no smoking" anywhere. But I don't go for that one at all. I think if some people couldn't smoke on the job, they'd be wrecks.

FLORES: I'm sure you don't like that one. Here's one you forgot: How about sponsoring a "kick the habit" program?

DEMONGEOT: Not all smokers want to kick the habit. Some of us enjoy it very much and are willing to take whatever risks there might be. As I said earlier, if we can't relieve tension through smoking, pressures will take their tolls on other parts of our bodies. We might become as irritable and unpleasant as non-smokers. Here's a good one. Instead of us kicking the habit, why don't you non-smokers join us and start smoking!

FLORES: Fun-ny!

RUTTENBERG: I'm glad we can laugh at this, but we still have the problem. And it is serious. I know about Lily because she has spoken to me. She said that the smoke is making her job unendurable, that she becomes physically ill. We can't ignore that. She said she's been thinking she'd have to give up her job if something isn't done. I'd hate to see that happen because she's a top-notch worker.

FLORES: I wonder if she did quit if she could slap us with a lawsuit. I know if we had collective bargaining, she could file a grievance. It would be interesting to see how an arbitrator would rule on the problem when the union would be composed of smokers and non-smokers.

RUTTENBERG: Well, fortunately — or unfortunately — we don't, so we have to solve the problem ourselves. But there's talk of unionization — for clerical staff and faculty.

DEMONGEOT: This is interesting. What if there was a union for non-professionals and an arbitrator ruled that smoking was prohibited, how would that affect the professionals who smoke? Would a union of faculty members have the same concerns? And if they did, what if they ruled differently?

FLORES: This is getting terribly complicated, but you're identifying some real problems.

DEMONGEOT: You see, I'm not at all sure what the relationship between management and a union is. Who's the boss when there's a union? I'm not at all clear on that.

RUTTENBERG: I think that as long as one employee felt strongly about smoking, the arbitrator would have no alternative but to rule that everyone had to stop smoking.

DEMONGEOT: Does that mean then that everyone—professionals and non-professionals, faculty and staff, union members and non-union members—would have to abide by the clerical staff's arbitrator's decision? Who would be the boss—management or the union? And which union. The staff's? The faculty's?

RUTTENBERG: I'll be frank. I don't really know what the relation is. I've never been a member of or worked with a union. But let's find out. It's almost certain apparently that the clerical staff of the college will unionize, and the library clerical staff will doubtlessly be invited to join.

FLORES: Well, we still have our problem here—without a union. What are we going to do? Are there other options in addition to those Blanche outlined?

RUTTENBERG: Isn't it interesting how problems compound the moment you set out to solve them! We started off with the smoking dilemma, and now we have the union and collective bargaining problem to look at, too. Since unionization is inevitable, it's incumbent upon us to know in advance what we're dealing with. In the light of none of us being sure what management's rights are when there's a union, I'm assigning you both the task of finding out!

FLORES: See, Blanche, the trouble you smokers cause! Now, we've got more work into the bargain!

DEMONGEOT: No comment.

RUTTENBERG: Okay, look, here's what I want you to do. I want you to find out what we as administrators and supervisors can and can't do under collective bargaining and union contracts—for staff and faculty. Some labor-management relations act or other must spell this out. As good librarians you both will have no trouble tracking down this information! And on the smoking problem I want next time we get together for you to present me solutions—not problems. It seems to me that if I'm going to make decision makers of you, you must take a stand in favor of one option over another. I think what we've done is fine—identify options. I'm not sure we got them all, but at least some were brought out. Now decide on one—each of you separately. Then have a "fall-back" one if we can't accept your first choice. And so on. I want each of you next time to select a solution and be prepared to defend it.

DEMONGEOT: When'll we get together?

RUTTENBERG: Same time a week from now. In case, by the way, you're thinking I'm passing the buck to you, I'm also going to try to solve this problem on my own. I'll present my solutions at the same time you do yours. Also, I'll look into the union/collective bargaining problem, too. We'll compare notes. Now, anything else you want to discuss?

FLORES: Not me!

DEMONGEOT: Me neither.

RUTTENBERG: Okay, I guess that's it. Bye.

21

THE ORDEAL OF ZACHARY TAYLOR PONDER, JR.

The day had started wrong for Zachary Taylor Ponder, Jr. First, he had slept light and slept badly. Then early in the morning it had begun raining—a cold, steady, autumnal downpour. And then he had nicked himself shaving, so badly that the styptic pencil had failed immediately to do its appointed task, delaying him so that he had to wolf down his breakfast, the eggs of which had on them a crust which he hated. As he stepped onto the porch on his way to the garage, he stumbled over a chair, upsetting a vase of flowers and soaking his trousers. He went back into the house, addressing his Maker in low agonized tones, changed, and started out again. This time he made it unscathed to the car.

As he drove to the library, he harkened to those busy inner voices filling his mind with ominous portents. Today—Friday—after four days as director of the Earnscliffe Public Library, he was to receive back from the town manager the budget his predecessor had prepared. His predecessor! He shuddered when he thought of the budget Dennis Baldwin had put together. The man had stayed on the job a mere month and a half—just long enough to do his damage. "Not your fault," Ponder tried to convince himself as he navigated the glistening slippery streets. Thereupon he rallied, and with an air of accepting the inevitable turned into the library parking lot and went to his office.

"Mr. Ponder," his secretary announced as he picked up the intercom, "I just got a call from the town manager's secretary. She said Mr. DeJong has looked over the budget and is returning it with a few comments and suggestions. She said he has to have it back in a week, with new figures if you're going to submit any. A week takes us to November 7th."

The something that had ached in Zach Ponder all week and which he thought he had finally quelled, started aching again. His pulse rate increased alarmingly. This is what he feared: changes and short notice. "Might as well face the music," he said resignedly. "Would you go over and get it, please?" He went back to the report he was reading.

Earnscliffe, an outsprawled town of 18,109, lies in a saucer-like setting of wooded hillsides in the northeast region of the country. It enjoys a relatively placid existence as a well-appointed dormitory for thousands of commuters to a large metropolitan area of 250,000. It is far enough from this core city (27 miles) to live independently; and while it does have some light industry of its own—mostly metal, lumber, and paper products—its unhurried atmosphere and quiet shady streets camouflage all signs of mercantile activity.

In the very center of Earnscliffe's small business district of conventional, suburban-type stores is the Johnson Memorial Public Library, a two-story brick and granite Victorian adaptation of Italian Renaissance design. Erected in 1872, it opened in 1873 when Eleazer B. Johnson, a wealthy landowner who established the city's first paper mill, cut the ceremonial tape and declared that "henceforth all who seek to educate themselves shall have the opportunity in this, Earnscliffe's public 'university.' "

Not unlike many municipalities in these inflationary times, Earnscliffe is feeling the pinch of a severely high general property tax—i.e., the tax on real estate and personal property, both tangible and intangible. For the present calendar year, it is set at $86.00 per thousand, 100% evaluation. Since the manager has predicted that it might increase another $11.00 next year, the finance committee has been charged by the community with the responsibility of trying to "cut corners" wherever it can. The manager himself has advised department heads to "try to hold the line" in his general guide to developing estimates.

With the federal and state government preempting the high-leverage taxes tied to growth in national income and to inflation, the city is left with a very slowly growing revenue base. In recent years, Earnscliffe's revenues have grown about 5 percent per year. (These are the costs of merely "staying even"—e.g., wage increases and price increases in purchased items.) And to make matters worse, retirees on fixed incomes, who are a somewhat heterogeneous aggregate—the people of Earnscliffe show a population-age distribution close to the norm for the state, with 11% 65 years of age or older—have recently presented the manager and selectmen with a petition deploring the soaring property taxes and asking them to exercise more constraint in preparing next year's budget. All in all, the financial picture in Earnscliffe looks grim.

It was against this background that Zachary Taylor Ponder's predecessor prepared the library's budget estimate for next year (Appendix I). Dennis Baldwin had started at Johnson Memorial in September of this year, directly from library school. He had worked part-time in a large city library while working on his degree, and had applied for the director's job in Earnscliffe in July—almost as a lark, for he did not think he had a chance of getting it. He was surprised and flattered when he was accepted. From what Ponder could gather he made an excellent impression on the trustees, who selected him over more experienced applicants because they felt they could work with him. To their chagrin, he was not on the job a month when he announced that he was leaving. At the same time that he was being interviewed for the Earnscliffe job, it appears he was also interviewing for a similar job on the west coast. The trustees of the west coast library were slower in reaching a decision, so he took the Earnscliffe job in case the other, which was his first choice, did not materialize. Town employees do not sign contracts in Earnscliffe; they merely exchange letters. Therefore he felt free to leave. But the manager and the trustees were livid.

Zachary Taylor Ponder, Jr. had been the Earnscliffe trustees' second choice for the director's position, and when they learned they would be needing another director they contacted him. He had been assistant director of a library comparable in size to Earnscliffe, but in that capacity had never prepared a budget. Hence his apprehension.

The secretary arrived back and presented Ponder with the budget. She lingered in the doorway of his office for a moment, while he gave it a quick glance. "Yipes!" he cried. "He's shredded it."

"Look bad?" Doris Suttie questioned, with simplicity.

"Terrible," was Ponder's reply. "Just as I suspected." He forced a smile. "I have a lot of work to do this week."

"I'll be more than happy to help in any way that I can," Suttie offered. "I can stay late to type for you, if that will help."

His smile broadened. "That means a lot to me, Doris. Thanks. Right now, though, I'd like to study it more carefully. I'm sure we'll be in touch a lot this week!"

Suttie took her departure, repeating the offer. Ponder gave her a friendly salute and resumed his examination of the document and the manager's letter (Appendix II). His face wore a look of studious concentration.

The annual town meeting, which is held each spring, is the principal governing authority of Earnscliffe. In the fall of the previous year, the process of budget preparation begins. Department heads estimate their expenditures for the coming year and submit them to the town manager, who approves or disapproves them. The manager's major task is to shape the individual requests into a combined budget and to measure the requests against expected revenues. He establishes priorities among the proposals and determines where cutbacks, if necessary, will be least painful. If a department's budget is approved immediately, it is incorporated in the combined town budget; if it needs to be amended, it is returned with the manager's suggestions as to how and where it could be changed. It is then re-worked by the department head and resubmitted. If the manager approves it this second time, it then becomes part of the combined town budget. If not, it is returned again and reworked until it is acceptable. And again, if necessary. The town manager's combined budget document is accompanied by a budget message, which explains the policies followed in its preparation, identifies significant items, and estimates the tax rate and revenue program necessary to support the proposed expenditures.

The next phase in the process begins when the finance committee receives the document. The committee's usual practice is to hold hearings at which department heads and the manager answer questions. The committee members are free to accept, modify, reduce, or add to any part of the budget. Their recommendations carry considerable weight with the citizens, and their final product as presented at town meeting is usually approved without major change.

In the case of the library budget, the director also secures guidance from board members. It has been their policy to require the director to submit a draft to them for review before submitting the final document to the manager. They typically modify it before giving it their approval. This year, however, due to time constraints and the fact that Baldwin left so precipitately, they were forced to submit figures they were less than satisfied with.

Thus it was not with surprise that the chairman of the board, Father Francis X. Banion, answered his telephone to hear Zachary Taylor Ponder, Jr. say:

"Father Banion? Zach Ponder here. I just received the library's budget back from Owen DeJong. He really did a job on it!"

BANION: How are you, Zach?

PONDER: Aside from the fact that we have to get this back to Owen by next Friday — fine! How about you?

BANION: Not too bad, thanks. Well, Owen isn't entirely pleased with what we submitted?

PONDER: That's for sure.

BANION: I'm not surprised. We all knew we were asking for too much, but we went along with what Dennis prepared because he was late in getting it to us and Owen wanted it before we had a chance to scrutinize it carefully. That Dennis! When I think of him, I ... well ... to put it frankly, cringe. It doesn't seem ethical to me that a person should accept a job and leave after a month and a half. It would seem to me that a person is duty bound to stay with a library for at least — the very least — two years. No matter how much more another job pays or how much more a person would like another part of the country or another job, the person should stay put for a minimum of two years. Well, that's not solving our problem. What do you plan to do?

PONDER: I thought I'd try to redo the whole thing. I don't like the justifications and I'm not sure some of the figures are realistic. Owen suggests in his letter that he doesn't see how we could ask for more than he's approved. I interpret this to mean he might be persuaded to approve a bit more.

BANION: You're optimistic, Zach. I don't. Those of us who have been around longer know that you can only increase your budget by about the same percent as previous years. What did we increase it by this time, percentage-wise?"

PONDER: Fifty-eight percent.

BANION: Good grief! Totally unreasonable. In fact, preposterous.

PONDER: Well, if I may suggest so, Father, I don't think you people should have approved it.

BANION: We had no choice. Dennis, after much pushing, finally got it ready two days before it was due in Owen's hands. We barely had a chance to look it over. We asked for an extension, but Owen said to send it over as it was. He said he had to have it to get a preliminary figure for the town's budget. He said *he'd* give it a careful going-over.

PONDER: Well, now he's giving *me* a week.

BANION: Well, you have something to work with, and you have Owen's suggestions. Can't you seclude yourself and do nothing but work on the thing for the week?

PONDER: That's my plan.

BANION: Good. Now here's my suggestion. You try to have something to show us next Friday afternoon. I think you should stay with Owen's figures, unless you can spot something obvious that should be changed. What you can do is find out, too, how we compare with other libraries in the Northeast in terms of per capita expenditures, circulation — everything. You'd know better than I what "everything" is. I'll call a meeting of the board and we can go over it then. I'll also call Owen and see if we can get an extension. Even a few days would help. If we could meet next Friday, and then again the following Wednesday we could get it to him for the following Friday.... Yes, that's what I'll do. I'll ask him for a week's extension. I'll call him now and get back to you.

PONDER: Okay.

BANSION: Bye for now.

PONDER: Good-bye.

A shock of resistance and antagonism went through Zachary Ponder. He was overcome by the sinking realization that he was going to have to work day and night to prepare something he could be proud of by next Friday. He arose and began walking the floor. "Better get to it," he said to himself, resuming his chair. He leaned toward the document and began to go through it page by page.

"I can do it," he said to himself, with a certain amount of aplomb which years of dealing with problems had given him.

The telephone rang. "This is Zachary Ponder," he said cheerfully.

"Father Banion, Zach. I spoke to Owen. He says he'll give us a week's extension."

PONDER: That's good news. It takes some of the pressure off.

BANION: He said again that we should pare it down to something much more in line with his figures. Perhaps you could do this by reevaluating some of the things Dennis felt we needed and by cutting down on some of the accounts.

PONDER: From my quick survey of the figures, I think that will be hard to accomplish in all cases. But I'll see what I can do. You know I do wish we didn't have to fit the library's budget into the town form. You know what I mean?

BANION: The form that all departments use?

PONDER: Yes. We all have to fit our special needs into the accounts on the form. For instance, you know that we put books under "Other Commodities?"

BANION: I agree with you, but what alternative do we have?

PONDER: Well, I wonder if I could do something different.

BANION: Meaning what?

PONDER: I don't know exactly. Call things by their proper names, perhaps.

BANION: Well, I tell you what. It's a good idea. Why don't you go along with the town form this time and afterwards, after we've submitted the budget and had it approved, work up something else. Other libraries must use line-item budgets and must have found a way around this.

PONDER: I also feel the justifications and the individual account descriptions which Dennis wrote could be improved upon considerably. I know I can't do everything I would like to in a week, but maybe afterward I could come up with something better.

BANION: Sounds good. In that regard, I'm not at all sure a line-item budget is best. I keep hearing about PPBS and zero-based budgeting. How would it be if after you get our budget in you look into the possibility of informing the trustees about other types of budgets, and showing us how they could be used by taking some aspects of our present budget and demonstrating the differences. Perhaps you could take an account — I don't know too much about it — and show us the difference under line-item, PPBS, and zero-based? Perhaps there are other possibilities, too.

PONDER: I'd be glad to. I think we need something else. Maybe we could set aside a couple of trustees meetings for this purpose.

BANION: Splendid! Oh, by the way, before I forget. What did Owen do about the bookmobile?

PONDER: He cut that out. Father, I find it surprising, to speak frankly, that even with the little time you had you would have let that go through.

BANION: Well, at least it made the manager aware of our need. You know of course — or maybe you don't — that suggestions for branch facilities have always been turned down over the years. We have a large area to cover here — 36 square miles. We've been talking about a bookmovile. Parking's a problem around the library, as you know. And we've been thinking a bookmobile would take the library to people rather than making them come to us. I know Dennis didn't do much of a job in presenting it. Now, there's another item for you to investigate. What sort of planning has to be done? How much do they cost? What's the upkeep? There must be all sorts of considerations which Dennis obviously didn't go into. There's another item for you for one of our regular meetings.

PONDER: I know I'll have to get to that question sooner or later. During the short time I've been here, people have broached the topic of a bookmobile with me.

BANION: Well, I wouldn't expect you to be detailed in your report in terms of where it would stop around town and where you'd park it! At this stage, we'd be interested only in knowing enough about them so that we could make an informed decision as to whether we wanted to even consider going after one. Right now, all the trustees know is that there *are* bookmobiles. We don't know anything about different types, or how one would go about planning for one, what has to be considered, costs. That sort of thing.

PONDER: I'll get to that, I promise! But right now I have a budget to work on!

BANION: There's no hurry, obviously, on the bookmobile question, but keep it in mind.

PONDER: Perhaps trustees' funds could be used for a bookmobile.

BANION: I'm glad you brought that up. This budget you're preparing is strictly the appropriation we're requesting from the town. It doesn't include reference to any other source of funding.

PONDER: Yes, I know that.

BANION: By the way, what are your thoughts on "padding" a budget?

PONDER: By that you mean putting in some expendable items, knowing they'll probably be eliminated in order to get more money? Well....

BANION: Don't answer that now. We should discuss it as a group. I'll let you get to work. If you think I can be of help, don't hesitate to call.

PONDER: Thanks. But I'll see how I make out. I'll keep you posted. I'm going to try to do a much more creative effort than Dennis did, within the confines of the town's budget format.

BANION: Sounds good. It would be very useful for us to have you offer a critique of Dennis's budget, where you think it's weak, making suggestions for a new proposal, and of course coming up with the actual figures you think we should submit now. I'm truly sorry about this ordeal by fire. But I want you to know we certainly appreciate what you're doing. We'd be lost without you.

PONDER: Thanks for the kind words. I'll be in touch.

BANION: Now don't forget I'm here if you need me. I'm as close as your phone. Call me if I can do anything. Bye.

PONDER: Bye.

APPENDIX I

JOHNSON MEMORIAL LIBRARY BUDGET
(as submitted by Dennis Baldwin)

Departmental Description and Background
The Johnson Memorial Library provides books and nonbook materials which will best serve the interests, needs, and backgrounds of people of all ages in the community as they seek self-education, build life-long interest in books and ideas, further formal education, meet informational needs, and find wholesome recreation.

The library implements these objectives through the effective organization of materials, through specialized service to children, young adults and adults through booklists, displays, and group programs. It reaches out beyond its four walls to support the educational, civic, and cultural activities of community groups and organizations.

Statistics
The figures below portray graphically the very significant growth and gains made in the library.

Library Circulation

Prior year	Last year	This year
139,876 (actual)	148,980 (actual)	16,900 (estimate)

Total Book Stock at End of Year

89,015 (actual)	93,714 (actual)	98,400 (estimate)

All Registered Borrowers

9,109 (actual)	11,001 (actual)	12,400 (estimate)

Volumes Cataloged

3,816 (actual)	4,029 (actual)	4,500 (estimate)

CLASSIFICATION	EXPENDITURES				
	Prior Year Actual	Last Year Actual	This Year Actual	Next Year Dep't Request	Proposed Manager Request
Personal Services	148,700	168,200	189,800	283,240	218,040
Contractual Services	28,070	29,880	33,260	37,230	35,230
Commodities	31,130	34,650	39,900	49,550	46,050
Equipment Outlay	700	720	830	47,090	1,090
Total Expense	208,600	233,450	263,790	417,110	300,410
Personnel					
Regular	10	10	11	17	12
Part-time*/Seasonal	10	11	11	16	13
Total Personnel	20	21	22	33	25

*Includes Pages

APPENDIX I (cont'd)

BUDGET JUSTIFICATION

1.1 Regular Salaries and Wages

The increase in the salary figure is accounted for by the following personnel changes.

Reference Librarian. The public continues to make increased demands on our reference services and personnel. We are proposing that Ms. Myers be changed from part-time to full-time so that our reference staff can be freed up for other important tasks such as community development, work with special groups, and readers' advising. No statistics are kept on the number of reference requests, but we know they have gone up.

Bookmobile Librarian. It is evident that we need some way of getting out to the public. Parking has become a problem around the main building and it would be difficult this year to find a suitable location for a branch facility. The bookmobile would meet this need to bring the library to the people.

Children's Room Circulation Clerk. Mrs. Kellogg, our Children's Librarian, is forced to spend most of her time at the circulation desk in the Children's room because she does not have the help she needs to administer that important part of the operation. The additional hours that Miss Hill would give us would mean that Mrs. Kellogg could function more as a professional librarian.

Assistant Custodian. It is imperative that we add an additional custodian to our staff. Mr. Shand works from 8:00 a.m. to 5:00 p.m. and gets some help from our male pages. He opens the library on Saturdays but does not stay during the day. The staff has to close the library at nine o'clock at night and this means having to go around and turn off all the lights and make sure the windows are closed. It is also at night that we have discipline problems with our young people and it would be nice to have a man around to help control them.

Cataloging Clerk. At the present time we are grossly understaffed in the cataloging department and our cataloger is forced to spend a good deal of her time performing clerical tasks. An extra person would mean that we could get rid of the backlog of books that continues to pile up.

Bookmobile Driver. The reason for the driver is self evident.

1.2 Overtime Reserve.
Quite often during the course of the year various emergencies will arise, such as accidents, sickness and sudden demands on the library. During these periods the part-time help is occasionally asked to put in extra hours to meet these emergencies. The salary levels for part-time personnel do not cover these unforeseen contingencies, so we are asking this year for a sum to meet this need.

1.3 Part-time

Circulation Clerk. Due to increased circulation, our circulation staff has been stretched to the limits of its resources. There are times now when we need two people on the circulation desk at the same time, but we have no one to assign.

Pages. This year we would like to raise the rate of page salaries from half the current minimum wage to the minimum wage. We are also asking for four additional pages. Use of our materials by the public, particularly periodicals and magazines, which are in the basement area and hence not open to the public, has

APPENDIX I (cont'd)

increased to such an extent that our present pages are finding it difficult to keep up with the daily demands made on them.

1.4 Seasonal
Summer help from college students has become a vital part of our operations. We have always taken on one summer student ($300) to replace desk personnel during vacation time, but this year we plan to undertake a complete inventory, clear registration files, and change the cataloging scheme in the Children's Room. Two additional college students ($800 each) would accomplish this.

2.1 Utility Services
Fuel $10,000
It is difficult to estimate fuel costs these days, but this should get us through the year.

Electric $8,500
With the fuel adjustment costs going up steadily this figure may well be conservative.

Water $50
We receive two water bills a year, each just under $25.

2.2 Communications
With a growing staff a few more telephones will have to be added.

2.3 Transportation
This covers the traveling expenses of the staff members to seminars, children's, young adult, and adult conferences, to state association meetings, and so forth. With a larger staff and increased participation in these functions additional funds will be needed.

2.4 Out-of-State Travel
This sum will cover attendance at the American Library Association meeting and the regional association meeting; the latter is attended by several staff members.

2.5 Advertising
This year we hope to do a good job of publicizing the library through posters and other such means.

2.6 Dues
This amount covers our contribution to the American Library Association and the local library association. This membership is valuable for it brings all the publications of the various sections and divisions. This opportunity enables the staff to keep abreast of professional developments.

2.7 Binding
With our collection growing the way it is and increased use being made of our

APPENDIX I (cont'd)

materials, more and more volumes have to be sent out for rebinding. Binding costs continue to go up, but it is still more economical to rebind than replace.

2.8 Maintenance of Buildings & Improvements

The following items make up this account.

1. Normal building maintenance and repairs	$4,000
2. Improve lighting in cataloging area	750
3. Replace skylight over main reading room	1,200
4. Carpet young adult room	2,000
5. Three display bookcases ($350 each)	1,050
	$9,000

Explanation

1. Normal building maintenance and repairs. This covers the costs of supplies which would be used by the custodial staff, i.e., paper towels, paint, light bulbs, floor wax, soap, mops, brooms, etc.

2. Improve lighting in cataloging area. The cataloger and her staff are located in a very dark corner of the building.

3. Replace skylight over main reading room. The skylight leaks and several of the panes of glass are cracked. Mr. Shand and I feel that it would be wiser to replace the whole window rather than repair it. To repair it would cost about $120.00.

4. Carpet young adult room. We are requesting this because we feel carpeting would help stifle the noise that sometimes emanates from this room. The staff also feels that the room needs to be made more attractive; bright carpeting would help. The area is 44x49 feet.

5. Three display cases. These are to be situated near the front entrances of both the adult room and the children's room. The idea is to draw attention to recently acquired books.

2.95 Other Contractual Services

Charging Machine Rental (2 at $180 per year)	$ 360
Charging Machine supplies	1,960
Postage Meter rental	130
	$2,450

3.1 Office Supplies

This account covers all the secretarial and office supplies needed by the adult and children's staffs during the year.

3.3 Operating Supplies

The costs of operating supplies (plasti-clear jackets, record jackets, maga-files, attaching tape, etc.) has gone up considerably in price in the past year. As we grow larger we need more of these supplies.

APPENDIX I (cont'd)

3.6 Repair Parts-Equipment

This account covers the costs of replacing parts in the audiovisual equipment—film projector, tape recorder, etc. The costs of maintaining our typewriters also comes from this account.

3.8 Minor Apparatus and Tools

The following items are requested:

1. A mimeograph machine (to prepare our own booklists, flyers, lists of holdings, etc.)	$ 800
2. Sign Printing Machine (to prepare our own posters, directional signs, display notices, etc.)	1,300
3. Electric typewriters (at $700 each)	1,400
	$3,500

Explanation

Items 1 and 2 are being requested because we feel that the library could be doing a much better job of publicizing its wares.

3. At the present time there are no electric typewriters in the library. I would like to get one for my secretary and one for the cataloging section, equipped with a special library keyboard. We feel that electric typewriters do a far better job than manual ones.

3.9 Other Commodities (Books and Materials)

Since we are forced to adapt library operations to the Town budget forms (which does not have a heading for books and materials) we put them in this account.

The prices of books and materials continue to mount. A look into the standards for public libraries would show us to be considerably below the suggested level for libraries our size in books. The public has come to expect that we will have a wide and varied selection of new material, which means a greater obligation to try to serve. The people of Earnscliffe have the opportunity to move the Johnson Memorial Library on to greater heights by granting the money to strengthen our collection. There comes a time in the life of any institution when it must forge ahead or, perforce, mark time, or, worse, retrogress. We cannot afford to mark time.

This account also covers the "Sundries" items (petty expenditures and postage), and $2,000 of the total is for sundries. (It has remained the same for years.)

4.1 Machinery and Equipment

Considering the far-flung nature of our city, the problems with parking around the main library building, the lack of branches, the need to bring the library to the people, we are requesting a bookmobile. We have looked into the prices of bookmobiles rather carefully and have concluded that the most reasonable expenditure would be $46,000.

APPENDIX I (cont'd)

4.2 Office Equipment

The following items are also requested:

1.	Book vans (3 at $90 each)	$ 270
2.	Additional magazine rack	350
3.	Rotating fan for cataloging area	150
4.	Slide projector	320
		$1,090

ANNUAL BUDGET
PERSONNEL DETAIL AND SALARY CALCULATIONS

	Current Budget	Dep't Request	Proposed Manager
Position Title & Name			
FULL-TIME			
Library Director Dennis Baldwin (P)	25,000	27,500	27,500
Assistant Librarian Jill Earle (P)	18,000	19,800	19,800
Children's Librarian Ruth Kellogg (P)	16,000	17,600	17,600
Reference Librarian Edna Lawson (P)	16,000	17,600	17,600
Reference Librarian Ethel Scott (SP)	13,000	14,300	14,300
Circulation Head Karen Prescott (NP)	12,800	14,080	14,080
Cataloger Gloria Payne (P)	16,000	17,600	17,600
Secretary Doris Suttie (NP)	9,500	10,450	10,450
Custodian Ralph Shand	11,200	12,320	12,320
Circulation Clerk Jean Godden (NP)	10,500	11,550	11,550
Circulation Clerk Rita Skelly (NP)	9,800	10,780	10,780

P — Professional
SP — Sub-professional
NP — Non-professional
*Change to full-time
N.B. — Staff benefits are not included since they are paid by the town.

(Annual Budget continues on page 264)

APPENDIX I (cont'd)

	Current Budget	Dep't Request	Proposed Manager
Position Title & Name			
PART-TIME			
Reference Librarian* Mildred Myers (P)	8,400	16,800	8,400
Circulation Clerk Grace Polk (NP)	4,900	5,390	5,390
Cataloging Clerk/Typist Amy Lang (NP)	4,800	5,280	5,280
Children's Room Circulation Clerk* Laura Hill (NP)	4,900	9,800	9,800
Pages	8,200	12,500	8,900
Summer Help	800	2,400	800
NEW POSITIONS			
Bookmobile Librarian (FT-SP)	-	16,000	-
Assistant Custodian (FT-NP)	-	10,900	-
Cataloging Clerk (FT-NP)	-	12,000	-
Bookmobile Driver (FT-NP)	-	12,000	-
Circulation Clerk (PT-NP)	-	5,390	5,390
Overtime Reserve	-	1,200	500
Total	189,800	283,240	218,040

P — Professional
SP — Sub-professional
NP — Non-professional
*Change to full-time
N.B. — Staff benefits are not included since they are paid by the town.

APPENDIX I (cont'd)

ANNUAL BUDGET

DETAIL

Ac.#	Account Classification	Prior Year Actual	Last Year Actual	Current Year Actual	Next Year Dep't Request	Proposed Manager
1.1	Regular Salaries & Wages	126,800	141,800	157,800	224,480	173,580
1.2	Overtime	-	-	-	1,200	500
1.3	Part-time	21,100	25,600	31,200	55,160	43,160
1.4	Seasonal	800	800	800	2,400	800
	Total	148,700	168,200	189,800	283,240	218,040
2.1	Utility Services	12,750	14,250	16,550	18,550	18,550
2.2	Communications	1,300	1,450	1,650	1,800	1,800
2.3	Transportation	350	390	450	650	650
2.4	Out-of-State Travel	700	700	700	700	700
2.5	Advertising	200	200	200	400	400
2.6	Dues	120	140	160	180	180
2.7	Binding	2,500	2,700	3,000	3,500	3,500
2.8	Maintenance of Buildings & Improvements	7,700	7,600	8,100	9,000	7,000
2.9	Maintenance of Equipment					
2.95	Other Contractual Services	2,450	2,450	2,450	2,450	2,450
	Total	28,070	29,880	33,260	37,230	35,230
3.1	Office Supplies	250	300	350	450	450
3.2	Food, Drugs & Chemicals					
3.3	Operating Supplies-Bldgs. & Improvements	2,500	2,800	3,100	3,500	3,500
3.4	Repair Parts-Bldgs. & Improvements					
3.5	Operating Supplies- Equipment					
3.6	Repair Parts-Equipment	80	80	80	100	100
3.7	Operating Supplies- Construction					
3.8	Minor Apparatus & Tools	800	870	1,370	3,500	2,000
3.9	Other Commodities	27,500	30,600	35,000	42,000	40,000
	Total	31,130	34,650	39,900	49,550	46,050
4.1	Machinery & Equipment	-	-	-	46,000	-
4.2	Office Equipment	700	720	830	1,090	1,090
4.3	Other Equipment					
	Total	700	720	830	47,090	1,090
	GRAND TOTAL	208,600	233,450	263,790	417,110	300,410

APPENDIX II

THE TOWN OF EARNSCLIFFE
INTER-DEPARTMENTAL MEMO

October 30th

To: Zachary T. Ponder, Jr.
From: Owen H. DeJong
In re: Budget for Johnson Memorial Library

I realize that you had nothing to do with this budget request, but I can't forebear remarking that I was amazed to see such an incomplete request for a bookmobile. Needless to say, I eliminated it. I would, however, be happy to discuss with you and the trustees the possibility of a bookmobile, but before we do there is a lot of "homework" to be done by way of preparation.

I have made several cuts, as you will see. If you and the trustees feel that some items should not be touched, I would be willing to consider your suggestions — *as long as you do not exceed my total figure.* In other words, feel free to work within that figure. The Finance Committee is not likely to view with favor the percent of increase my figure represents over last year (13%), but I think I can get them to accept something close to it. I make no guarantees, however. And I'm not sure, given the fact I must have your resubmitted budget back by November 7, that you will have time to do much more than accept what I have proposed.

The descriptions of and justifications for the various items leave a lot to be desired. I would appreciate it if you would begin to think of how the supporting data and justifications could be strengthened.

Personal Services. I don't think the circulation figures warrant the additional staff being asked for. Could you not attempt to streamline operations and undertake time and motion studies? If we are getting pages at the rate we are paying them, is there any need to up their pay? I know we have no trouble recruiting pages, and I'm sure we're not obligated to pay them the minimum wage. You might check that. Could you not keep a tally of the number of reference requests so we could have something to go on? Is there enough work to justify a second custodian? The library has been able to get along fine with one for a long time. Why a second all of a sudden? The reason given is weak.

Maintenance of Buildings & Improvements. I don't think carpeting would accomplish the stated purpose. Eliminated.

Minor Apparatus & Tools. Why not use our mimeograph machine? After all, we're only a short block away. Ours is not used all the time and I'm sure one of your staff would not lose much time running things off here. Eliminated. Why not get one electric typewriter this year and request another next year? I have eliminated one.

APPENDIX II (cont'd)

Other Commodities. I would rather keep this item more in line with the previous years' increases. We have a pretty good collection on what we have been allocating for books and other materials. I have taken $2,000 from this account.

I have tried to be reasonable with the request. My budget represents a 13% increase over the present year, which is not bad compared to some of the other town departments this year. If you can pare it down, however, I feel we will encounter less opposition from the Finance Committee. As it stands now, the library budget will represent 2.9% of the operating expenditures for the town. I think the per capita support is excellent.

OHDeJ/ct

22

GIFTED CHILDREN AND OTHER CONCERNS

In 1793, Hurley Barnes and his family sailed down the Lewark River in a small boat. Stopping a few miles north of where the Lewark meets the great Modoc River in what is now called the American midwest, they constructed a humble cabin and began trading with river men and friendly Indians. Before long the tiny settlement attracted wagon caravans from as far as 100 miles distant, and the town of Middlebourne was formed. But it was the railroad that brought Middlebourne to life. This, coupled with its ideal location at the confluence of the two rivers, predestined the town to become important as a distribution and shipping point and also a manufacturing center. The years from 1850 to 1900 witnessed Middlebourne's growth from a community of 10,000 to a city of 40,000, its present size. (A profile of the City of Middlebourne and the Middlebourne Public Library, which is given to all new library employees, is in Appendix I; Appendix II is the American Library Directory entry for the Middlebourne library.)

Carol-Lyn Hungerford was considered to be a leader in Middlebourne. She had stepped down as president of the League of Women Voters several years ago, and for the last year has been serving as a member of the board of trustees of the Middlebourne Public Library. So significant were her contributions to the library and the board that last night at their annual organizational meeting the trustees elected her president, this in spite of the fact that several other members with longer periods of service were interested in assuming the role. Nonetheless, her election was unanimous.

The next morning, library director Nicholas R. Magro, sat in his office musing over the previous evening's activities; he was pleased that Hungerford had been elected. And yet, could an eavesdropper have participated in the secret operations of his mind, the eavesdropper would have perceived that Magro had uncomfortable qualms of apprehension. The reason? Carol-Lyn Hungerford was the mother of a precocious seventh grader named Steven, who, as she enjoyed pointing out on more than one occasion, had demonstrated an IQ of 145, thus placing him intellectually far ahead of his co-students. The proud mother, as a result, had been a leader in the fight to establish a program for the "gifted and talented" in the public school system, and on several occasions had suggested to Magro that the public library should offer some sort of "gifted and talented" program. Magro was on record as subscribing to the view that the public library as a democratically based public institution had no business using a disproportionate amount of its resources to support an elitist program for a tiny minority of the community. He was sure that he would be hearing more about the gifted and talented, but he also believed that he was not the only decision maker in the library. Therefore, he decided to discuss the problem at an upcoming meeting of department heads scheduled a week hence. He issued a memo indicating his desire to add the subject to the agenda which already contained three items: fines, programming, and information and referral. He asked department heads to "carefully consider" whether a program for the gifted and talented at the Middlebourne Public Library might reasonably be developed. He further suggested that in preparation for the meeting they prepare themselves by "dipping into" the literature of the subject. After all, he thought to himself, "I may be making a mountain out of a molehill in this thing. It may not be as bad as I see it."

The appointed time for the meeting arrived. The following were seated around the circular, glass-covered table in the "Trustee's Room": Glenn Alvey, head of reference; Carlis Marr, head of circulation; Sheri Prince, head of branches; Cathy Sabo, head of adult services; Audra Vanek, children's librarian, and newly appointed (two days) administrative assistant, Judd Mesbacher. (Frances Lowell, head of technical services, was absent due to illness.) Magro had set up an easel with a large paper pad on it in one corner of the room.

The director welcomed Mesbacher, who was attending his first staff meeting, and reminded everyone that the new appointee had for the past three years been a reference librarian in a public library in a community of 20,000 in a neighboring state since graduating from library school.

NICK MAGRO: You've all received the agenda as amended. Since this will likely be a long meeting, I suggest we postpone approving the minutes of our last meeting. The sequencing of items on the agenda is of no particular importance, but I would like to suggest that since two of the four items are trustee initiated we might start with them. Can we zero in on the "gifted and talented?"

Hearing no objections the director continued:

I want you to know that for some time Carol-Lyn Hungerford, who incidentally was elected board president last week, has been suggesting that we start some kind of a program for the "gifted and talented" at the library. I've never followed up on her suggestions, but now that she is president I suspect we'll be hearing more about it. Carol-Lyn makes no bones about the fact that she's interested in providing opportunities for her son, Steven, but to her credit I know she's genuinely interested in all kids in town with Steven's abilities. Steven's in the "gifted and talented" program at school and apparently is often bored. It's too bad because, as many of us know, Steve is a really nice kid. The reason I've never done anything about his mother's suggestions is that I have a gut feeling that such a program does not belong in a public library. But I know we're soon going to have to either refuse to get involved on the basis of some pretty strong arguments, or develop a program.

AUDRA VANEK: Well, why not do something, Nick? I thought the public library existed as a resource for all people in the community. It puts on programs for film buffs and young adults; why don't we do something for the intellectually superior? After all, it seems to me that the Library Bill of Rights says something about selecting materials for all people of the community.

GLENN ALVEY: At least the schools do one thing right, in my opinion. They do try to provide "enriching experiences" for these kids rather than make them skip grades. A 12 year old in college is kind of lost. And we at the library are in a position to provide something extra.

CATHY SABO: Some kids are more "equal" than others, Nick. Why not recognize this fact and help where we can. But not everybody agrees with you, Glenn, about enrichment being better than having kids skip grades. I remember reading recently about Michigan State University accepting a 12 year old student.

CARLIS MARR: I read something that Bruno Bettelheim said about this. He contends that gifted children are perfectly capable of taking care of themselves, and if they can't then they aren't gifted.

MAGRO: That's an interesting thought. Well, since I asked you to do a little homework on the subject, I thought I might do some too. I called Dr. Coup, the superintendent of schools, and asked him how a child got into their gifted program, and what they did with these kids. He told me—somewhat apologetically I think—that students are selected by their score on an IQ test. If they achieve around 130 or above and have the recommendation of two teachers, and their parents are willing, they're in. He said they try to arrange special visits to cultural institutions and attend concerts, and that the kids have an opportunity to speak with people connected with the event afterwards. This sort of thing happens about four times a year. Also, the students are encouraged to explore subjects of interest to them in their school libraries and report on their investigations, either orally or in writing, to a teacher who serves as a kind of counselor or mentor for the project.

MARR: Well, I see a problem already, or rather several of them. I think IQ tests are pernicious. I don't trust them. For one thing, whether or not they accurately identify bright WASP kids, it's a known fact that they're grossly deficient in identifying talented minority children and, for that matter, girls. They help perpetuate racism and sexism. For another thing, to the best of my knowledge IQ tests do not differentiate between different kinds of giftedness. Believe it or not, success in school is not the only kind of success possible or even desirable in this world.

VANEK: I think you've made some important points, Carlis. If I'm not mistaken the military decided some time ago that IQ tests were a poor predictor of leadership qualities.

SHERI PRINCE: I thought that a formal definition of "giftedness" might be helpful. Actually I came across several, but I'll give you the one which was established by the U.S. commissioner of education. It reads:

> Gifted and talented children are those by virtue of outstanding abilities capable of high performance.... Children capable of high performance include those with demonstrated achievement and/or potential in any of the following areas, singly or in combination: (1) general intellectual ability, (2) specific academic aptitude, (3) creative or productive thinking, (4) leadership ability, (5) visual and performing arts, (6) psychomotor ability.

ALVEY: That's a definition that makes some sense. I like the idea of broadening the definition well beyond the limits of academic performance. I guess the problem is, how does one identify potentially high performance in these other fields? The schools really have a problem.

MAGRO: Perhaps since they have only an inadequate measure of only one of the five characteristics, the schools ought to recognize their inability to deal with the problem and give up. If the schools can't do a half-way decent job, how can the public library be expected to contribute anything constructive?

ALVEY: You know, another thought's been running through my head, now that you mention a relationship between us and the schools. It seems to me that one of the strengths of the public library insofar as attracting patrons is concerned has always been that it was completely free from the constraints of structured formal education. We're the "people's university." To ally ourselves with formal education in this or any other way might possibly compromise this position. Even though we were asked to by the truant officer we don't even report school age children who are in the library during school hours. If by being identified in the popular mind with a few gifted youngsters we compromise our ability to attract blue collar workers, for example, I think we'll have done ourselves irreparable harm.

VANEK: Who knows if that would actually occur? It's anybody's guess.

PRINCE: You know, one theme seems to surface again and again in the little reading I did, which may tie in with the previous thought. Many writers seem to spend a fair amount of time either accusing "gifted and talented" programs of being elitist, or defending them from such a charge. You find school board members announcing that it's simply not the responsibility of the public school system to deal with this kind of child, and you find a PTA in an east coast community, whose public school system has close ties with a highly prestigious graduate school of education in the area, giving money to a "gifted and talented" program only on the condition that the program be open to all. But what really bothers me about the whole idea is that by labeling some kids gifted the schools are also ipso facto labeling others as being less gifted. I remember reading about a program out west where the gifted formed an elite class with special privileges. They were taken out of school for special trips while the other kids had to remain. You can imagine how those who couldn't go felt, many of whom worked as hard or harder than the privileged few. It was almost like predestination, and predestination stinks. The author of the article saw an element of self-fulfilling prophecy in the program.

MAGRO: I must say I like the idea of programs for the gifted which are open to all. Teachers should broaden all children's knowledge and understanding, not just a select few. I agree with those who say that an educational system should provide opportunities and rewards for individuals of every degree of ability so that all will achieve their potential.

SABO: Yes, the world contains a great diversity of people, children with adult mentalities as well as adults with juvenile mentalities, and perhaps we need to recognize this and serve both groups as best we can. This kind of philosophical basis makes a lot more sense than the idea that we must nurture the gifted child today because he or she will become the leader of tomorrow. This bothers me on two counts, one because it smacks of exploitation and, two, because a fair number of the world's leaders, for better or worse, Winston Churchill, Albert Einstein, and Adolph Hitler to name but three, were remarkably successful as leaders in spite of less than outstanding academic records. Which goes to show that talent for academic work is only one variety of giftedness.

MARR: You include Hitler?

SABO: I said for better or for worse, Carlis.

MARR: OK!

PRINCE: I read a really fine article by a man who argued that all children are gifted and that the purpose of education is to promote excellence in as many forms as possible. I buy that. It seems to me I picked up somewhere the idea that Japan has a national policy of encouraging creativity, and the upshot is that Japan is now called a country of 115 million overachievers. It's perhaps like applying the Pygmalion theory nationally; if you assume everyone will perform well and do your best to help them to do so, lo and behold! everybody does perform well, or nearly everybody. The literature of education and management doesn't lack instances of the Pygmalion theory working.

MAGRO: Well, we've certainly had an interesting discussion, but we really haven't related the problem to the library and Steven Hungerford. We've discussed educational theory because it's the school system that, for better or worse, is selecting the students. The question is, what do we at the library want to do? What can we do? As a matter of fact why don't we consider the kinds of things we might possibly do without worrying too much about philosophical bases. When we've developed a list of possibilities, we can go down it and relate particular activities to whatever philosophical basis seems reasonable.

In due course, the following 19 ideas were found scribbled on six sheets of paper which were taped to the walls of the room. The process of originating ideas was based on the "immediate suggestions" segment of a George Prince "synectics" exercise. Magro asked Mesbacher to copy them down and said that he would explain later what he wished his new staff assistant to do.

    1) Allow all students access to entire library; remove age restrictions.

    2) Guarantee quiet, undisturbed carrels for independent study.

    3) Make it easy for students to use area specialized and higher education libraries.

    4) Strengthen collection of "how-to-do-it" books and programmed materials for individual instruction; keep some on reserve.

    5) Strengthen collection of games, riddles, etc.

    6) Work with student to prepare individualized reading program.

    7) Offer instruction to students on techniques of developing an individualized reading program.

    8) Student could sign a contract with public library (or media center, or teacher) that a particular subject will be investigated using public and other libraries.

    9) Library works with history teacher and students to develop local oral history tapes for public library collection. Students interview townspeople. School media specialist and public library media librarian provide expertise.

    10) Library sponsors a mini-course for students on how to use a public library in order to find answers to one's own questions.

11)   Library sponsors a book club to encourage the reading of fiction or nonfiction generally or in specific interest areas.

12)   Through reading club library encourages the development of a critical approach to reading.

13)   Library sponsors a creative writing club.

14)   Library sponsors a special interest club (e.g., puppets, drama, video, film).

15)   Students can help review and select materials for the public library.

16)   Student group prepares with help of public library staff a slide/sound or videotape presentation on some subject (e.g., how to find what you want in the public library).

17)   Students can produce bulletin boards, posters, displays, games, etc. for the public library.

18)   Public Library can arrange expeditions at reduced cost to museum exhibits, concerts, etc. It can also arrange for crafts people, authors, etc. to be visited by students.

19)   Public Library can develop an individual learning program whereby it matches up students who want to teach something with students who have a yen to learn something; library serves as a clearing house.

After a brief coffee break the department heads resumed their seats.

MAGRO: Well, let's get started again. Programming's on the agenda because one of our trustees objected to the program Sheri Prince did at the Wayne branch on sex education. He wonders why we do any programs anyway. He convinced our new president to have the board discuss the advisability of programming at all, especially since we had a film showing last month that drew only three people. We certainly lost keeping the building open for that program. Just for the record, last year we put on 97 adult programs with a total attendance of 1,788, and 231 children's programs which attracted 3,634 kids. A total of 87 non-library meetings were held in our hall by a variety of community organizations.

VANEK: Programs are vital to working with children in the library. A child's attention span is short. We need to interest them. We need to get them in and keep them. The programs we devise come from my agreement with the philosophy that children's library services should be to some degree socially oriented. This includes books of course, but programming efforts should meet the needs of Middlebourne's children. The children love the puppet shows, the movies, story hours, contests. The shows from the Kissippi Children's Zoo are always well attended. We have pet shows, book discussions, crafts, almost whatever is requested or thought of. The idea of stopping programming for children is ridiculous!

PRINCE: There's no way I would favor doing away with all programming. The children's things Audra puts on at the branches are well attended. The adult programs at both branches seem well received by the area people, though some are attended by the same group of people all the time—book discussions, for instance, and the crewel group. No one new ever seems to show up no matter what publicity goes out. They're like clubs.

MARR: We have no coordination with programs—no plan. I think "one shot" programming only works for a time. If we're going to program to any significant degree beyond occasional children's work, we may be at the point where we need to discover what the city wants and needs and put together a rationale for programming.

ALVEY: What is the purpose of programming? When we did the genealogy programs for people with German ancestry a couple of years back, I read that programs could be given either to get people into the library to interest them in traditional services, or get them in as an end in itself. Are we interested in programs oriented toward books, or programs for their own sake?

MAGRO: When the library gets deeply into programming, funding becomes a problem. Often such things need to be funded through foundations or local businesses. Glenn's genealogy programs were funded by Schmidt Cement; they had good publicity, and were well received. Large amounts of programming would eventually probably have to be part of the budget.

SABO: In whatever form and however funded, programming is part of today's library services everywhere. We need to question how much we need here. Carlis' thought that we could do better with our programs if we had a system should be considered. We all go off on our own. I'd like to see more coordination. According to some report I read, one-third of all public library adult programs done back a few years in an eastern state were cancelled due to lack of attendance. Maybe a system would have helped in some of those cases.

MARR: Even though I mentioned a system, I really don't feel we should do much more than we do now. Just systematize our present efforts. Library users and non-users don't know what to expect from a library when it does too much. I can think of one large city library in this country which at one time concentrated so much on cultural activities that it left itself with severely weakened traditional service at its central library. Let each organization concentrate on what it can do best.

MAGRO: I think we better push on to the next topic. Judd, I'll be asking you to develop a rationale, as Carlis suggests, for programming that I can present to the trustees, and to devise a plan for coordinating programming activities. I think I'll avoid any reference to the sex education program; if the trustees bring it up again I'll deal with it then. Now, I put "fines" on the agenda because as many of us know Audra feels they're working to our disadvantage in the children's room, and perhaps in the rest of the library as well. Audra, why don't you take it from here?

VANEK: Well, the problem is just that I know our five cents per day fine for overdues is keeping a lot of kids from using the library. Last week I went down the delinquent borrowers list and found 371 youngsters who owe us $25 or more, and therefore are prohibited from using the library. And what really hurt was that one of them lives on my block and is in no way what you would call a "delinquent" child. In addition we had a father come in last week with his boy and pay the kid's $2.50 fine, and then tell him that if he couldn't keep track of his library books any better than this he'd be denied permission to use the library at all. I know this goes on more than we'd like to think, especially with some of the kids who live near Wayne and lack some of the "advantages" we enjoy.

MAGRO: Well, one thing's for sure. With the $4,079 we collected in fines last year going right back to the city we don't get much monetary advantage from charging fines. I suppose you could argue that this practice allows the city to appropriate that much less for us next year, but I suspect we'd get it anyway. So our time, money, and effort could certainly be better used from that point of view. Another point is that even if you assume that that money ultimately comes back to us from the city how much did it cost us to collect it? We don't have any idea, but I'll guess plenty, and probably more than the amount we collect.

ALVEY: And any time staff spends accepting fines, making change, and keeping records is time devoted to offenders rather than providing service to that larger group of honest patrons.

SABO: That's quite true, but I do think we go a bit too far when we call these people "offenders" and "delinquent" and accuse them of not being honest. In many cases, they're simply absent-minded and I think this should be recognized. There's a big difference between returning a book late and not at all. Perhaps our insistence upon punctuality is a bit paranoid. In my experience life has many crises that could legitimately keep an adult or child from returning a book on time.

MARR: It's possible that a no fines policy at Middlebourne could be a real money saver. I think both supplies and postage could be cut. For one thing, three notices plus a bill, which we currently send, could be reduced to one notice plus a bill. And fewer files, supplies and less space would be needed for record keeping. Work flow might even be smoother because there'd be no need to examine each book the moment it's returned to see whether or not it's overdue. And I don't want to make any promises, but it's even possible we could get away with one less staff member in the department, for a saving of eight to nine thousand dollars.

PRINCE: Also, our system is not quite fair in that it doesn't treat all equally. The conscientious borrower with a fine under $0.75 who comes to the desk will pay his fine, while the person who drops his book in the book return box outside will pay nothing because we don't bother to write up fines for less than $0.75. I'm sure, too, that Carlis will agree with me—and no offense, Carlis—that on occasion we do make clerical errors and dun the wrong person.

MARR: You're right, Sheri, and no offense taken.

VANEK: I think one of the things we must look into is what effect a no fines policy has on the promptness of return and whether or not materials are finally returned at all. If I remember correctly there's some evidence that fines have little effect on the promptness of return. However, other people say that with a no fines policy materials are returned somewhat more slowly than when patrons are fined, but the big advantage is that ultimately fewer books are permanently lost. And of course in the meantime both adults and children can use their library. I think this is a subject we could well investigate further.

ALVEY: You know, some parents have actually become upset when their local public library gave up charging fines because somehow the library by charging fines was promoting responsibility. I think this is hypocrisy. Responsibility should be taught for the right reasons — the needs of others rather than the fear of punishment. I think a much healthier relation with patrons will exist when the library is seen as a service organization rather than as a disciplinarian. And we'll help keep our patrons honest, too; with a no fine policy there'll no longer be a need for patrons to sneak books back on the shelves after they're due and then pretend they were there all the time.

MARR: And not collecting fines will certainly improve our image. "What do librarians do all day? They collect nickels and dimes." I cannot tell you how happy we in the circulation department will all be to put an end once and for all to the smiling delinquent patron who rejoices in paying his fine because he is thereby "supporting a worthy cause."

PRINCE: I think the point needs to be made, if we do decide to recommend to the trustees that fines be eliminated, that we're not totally abandoning the ship. I would think that we would still charge for lost and damaged books and that we would revoke borrowing privileges of chronic offenders, or whatever we decide to call them. There seem to be some different practices regarding fines. Many libraries have had fine free days or weeks in an effort to entice strayed material back. If a child doesn't have the money to pay a fine at least one library lets the child work the fine off in the library. Can't you just see some indignant parent working his fine off shoveling snow from the library steps! Another library uses its fine money to support a foster child in a foreign country. One library with a no fine policy still charges a stiff daily fine for overdue seven-day material; if you dont respond to an overdue notice in 30 days you get a bill for the material plus a $5.00 service charge per item. And if you don't pay you don't use the library. Or one could institute a no fine or low fine policy for patrons who have problems paying, such as children, the aged, the institutionalized, the poor, if you could ever figure out who qualified.

MAGRO: Judd, you haven't said much during this discussion but I see you've been taking notes. Could you come up with a study, based upon any reading you might think necessary as well as any investigations you might want to do at the library, which would help us to formulate a reasonable recommendation for the trustees? You might want to consider such things as the effect of either policy on the patron and his or her use of the library, the return and non-return of materials, likely numbers of overdue materials, promptness of return, total costs involved and amount of staff work, as well as any other ideas that may occur to you. Feel free to do a systems analysis of our present fine procedures complete with flowcharts and cost benefit analysis, but I'm sure you won't forget that a major component of this problem is psychological and therefore almost impossible to quantify.

MESBACHER: Be glad to. I'll see what I can do.

MAGRO: Splendid. Now, "information and referral" was put on the agenda at Glenn's request. Glenn, do you want to get us started?

ALVEY: Well, the time is late, but I'd like to raise the issue. I feel we should begin discussion of the possibilities of information and referral at Middlebourne because we in reference are getting more questions relating to social service information. "My apartment has no heat; who do I call to complain when my landlord doesn't do anything?" is one such question. "Is there some organization that could find a sitter for my invalid brother so I could get out sometimes? I can't afford a nurse," is another. We can answer or try to answer such questions individually and have started a file of agencies. If this is an important service, shouldn't we be considering whether a full I&R center is needed?

PRINCE: When I saw the item on the agenda, I looked for available information. One definition which appealed to me is "linking people in need with the appropriate agency or service designated to alleviate that need." I also found a pamphlet which indicates the steps the library takes in providing the service. The steps on identifying the information really needed and locating the resources are much like what we do in general reference work anyway—interpreting the question and finding the sources—except that in the case of I&R the source is an agency name and subject file produced by the library. From there on, the library connects the patron with the resource by just giving names and phone numbers or making an appointment, talking to the agency on behalf of the patron, arranging transportation or whatever the library's planning has indicated will be the library's role. Follow-up to see whether the patron was satisfied could also be included.

ALVEY: The literature available makes it very clear that staff training is extremely important, for all staff, from director to custodians. The question, "How can I get from Central to Wayne on the Jitney?" should be part of I&R and everyone should know where to send the questioner.

MARR: Why should information and referral be headquartered at a public library rather than somewhere else? I know that England has Citizens Advice Bureaus which are privately run and government financed.

ALVEY: One of my sources suggested that the public library is safe and neutral, versatile, accessible, and the librarians have the necessary skills to do the job; also, public libraries are not forced to limit the kinds of information they provide, thus making them naturals for I&R. I don't know anything about the English service.

MARR: It seems to me that the economic factors could be considerable. How would you go about determining whether the results were worth the input? Judd, perhaps you might come up with some ideas on this. For example, what would we need to do? As we discussed earlier we certainly need to know what our focus is. I tend toward the traditional approach and so feel that if the library basically supplies materials and traditional information, delving into social work dilutes the library's effectiveness. I don't want to see books becoming an afterthought. When one large city library returned to the basics of reference and book collection and promotion, circulation at the main library went up 10% and reference went up 40%. Causes could tend to make us try to go off in too many directions at once. However, if an I&R service is really needed here I wouldn't oppose making a start, but only a start at this point.

SABO: We could begin such a service by adding to the directory of social services in Middlebourne done by the League of Women Voters a couple of years ago.

MAGRO: We need Frances Lowell's input here, as making a card file and subject headings would involve her staff. They complain of backlogs now. Before starting in earnest, we should discover if anyone else is doing or contemplating doing such a thing and take on Carlis' question. Does it relate to our goals as a public library? No doubt the greater the investment a library would make in I&R the more effective the service would be likely to be, but what level of service would be most cost effective?

VANEK: Glenn, what are some ways libraries provide information and referral?

ALVEY: Some libraries provide only a directory of services and agencies. Some give out information but don't contact agencies. Some do the total I&R as discussed here, and some do part or all of it using computers. There are two definitions in one source I read which may be of interest here. "Steering" is used in I&R to mean giving information about which resource can help a patron. "Referring" means making contact with the resource on the patron's behalf.

VANEK: If we decide to take on making up an agency/subject file there'd be a lot of footwork even if we use the League list as a basis. We'll need community volunteers to find the information and perhaps to use the finished file. There might be some difficulty with agencies who see us as "horning in" on their territory. Our PR before we even begin a service must be right.

MAGRO: Judd, this is a doozie of a way to introduce you to Middlebourne, I admit. But we're a bit under the gun because of trustee interests, either expressed or anticipated. I'd like to ask you to guide our examination of these four subjects. I appreciate the fact that time is a problem here, but I'd like us to be prepared to discuss the "gifted and talented" and "programming" questions by the next board meeting in three weeks. I don't think it's likely the trustees would want to consider "fines" and "information and referral" at the same meeting, but I'd like us to have recommendations prepared on these two subjects in time for the following trustees meeting in seven weeks. What I'd like you to do, Judd, is to analyze each of these questions somewhat as mentioned at the conclusion of our discussion on fines. I think it will be possible for you to determine which way we want to go based on our discussions of the gifted and talented, programming, and information and referral. If you're in doubt, please feel free to talk with anyone you wish. I think the next step will be to determine what further information is required and then to take steps to obtain it, either from the literature or from any studies you may wish to conduct. Finally, we need an outline of what needs to be done in order for us to take action. We need to consider, for example, who's responsible for doing what. It wouldn't hurt to examine any proposed list of activities against one of the established checklists of management functions such as Gulick and Urwick's POSDCORB or Louis A. Allen's classification of.... Yes, Susan (the secretary entered the room), what is it?

SUSAN COOK: There's a fire in the chili parlor next door to Lyon and the fire department's there.

MAGRO: Let's go, Sheri! Meeting adjourned.

APPENDIX I

PROFILE OF THE CITY OF MIDDLEBOURNE
AND THE MIDDLEBOURNE PUBLIC LIBRARY

An impressive lock on the Modoc River, a spectacular view of the confluence of the two rivers, a scenic state park, an exciting ferry ride across the Lewark, and the birthplace of a civil war general all combine to attract tourists in the summer. Fall and early winter duck hunters swarm to the banks of the Lewark River.

Inchworm Tractor Company has a branch factory on the edge of town manufacturing earthmoving equipment. There are also small plants making livestock feed, industrial fans, and construction and radio equipment. There are 61 manufacturing and processing plants registered with the Chamber of Commerce.

Many small businesses service the city, the area farms and the declining Two Rivers Air Force Base to the northeast.

Bethage College, a private, four-year liberal arts college on the bluffs overlooking the Lewark River, was founded in 1905 by the Methodists. It is no longer affiliated with the church. For many years it has been a well-respected college with about 800 students from all over the country. Though its endowment is adequate, Bethage is having the same fiscal problems facing other such institutions throughout the country.

Middlebourne, the county seat, is serviced by three major highways: U.S. routes 33 and 12, and state route 106. A Midwest and Southern Railroad spur carries freight and farm goods to Middlebourne and towns west. Two bus lines, one national and the other, Tinkerbell, an area carrier, arrive and depart at Middlebourne's Union Bus Terminal. Passenger trains are available at Kissippi, 40 miles south on Route 33, and Kissippi Regional Airport is serviced daily by Tinkerbell Bus Lines.

There are two modern motels on Main Street downtown at the U.S. route 33, state route 106 bridge over the Modoc. Other tourist accommodations are located on U.S. route 12 to the north. There is also a tourist lodge and cottages, and tent camping available at the state park on the southern edge of the city at the confluence of the Modoc and Lewark Rivers.

Middlebourne's cultural activities include a historical museum and the General Lewes homestead. A four-program series is presented each year by the Middlebourne City Concerts, a private group affiliated with a national concert booking organization. These concerts are held in the Main Junior High School auditorium. Bethage College holds several lectures and programs each year which are open to the public. Movies are available at the Northside Shopping Center and a drive-in theater near Inchworm Tractor Company. An occasional show at Two Rivers Air Force Base welcomes local residents.

Middlebourne has amateur baseball, softball, and soccer leagues for children and adults, and the park department also runs an ice skating rink, an outdoor pool, an 18-hole golf course and a summer recreation program at Long Park near downtown and at Southeast Park near the ferry docks.

In 1893 a descendant of Hurley Barnes decided there should be a quiet place where gentlemen and ladies could obtain the finest literature of the ages, and so a library was formed. By 1896 a large collection of donated books was on hand, a room on the third floor of the new city hall was set aside, and Agnes Millweather

APPENDIX I (cont'd)

was hired as librarian. Two years later the Middlebourne Public Library became a part of the city.

In 1905 the first public library building went up in Middlebourne. This small Indiana limestone building on Main Street now houses the Barnes County Historical Society and Museum.

July 1967, saw the opening of the Middlebourne Public Library's present central building on State Street between a city parking lot and the police station, and across from city hall. The building has two floors with a total of 22,000 square feet of space. The Gaylord circulation system was installed in the main library and in the children's room for the opening of the new central building. There is a small, well-used auditorium for community use and a story hour room in the children's area.

Middlebourne Public Library has two branch libraries. Wayne branch at the corner of U.S. routes 12 and 33 is situated in the Northside Shopping Center, which opened two years ago. Lyon branch is an old store front building in a small shopping district now serving the newer housing areas on the northeast side. Complaints are heard that this branch is now too small and not well situated. Both branches serve mainly as recreational reading centers, but have small reference collections and provide children's books and programming.

Parking is easily available at Central and at Wayne, but Lyon has on-street parking only. All library buildings are on routes of the Middlebourne City Jitney Bus Company, which runs infrequently. Middlebourne has no bookmobile service. There are small paperback collections housed at the county jail, Memorial Hospital, and the common room of Jeffrey Housing for the Elderly, named for the former mayor who arranged for the federal funds that helped build these apartments.

Middlebourne Public Library is governed by a board of trustees numbering nine, who are appointed by the mayor to three overlapping terms. Soon after the library moved into its present building the trustees formally approved the following objectives for the library:

> The Middlebourne Public Library exists to serve all persons, regardless of age, sex, race, economic or occupational status. The objectives of the library are to:
>
> 1) help people know more about themselves and their world.
>
> 2) supplement formal study and encourage informal self-education.
>
> 3) meet the informational and recreational needs of the entire community.
>
> 4) stimulate thoughtful participation in the affairs of the community, the country, and the world.
>
> 5) give access to a variety of opinions on matters of current interest and encourage freedom of expression.
>
> 6) support educational, civic, and cultural activities within the community.
>
> 7) aid in learning and improving job-related skills.
>
> 8) assist the individual to grow intellectually and spiritually and to enjoy life more fully.

APPENDIX I (cont'd)

The Middlebourne Public Library is a member of the Muddy Rivers Library System, part of a state-supported group of cooperative systems including primarily public libraries, although thought is being given to encouraging participation by other types of libraries. Headquarters of the system are in Blackland, a city about the size of and to the north of Middlebourne on the Modoc River. The Kissippi Public Library is the reference and interlibrary loan center for the system.

There are a few other libraries in or near Middlebourne besides the media center for the Middlebourne Public Schools. The library at Bethage College holds about 145,000 volumes, receives 800 periodicals and has joined an automated cataloging network. Memorial Hospital has a small medical library of approximately 1,000 titles. Inchworm Tractor has a reading room for its management personnel to look over the technical periodicals it receives specifically regarding its business. Inchworm and other businesses in Middlebourne depend on the business collection and reference department of Middlebourne Public Library.

Middlebourne Public Library and Bethage College Library have liberal interlibrary loan and in-house use agreements.

Two Rivers Air Force Base, which is in an unincorporated area of Standard Township, has a recreational reading room for its men and women.

Standard Township is one of the many taxing bodies common in some areas of the Midwest. Barnes County collects all real estate and personal property taxes. The county runs the courts and the jail, assesses and collects taxes, and has charge of county roads. The township, in which Middlebourne is also situated, is concerned with the administration of unincorporated farm areas and two unincorporated villages, Downland on Township Road 186 connecting with Middlebourne by the ferry in the summer, and Springdale, north on U.S. route 33. The township also has charge of its roads, a volunteer fire department headquartered in Springdale, and the Springdale Covered Bridge over East Branch Creek. A levee district headquartered in Middlebourne pays for the upkeep of levees on both rivers in the city and on farmland from just north of Kissippi through Blackland.

Middlebourne itself has the usual city services to support. Tax support for both the public schools and the public library come from property owners within the city limits. The value of all the taxable property in the city, as assessed by the Department of Local Government Affairs is $175,654,000; the Middlebourne Public Library is currently funded at .146%, the state mandated limit with referendum being .30%.

With personnel at Two Rivers Air Force Base steadily declining in numbers rumors recur that it will close. Though the government claims no such plans, much of the land is no longer used and Middlebourne's mayor and city council have discussed the pros and cons of annexation to provide an industrial park for the city.

APPENDIX II

ENTRY FOR MIDDLEBOURNE IN
THE AMERICAN LIBRARY DIRECTORY

P   MIDDLEBOURNE PUBLIC LIBRARY, 246 Main St. Founded 1898.
      Dir Nicholas Magro. *Admin Asst* Open. *ILL* Edna Stanski. *Ad Serv*
      Catherine Sabo. *Cir* Carlis Marr. *Ch* Audra Vanek. *Tech Serv* Frances
      Lowell. *Ref* Glenn Alvey. *Br Libs* Sheri Prince. Staff 27 (prof 7, cler 18)
      Pop. served 40,000. Circ 290,660.
      Income $300,160 (city $255,136, other $45,024)
      Bks $46,435. Per $5,406, Bd $1,077. Microform $1,482. A-V $4,362.
      Sal $219,424 (prof $89,480, cler $120,517)
      Bk Titles 82,528, vols 112,135; Per sub 283; Microform--Reels 1,077, Fiche
      256; A-V--Recordings 4,689, Audio tapes, Films, Filmstrips, Maps, Art
      reproductions. Vertical Files.
      Special Subjects: genealogy, history of two rivers area (Member of Muddy
      Rivers Library System)
      Branches: 2
      Lyon, 4320 E. Mason. Vols 4,224
      Wayne, 1575 N. Monroe. Vols 6,572